D1380470

C334516328

TO BE
SOMEONE

Patron
Alan Davies

TO BE
SOMEONE

IAN STONE

unbound

This edition first published in 2020

Unbound
6th Floor Mutual House, 70 Conduit Street, London W1S 2GF

www.unbound.com

Text Design by Ellipsis, Glasgow

A CIP record for this book is available from the British Library

ISBN 978-1-78352-766-3 (hardback)
ISBN 978-1-78352-768-7 (ebook)

Printed in Great Britain by CPI Books

1 3 5 7 9 8 6 4 2

To Rosie

And in memory of Helena Stone (1938–2020)

Contents

Foreword

I first heard The Jam when I was fourteen. It was on John Peel's late night show on Radio One. On this particular evening, he was playing slightly more esoteric stuff than normal. There may have been something vaguely Nordic and shouty, it's hard to recall but I was thinking of turning it off. And then he announced, in those flat, Scouse tones of his, 'This next tune is "In The City" by The Jam.' Paul Weller's impatient, angry guitar started up, Bruce Foxton came in behind with the bass and Rick Buckler kicked in with the drums. I felt like I'd been smacked in the head. That energy, that power, that noise. Nothing has ever come close.

From that moment on, I bought every record they ever released and every magazine with their picture on the front cover. I had Jam badges on my jacket, Jam posters on my wall. I played their singles and albums constantly. I knew every word, every hook, every beat. When I finally persuaded my mother to let me go, I criss-crossed the country to see them live thirty-two times and watched as they grew into one of the biggest bands in Britain.

They wrote some of the best tunes I've ever heard. The look was cool as fuck, the attitude was defiant and angry. They played fast and loud and they were not much older than I was. The lyrics were beautiful and honest. They talked about youth and young ideas and they seemed to be about and for me. It was a turbulent and divisive time to grow up in Britain and Paul made sense of it all. Through The Jam, I started to see more clearly what was actually going on.

Five years later, when I was nineteen and ostensibly a grown-up, Paul Weller announced that the band were splitting up. I was devastated. I'm just about over it now. This book is my story of that time. Those five years from 1977 to 1982 when three young lads from Woking stretched my (and thousands of others,) hitherto limited horizons way beyond anything I'd previously imagined. When I was, when we all were, in the presence of, as John Weller correctly put it, 'the best fucking band in the world'.

Chapter One
Ain't that a kick in the head

It's late 1979. I'm sixteen years old and I'm on the top deck of a 253 crawling along Green Lanes on the way to the Rainbow Theatre in Finsbury Park in North London. I love this venue. I've seen The Jam here more than once. But tonight, I'm going to see Sham 69, a punk, pub rock band who've somehow captured the imagination of a certain sort of disaffected male youth. Namely white, violent and often racist. And also, for reasons I could not articulate at the time, me. This doesn't concern me as much as it perhaps should.

The truth is I don't even like Sham 69 that much. Jeremy Goldman, a friend from the year below me at school, had managed to get a couple of tickets and asked me if I wanted to come along. Aside from listening to my parents shout at each other, which I can hear any evening of the week, I've got nothing else on so I say yes.

I've just left Pete Bernstein's house in Clapton. I've been there most of the afternoon. It's a school day but we had Maths and double Religious Education, presumably because the school considered made-up stories from two thousand years ago twice as important as Maths, so we made an executive decision to bunk off and listen to records. At some point, his mum came in from work. She didn't seem in the least bit surprised or annoyed that we weren't at school. She just made us a sandwich and left us to it.

The bus moves slowly towards Manor House. It's an oppressively warm Friday evening. The top deck smells of cigarettes. It always does. I look out of the window to my left. We're passing a council estate. A young guy is strolling down the street towards four other guys sitting on a wall. I see that they've spotted him. One of them stands on the wall and as he passes, kicks him hard in the face. He goes down. The four boys run away laughing. I look around the bus. No one else has seen what happened. The bus moves slowly along. I keep looking at the young guy. He slowly gets up. There's some blood and he wipes it with his sleeve. The bus goes round the corner at the junction and he's gone.

I get off the bus at Finsbury Park under the bridge on the Seven Sisters Road. It's a lively part of London, at least compared to West Hendon where I live. I've been coming to the Arsenal stadium just up the road since I was seven so I know it well. On match days it's dangerous enough but tonight is off the scale. There are skinheads everywhere. People are tense. I keep my head down and make eye contact with no one. I think that I can't believe my mother let me go to this. And then I remember that I didn't tell her, at least not in detail.

'I'm going out after school.'

'What time will you be back?'

'Late.'

I slammed the door before she had a chance to say anything else. She didn't need to know any more than that. Because if I'd said, 'I'm going with another Jewish boy to watch a band that have a violent, racist skinhead following and it's more than likely that it will kick off', she might have been reluctant to let me go. I'd have gone anyway but who needs the argument.

I can see the Rainbow on the other side of the road. It's the best music venue in London. Everyone has played there: The Who, Michael Jackson, David Bowie. Jimi Hendrix burned his guitar there. I could of course walk fifty yards up the road and cross at the traffic lights but I'm sixteen years old so I run straight out into the road. An articulated lorry is coming the other way and I realise that I might not make it. I turn back towards the kerb and I'm hit by a car. There's a screech of brakes but he can't stop in time. I bounce onto the bonnet and then roll off. I sit up and check myself. There doesn't appear to be any lasting damage. A small crowd has gathered. They look concerned. The man who was driving gets out of the car. He looks at the car first to see if there's any damage. Then he looks at me.

'What the fuck do you think you were doing?' he says. I was expecting a touch more sympathy from the man who has hit me in his car.

'Sorry,' I say.

'Are you OK?' he says realising that his paintwork is fine but I might not be.

'I think so,' I say using all my years of medical training. I don't think there's any major head trauma. Although trying to cross the road at Finsbury Park when I wasn't at traffic lights suggests that I already had one.

He helps me to the side of the road.

'That was an incredibly stupid thing to do.'

'I know. Sorry.'

He gets back in his car, drives off and the crowd dissipates. I check myself again. My leg is throbbing and I'm a bit shaken up but other than that, I seem fine. I decide to go to the gig. I limp up to the traffic lights and cross when it's safe to do so. I see Jeremy Goldman waiting for me outside the venue. I limp towards him.

'You alright?' he says.

'No. I just got hit by a car.'

'Shit.'

'I'm alright,' I reassure him. He looks doubtful.

'Have you got the tickets?' I ask him.

'Yeah, it's a bit early though. Let's hang about for a bit.'

We hang about for a bit, it's what teenagers do. It's tense. There are thousands of skinheads milling about. They all look extremely angry and aggressive. It's their default position. There are a lot of Nazi salutes. It occurs to me that I've never been in a place with so many people doing Nazi salutes although to be fair, boys who attend a Jewish school tend to move in very different social circles. I'm getting some funny looks. I become very aware of my nose and the fact that only thirty-five years before this, actual Nazis would've been doing much more than giving funny looks to people like me. I stare at the floor to make myself less conspicuous.

There are a lot of violent conversations.

'. . . beat up this bloke the other day'.

'So I said to him, "Fuck off you cunt!"'

'. . . almost got my head kicked in.'

'fuckin' Paki bastards . . .'

These skinheads don't seem to get on with anyone. I look at Jeremy. 'Maybe we should go in.' Jeremy nods his agreement.

It's safer inside, but it's a fine distinction. Unusually for a gig, we decide to watch from the balcony. Normally, we'd be in the mosh pit as close to the front as possible but this doesn't seem like our sort of crowd. We get seats right at the front and we've got a great view. From our vantage point, we gaze down in open mouthed wonder at the carnage below. Hundreds of Nazi skinheads are shouting, drinking and sieg heiling. It looks like a Nuremberg rally interspersed with pub rock tunes. I can see bald heads and sweat and checked shirts and braces and boots. Fights are breaking out all the time. It's insane. There's a support band on stage called Oy You Cunt or something like that. They thrash about for a bit but no one pays them much attention. The audience are too busy fighting.

There's a brief interval while they reset the stage. The fighting continues unabated. Finally, Sham 69 appear and a big fight breaks out to welcome them. The band patiently wait for it to subside and then launch into 'Borstal Breakout', a song about escaping from a young offenders institute which, by the looks of the audience, some may have felt was autobiographical. The end of every song is met with cheers, fights and more Nazi salutes, not necessarily in that order. The gig is broken up three times when the violence gets too out of hand. Each time it happens, Jimmy Pursey the lead singer takes a break from 'singing' and pleads for calm. He might as well have asked for everyone to sit cross legged and start meditating. After he's implored us to chill out and there's a temporary cessation of hostilities, he launches into another song about sticking the boot in or punching a cat.

They play eight songs in total. There's 'Hurry up Harry' which is a song about trying to get Harry to hurry up because they're all going down the pub. There isn't a lot of subtext with Sham songs. There's one called 'George Davies is Innocent'. I had no idea who George Davies was but if he's at the gig, he's pretty much the only one who is.

Then they played 'If The Kids are United'. It may have been the most ironic moment of the evening. Halfway through the song, an enormous and very fat skinhead, who is definitely not a kid, jumps up on stage and starts stomping about. No one tells him to stop or get off the stage. No one dares. He accidentally-on-purpose puts his foot through the drum kit. This ruins the gig but is a blessed relief for music lovers who might have been attending. The song comes to a grinding halt. There's a pause as he inspects his handiwork, he gives a Nazi salute and then for an encore, he attacks a black bouncer. The bouncer appears to be trained in martial arts and kicks him in the head. Before this evening, I've never seen a single person kicked in the head, now I've seen two in a couple of hours. A riot ensues. Jimmy Pursey bursts into tears and starts ranting at the Sieg Heiling Nazis. Bottles come flying towards him. He's dragged off stage by security. (It's the last gig Sham 69 do for eight years. It was probably right for them to take a bit of a break.) The safety curtain thuds down, the houselights come up and that appears to be the end of the evening's entertainment. No one can say we didn't get our money's worth. A large bouncer taps me on the shoulder.

'I think you lads should leave now.'

We weren't about to argue. Welcome to Britain in the late 1970s.

Old Ian versus Young Ian

Things We Didn't Have in the 1970s

Part One

Health and Safety

Many people decry the nanny state and how health and safety regulation has constricted people's lives. To give but one example, I could safely and healthily drink a cup of hot coffee without a lid on the cup but nowadays, takeaway coffee must be served in a cup with a lid on. I once protested that I'd be fine. The lady serving looked at me.

'Well you say that, but what if you pour the coffee all down your face?'

'Then I'm a fucking idiot,' I said. 'And I deserve a burnt face.'

She stared at me.

'More than that,' I continued, 'I resent the inference that I might.'

I feel like I was walking towards the coffee shop and they were looking at me and whispering to each other, 'Get the lids out. This bloke will hurt himself.' She was unbending. I removed the lid as soon as I left the shop, like the maverick that I am.

In the 1970s, we had both health and safety but they weren't considered a joint enterprise. Consequently, the most innocent of activities involved a degree of danger. Children's playgrounds were built almost entirely on concrete. If you came off the swings and landed on your head and got brain damage, it was seen as natural selection. That was how we weeded out the stupid people.

Chapter Two

But you'd better listen man, because the kids know where it's at

'You dirty fucker.'

Like a lot of teenagers back then, hearing these three words, uttered on an early evening TV show in late 1976, changed my life. I'd heard swearing before of course. I went to an inner-London comprehensive school. I went to football most weeks. I also lived with my parents. But I'd never heard swearing on live TV just after six o'clock on a weekday evening. It wasn't considered suitable to broadcast someone calling someone else a dirty fucker, even if he probably was, while people were having their tea. It still isn't. I never normally watched the *Today* programme but for some reason I'd decided to tune in and I was tremendously impressed. I thought that I may have to watch it more often. As someone who was just starting out on my swearing career, it was a huge shot in the arm to see people not much older than myself swearing on national telly at teatime.

My mother was also watching and she wasn't quite as impressed as I was.

'That's not nice,' she said.

What she couldn't see was that that was entirely the point. That was why I liked them. Because they upset my mother. She tutted loudly and then went back to her *Woman's Own*. If she could have been bothered, she would've changed channels but the programme finished straight away. Our TV was tuned to ITV most of the time anyway and there was nothing much on the other side. Plus turning the TV over involved getting up from the sofa and pushing a button on the telly, so ITV was where it often stayed.

In hindsight, it's easy to see how things went so wrong. Bill Grundy was a mainstream TV presenter who was used to fronting an early evening magazine programme presenting upbeat little items of 'news' from around the country. Stories about a farmer who, after his combined harvester had overturned had walked away without a scratch; that sort of thing. He would never have encountered anything like this. He was meant to interview the band Queen, which would've made interesting telly in itself. Bill Grundy and Freddie Mercury would not be soulmates. But Queen cancelled and The Sex Pistols stepped in at the last minute. The band turned up drunk and could barely contain their contempt. The feeling was mutual. They had an entourage which included a man wearing a swastika armband, another thing my mother thought was not nice; she may have had a point there. Also with the band was a very young Siouxsie Sioux, who said to Grundy that she'd always wanted to meet him. He said they should meet afterwards. It looked predatory enough then but now it's positively creepy. The interview rapidly descended from there, with Grundy encouraging the band to use worse and worse language. It ended with the credits rolling, the entourage dancing to the theme tune and Steve Jones calling Grundy a dirty fucker.

The reaction the next day was predictable. The newspapers were apoplectic. These people had to be stopped. Filth seemed to be the operative word. There were headlines like 'The Filth and The Fury' and variations like 'TV Fury at Rock Cult Filth'. (It was only eight years after Charles Manson so everyone was still a bit on edge for anything that might seem a bit cult-like. To me, there's a world of difference between smoking, drinking and swearing on daytime TV and human sacrifice, but perhaps that's how it starts.) It was reported that a man was so incensed by the language that he had put his foot through his television rather than listen to 'that filth'. I imagine that when he calmed down and surveyed his smashed up TV, he might have uttered the odd filthy word himself.

As the scandal rumbled on, there were earnest articles tutting over the bad language and moralising about the drop in standards. Meanwhile, teenagers everywhere bought the Sex Pistols single 'Anarchy in the U.K.'. And the record companies, suddenly alert to any possibility that might make them money, rounded up any group of pissed-off looking young men with even a modicum of musical ability, and quite a few without even that, and shoved them into a recording studio.

The whole thing was a massive shock to the music business. It needed it. Finding good music back then was much more difficult than it is now. I lived in a musically illiterate house. My mother didn't listen to music much by then. My father liked musicals and was a big fan of the tenor Mario Lanza. If I think hard enough, I can still hear 'Only a Rose' blasting out of the stereo.

I had an eclectic collection. 'Mary Had a Little Lamb' by Paul McCartney and Wings was the first record I ever bought. (Give me a break, I was only nine.) I had 'Tiger Feet' by Mud, 'Ballroom Blitz' by Sweet and 'California Man' by The Move. I bought all the Slade singles and I still listen to some of them today. I had a couple of the *Top of the Pops* compilation albums. These were collections of hit songs recorded by cover bands. There was a sexy young woman on the cover wearing hot pants or another fashion item of the day. I'm prepared to admit that I might have bought the albums because of that.

Mainstream shows like *Top of the Pops* (and we only ever watched mainstream shows in my house) churned out a mixture of classic soul tunes and all sorts of terrible rubbish. Brass bands, girls' school choirs, someone called Lieutenant Pigeon. 'Save Your Kisses for Me' by Brotherhood of Man had been number one for what felt like my entire childhood. The radio stations were not much better. Radio 2 played easy listening tunes. I didn't find them easy to listen to at all. Radio 1 played chart hits. That meant a constant diet of anodyne, saccharine rubbish interspersed with the odd decent tune. Plus you had to put up with the DJs who were for the most part wankers, or in some cases, much much worse. Simon Bates, who I later met at a gig and turned out to be a very nice bloke, had Our Tune. He told incredibly sad stories about people with terminal illness (it's possible that there aren't many happy stories about people with terminal illness), some of whom would no doubt have been happier to die rather than listen to any more stories about other people with terminal illness. And the tunes they'd request would be maudlin and sentimental nonsense like 'I've Never Been to Me' by Charlene ('I've been undressed by Kings and I've seen some things that a woman aint s'posed to see' might be my favourite ridiculous lyric of all time), or 'Seasons in the Sun' by Terry Jacks. Personally, if I'd suffered a bereavement, I'd want something a bit more upbeat. Noel Edmonds presented the Breakfast show and he thought he was much funnier than he actually was. So did Dave Lee Travis. He had a jingle that went 'Quack Quack Oops'. No wonder there was social unrest.

The only show that was really worth listening to was at ten in the evening. John Peel was different from the other Radio 1 DJs. He didn't seem to feel the need to sound enthusiastic. If he liked something, he said so but he didn't make a big deal about it. He didn't have any of the 'please like me' neediness of the other DJs. We could like him or not like him, it was entirely up to us. I liked him enormously.

With the eight pounds I was earning from a Saturday morning job stacking shelves in the local Co-op, and fired up by Steve Jones's sweary appearance on telly, I'd go into Our Price Records in Camden and hoover up music by all sorts of bands that John Peel introduced me to. Some of the songs he played were a bit out there but every so often you'd hear a gem and think, 'I MUST get that'. He played 'New Rose' by The Damned. I loved the 'huh' shout at the beginning. He played The Sex Pistols, The Clash and The Stranglers. He played X-Ray Spex. DLT was not playing X-Ray Spex. Basically, I was into anyone who sounded as pissed off as I felt. And none of it was nice.

When I first heard The Jam on his show, I vividly remember thinking 1) *This* is the band that my friend Simon has been talking about and 2) *I had to go* and see them. I suggested this to my mother. She was having none of it.

'You're too young. It's dangerous in town in the evening.'

'How do you know? You never go into town.'

It was ridiculous. I was travelling up and down the country watching Arsenal away games. That was actually dangerous. I'd once been chased down a dual carriageway in Stoke, and come very close to being killed on a number of other occasions. But whereas my mother deemed this acceptable, possibly because she didn't know how bad it actually was, she put her foot down when it came to going to The Marquee in the centre of London to see The Jam. I think it was purely because it was in the evening. I was livid. I don't think I said more than two words to her for about six months. I was a very teenagey teenager.

My mother was reading snippets about the new punk scene. It was all a bit hysterical. So was she. I tried to tell her that The Jam were mods, not punks, but it fell on deaf ears. She wasn't interested in the fact that the press, in an effort to pigeonhole them, lumped The Jam in with the punk movement. It was all the same to her. I could see that Paul Weller was not a punk and he was never nihilistic in the way The Sex Pistols said they were. 'Get pissed, destroy!' was not a lyric that Paul would ever have written. The things that Paul sang about were much more relatable. More authentic. There was none of the Kings Road art school poser type thing with him. He was the real deal.

Paul got The Jam to wear suits. Unless he was appearing in court, one couldn't imagine Johnny Rotten in a suit. The clothes were a big part of it. The look was as important to Paul as the music. This meant a lot to working-class kids like me. I used to see the punks with their ripped clothes and their safety pins and while I liked the 'fuck off' nature of that look, I could never do that myself. It might be fine for middle class kids who wanted to dress down, to make a conscious effort to distance themselves from the establishment of which they would one day become a respected part, but it was different for us. We tried to dress up, not down.

There was no doubt that Paul's voice was rough around the edges and he definitely shouted a bit too much on the first album. As my dad said, 'He's no Matt Monro'. I couldn't disagree. He wouldn't be singing a James Bond theme anytime soon. But I didn't want Matt Monro and nor did any of the fans I talked to. Paul might be shouting a bit but it was what he was shouting about that got us going. It was angry, it was focused. It crystallised exactly what we all felt.

The first chords of 'In The City' thrill me every time I hear them. And when Paul said that he's got a thousand things to say to us, I believed that he did. It took me a few listens to realise that the song was about police brutality, a theme that Paul would return to on more than one occasion. I was aware that it happened. Even the tabloid rags my father read occasionally had stories about young men dying in police custody. My mother thought that a song about police brutality was also not nice. She was right, but I tended to think that actual police brutality was worse. She didn't appreciate it when I pointed that out.

I knew that the relationship between the police and the general public was at a low point. There was very little respect on either side. There were deaths in custody. There was stop and search and arrest without trial and internment in Northern Ireland. The Yorkshire Ripper was on the loose and the police seemed to be unable to find him. There were also rumours of the police regularly making up evidence to convict people for things they hadn't done. These rumours turned out to be true.

The public probably didn't help. Quite a large minority regularly called them filth or pigs or suchlike. I briefly had a poster on my wall of a pig wearing a police helmet. My mother hated it and asked me to take it down.

'Who's going to see it?' I asked her.

'I will when I go in your room.'

'Well, don't go in my room.'

'What if a policeman comes round?'

'Don't be ridiculous. When's a policeman ever going to come round here?'*

Aside from the energy of the song, what got me more than anything were the references to youth and young ideas. This felt like music and lyrics written specifically for us. For me. This was what I'd been looking for. The fact that up to that point, I didn't know I was looking for it was neither here nor there. Paul Weller knew, and I was an instant disciple. When he said that the kids know where it's at, it was the most empowering thing I'd ever heard.

'Yes', I thought to myself, 'the kids do know where it's at.' Not me though, or anyone I knew; I didn't have a clue what *it* was let alone where to find it. But I figured Paul Weller knew what was what. That was enough for me. I was hooked.

---

* Little did I know what my dad was planning.

Things We Didn't Have in the 1970s

Part Two

Much in the Way of Entertainment

I realise things are relative. When my parents were growing up, there was almost no entertainment at all. People would have had to 'make their own entertainment'. What that consisted of I have no earthly idea, but no one looked particularly entertained. By the 1970s, things were marginally better but the paucity of decent things to watch on TV or listen to on the radio was still bordering on criminal. For kids, the most wholesome show was *Blue Peter*. I recently watched a clip from the early 1970s and it featured a woman wearing a football kit (including boots) whistle a song. She was a very good whistler. Why she was wearing football kit was never mentioned. Later in the decade, the most popular kids' show on BBC TV was presented by a paedophile who made children's, and no doubt his own, wishes come true. All three TV channels stopped broadcasting around midnight. Most evenings, it was a relief.

We had board games, although the idea of my mother and father playing *Cluedo* (a popular Whodunnit game) does not bear thinking about. I think even the thought of murdering someone with a lead piping in the kitchen might have given my mum too many ideas. Sometimes we went out. Living in London, there were choices. There was theatre and opera and ballet and probably modern dance if you looked hard enough but we never went to any of them. We went to the cinema once or twice but as my parents couldn't go five minutes without screaming abuse at one another, we'd barely get through the trailers.

Chapter Three
David Watts

I attended JFS (the Jewish Free School), a co-educational comprehensive secondary school with 1,500 kids in Camden, North London. My parents wanted me to go to a Jewish school, so it came down to a choice between that or the much more religious Hasmonean High School in Hendon. Our family had recently moved into a housing association flat in West Hendon, a nondescript area off the Edgware Road. (Two thousand years beforehand, the Roman army would've marched almost past my house). My mother had very sensibly turned down the chance of living in a slightly bigger place on one of the most violent estates in London, Chalkhill in Wembley. It would've been handy for cup finals but I may not have made it to my eighteenth birthday. West Hendon was a brisk forty minute walk to Hasmonean, but our religious beliefs, never strong to begin with, dissipated through the 1970s and so my parents opted for me to take the bus, train and bus journey to Camden. It was one of the few decisions they made that I agreed with.

Camden was not the entertainment hub that it's become in the last twenty-five years. Like most of Britain in the late 1970s, there was an air of sleazy decay about the area. The market was vaguely trendy, but this was before enterprising hippies started flying off to India and coming back with cheap trinkets they could sell for 1,000% mark-up to unsuspecting tourists. Mainly because there were very few tourists.

The residents were a motley collection of Londoners. There were four men who lived in the streets around the underground station entrance. We would've called them tramps, which at that time described a very particular type of person. (Although there are a lot more homeless people now than there ever used to be, one sees very few 1970s 'tramps' any more but they were a regular feature of London life back then.) Men (and it was always men) with matted hair, wearing clothes that they'd not taken off for several years and giving off an odour that would stop a train. Which presumably was why they weren't allowed on the platform. They didn't even beg. Most people wouldn't (and because of the smell, couldn't) go anywhere near them. I have no idea how they fed themselves but they didn't seem to be emaciated so they must have been eating. Although it might have been the eight layers of old newspapers they used to keep themselves warm. For amusement, they used to drink heavily and bark – actually bark, like big Alsatian dogs – at schoolchildren as we walked past them. You've got to have a hobby. I guess when people look back to days gone by and talk about having to make our own entertainment, this is what they mean.

I never mentioned it to my mother. She may well have regretted sending me to JFS if she knew I'd have to run the gauntlet of barking tramps. The first time it happened, I almost wet myself. The tramps' barks were very realistic. I honestly felt like I was about to be attacked by an enormous and incredibly malodorous Alsatian. They laughed their hearty tramp laughs and from then on, I was fair game. It happened so often, I was crossing the road to avoid them.

★

Our school was next door to Camden School for Girls, a grammar school that was slowly transitioning into a comprehensive. It was full of impossibly tall and willowy middle class girls with double-barrelled surnames and first names like Vanessa or Chloe or Virginia. They all had cheekbones and good teeth and looked healthy and well-bred and no doubt took part in eventing competitions at weekends. They looked upon us, running around in our playground, with our outsize noses and Coke-bottle glasses, as the aristocracy look upon people who do manual labour. They paid us absolutely no attention whatsoever.*

Further up the road was Holloway Boys School, a famously tough inner city comprehensive whose alumni include one Charlie George, bad boy striker for Arsenal and one of my earliest heroes. The Holloway boys were a fearsome lot. One imagines that their school reunions would have been decimated by enforced absences due to the actions of the criminal justice system. As well as terrorising any kids who had the temerity to walk past their school just because they happened to live near Holloway, their regular lunchtime entertainment was to wander down the road to our school, stand in the street where we could see them and make gas noises and Nazi salutes. Even writing this sentence is shocking to me. Nowadays, I could see it happening perhaps once or twice before the authorities got wind of what

---

* Except for Martin Cohen, who was a very good-looking guy. He told me one day that he'd started going out with one of the girls from Camden Girls School. He was meeting her later on and did I want to tag along. Later that day, Martin and I got the bus to the station and in order to look like he didn't go to our school he took off his school blazer and tie when we got there. Vanessa or Chloe or Virginia turned up shortly afterwards and they kissed. I was introduced. She gave Martin a look that said 'what are you doing hanging out with one of those kids from the Jewish school?' It was a fair question. I went home shortly afterwards.

was going on and firmly put a stop to it. This abuse went on for years. It probably went on longer than the Second World War. It happened so often, I think it became part of the curriculum.

'What have you got today?'

'Geography, chemistry and double anti-semitism.'

We didn't take it completely lying down. There used to be abuse flying back and forth across the fence and the teachers would shoo us over to the other side of the playground. They should probably then have had a word with the hooligans, but they were more terrified of them than we were. Except for our history teacher, Mr Waterman. He was already a legend after one fantastic incident during one of his lessons. We were in a classroom on the fifth floor of the main building. He crashed in. He was not in a good mood.

'Sit down everyone.'

We sat down.

'I'm going to turn round,' he said in his distinctive Welsh accent. 'If I turn back and there is a bag left on the desk, I'm going to chuck it out of the window.' He then turned round.

Now all teachers have their own eccentricities. Some detest chewing, others cannot stand even the merest hint of talking in class. PE teachers don't like children. Mr Waterman was famous for having an irrational revulsion for anyone who kept their bag on their desk, so even though we were five floors up, we thought he actually might do something that crazy. We cleared our remaining stray bags from our desks.

He turned back, saw a bag on a desk and stared at us.

'Whose bag is this?'

No one answered. There was a heavy silence in the air. He picked it up and without a moment's hesitation threw it out of the window. I did wonder whether an unsuspecting child was taking his last breath before being killed by a bag falling from the sky. That would have been an unfortunate way to go and very likely the end of a promising career in teaching. We all looked at Mr Waterman. Personally, I have never been so scared in my life. No one said a thing. 'Oh Shit!' he said and then without warning, ran out of the room. We waited. It was strange. Was the lesson over?

After a minute or two, he ran back in carrying a battered looking case. He was out of breath. He looked at us and said, 'That was my fucking bag.' The laughter kept going for a good five minutes. What a man.

Now anyone who, even by mistake, was prepared to throw his own bag out of a fifth floor window, was certainly not going to tolerate Nazis outside the school gate. He was livid. Being a history teacher, he was perhaps even more acutely aware than the rest of us of the cultural significance of sieg heiling at a Jewish school. He was ranting at them.

'Fuck off, you Nazi wankers!' he shouted. One didn't hear a teacher swear that often.

They just laughed at him.

'There are black kids doing Nazi salutes,' he said to no one in particular. 'How the fuck can you have black Nazis?' It was a fair question.

'Fuck this,' he said and ran off. He came back a few moments later armed with a cricket bat, opened the gate and ran straight for them.

'Come on lads,' he said. 'Let's give the bastards what for.'

This whole episode had taken a turn I wasn't expecting. I'd been hitting a tennis ball against a wall so I kept hold of my tennis racquet and followed him out. I'm not sure it would've been much use in a fight even though I had a decent forehand. But it didn't matter. The Holloway boys took one look at this wild eyed, cricket bat waving, moustachioed Welshman and ran. It was glorious. They tried once or twice more after that but their hearts weren't in it. I wish he'd done it earlier on. One by-product was that any lessons he took after that were incredibly well behaved.

Not that I attended lessons that much. I just thought that most of what they were teaching me was nonsense. I wasn't interested in glaciers or the function of the pituitary gland.* By the last year at school, I used to take regular afternoons off. I'd walk purposefully along the corridor like I was rushing to get to my first lesson after lunch. And then when everyone was inside their respective classrooms, I'd scarper. The caretaker often saw me leaving but he never tried to stop me. He nodded imperceptibly, giving me a look that suggested that he thought it showed initiative. Although he might have been thinking that with my attitude, I may end up as a school caretaker.

I'd take a desultory wander round the shops of Brecknock Road. There wasn't a lot to see unless you liked hardware stores, bookmakers and takeaways. Some of the more grown-up-looking kids would hide their blazers in their bags and venture into the pub or the betting shop. In the pub, there was always the risk of bumping into one of the teachers who regularly drank in there, even when they had lessons that afternoon. I can't say I blamed them. If I had to teach me, I'd have been drinking as well.

I didn't have many friends at school. I met Simon and Robert when I was around twelve. They were both in another class, in another house, but we hit it off. They were mates and we got chatting one time in the playground. They were both Chelsea fans but I didn't hold it against them. Robert had a nose almost as immense as mine but no one said anything to him about it because he was already over six feet tall. He was taller than everyone in the class and most of the teachers. He was the tallest

---

* Simon told me that in his Biology 'O' level exam, one of the questions was 'Why is the pituitary gland known as the conductor of the orchestra?' And he answered 'Because it looked like Andre Previn.' Still tickles me.

person I'd ever met. I used to go round his house. He lived with his sister and his parents in semi-detached middle class splendour (to me) in the posh part of Hendon. They were all very tall as well. I was impressed. His house had a drive. It had central heating. It was always warm. His mum was very proper but she was sweet with me. She'd make me food and listen indulgently while I chattered away.

Simon was also a couple of inches taller than me, and he was way more confident in his opinions. He was, and still is, one of the funniest mates I've got. It's ever so slightly annoying how quick he is sometimes.

Simon lived in Edgware in a flat with his mum, Carole, and his sister, Jackie. They didn't have much more money than we did but their flat was more comfortable than ours. Carole was glamorous. She laughed at all my jokes and made me food. I loved going round there.

Later on in life, Simon was the first of my mates to have a car. He was also the one who organised most of the things we did together. The only reason we had a football team was because he used to ring round. I don't think we thanked him enough. Every friendship group needs a Simon.

In our final year, Simon and I often decided to forgo the delights of double religious knowledge and some cock-and-bull story about plagues or floods and wander down to the centre of Camden instead. We spent half an hour browsing in the Doctor Martens shop by the station. In a side street, there was a film crew shooting an episode of *Minder*; I was a big fan. Arthur Daley was a truly brilliant character and there was something great about watching a TV show and recognising locations. There was a crowd of twenty or so people watching it happening, most of them pensioners with nothing better to do. Dennis Waterman and George Cole were discussing the forthcoming scene with a guy who I presumed was the director. He was talking animatedly about what he wanted while the crew waited patiently. It was a nice day so no one seemed to mind.

At some point, the director strode purposefully back behind the camera, put on his headphones and said 'quiet please'. A hush descended. He then shouted, 'Action' and the scene began. Ten seconds after it began, an old lady in the crowd said, ''Ere, it's Richard Burton innit?'

On one of our many afternoons off, we were browsing in the record shop and we came upon the *In The City* album. Simon told me I should listen to The Jam. He looked serious and he was very insistent but no matter how enthusiastic someone is, it's hard to convey what a band sounds like without you hearing them. I said I'd check them out, but I guess I never got round to it until John Peel played them on his show. Then the penny dropped.

When Simon wasn't available for midweek post-lunch trips out of school, I would go to the pictures on my own at my local cinema in Hendon Central. One time, I went to see *Eraserhead*. My teenage brain was nowhere near ready for the surreality of David Lynch. At one point, I started laughing at a dead chicken dancing on a stage. The man in front of me tutted loudly presumably because the film was making a serious point I'd failed to grasp. Forty years later, I still don't understand what the fuck that point might have been. I also saw *Capricorn One*, a film about a shadowy government agency that faked the Mars Landings. I was getting a decent education but not in core curriculum subjects. I went to see *Rocky* and ran all the way back home from the cinema shadow boxing. For a moment, I contemplated a career in boxing. I mentioned it to my grandmother. She started laughing and said that my nose was too much of a target. She was right.

There wasn't much I engaged with at school but I liked PE. I never bunked off for that. I was physically capable, no mean achievement in a Jewish school where some of the kids could barely walk ten yards without feeling faint. I was a very fast runner, something that had come in handy when I was trying to escape the attentions of the Holloway boys. I ended up running the one hundred metres for my school house along with a boy called Adrian Grant. Adrian was the most accident prone boy in the school. He had a briefcase that regularly fell open for no reason; once it did so at the top of the staircase and spilled its entire contents five floors down the stairwell. I can still hear his plaintive 'Oh no!' as it happened. In Chemistry, if he was handed a Bunsen burner, we'd all step back a couple of paces. He'd catch his blazer on a door and rip the pocket. If he was using a compass, it would end up in his leg. He once wet himself in class.

We lined up at the start of the race, the gun went and we hared down the track. When I crossed the line, I turned round to see where he'd finished. Adrian and another boy were having a fight halfway down the track and the games teachers were running towards them to break things up. One of Adrian's plimsolls had come off halfway through the race, he'd stumbled and taken down the boy next to him. I wish I'd seen it happen.

I never learnt to swim, though. I was following a long tradition of Jewish non-swimming. There's not a lot of call for swimming ability when you're wandering about in the desert for forty years. Even when we did get to the seaside, we'd only go in when God had parted the waves. My ancestors really didn't like swimming. As a child, the water was not my friend. I had hundreds of swimming lessons but it never took. Sometimes, it was the teachers. Mr Duncan, my angry PE teacher* standing on the side of a pool shouting 'Swim for goodness' sake, swim' was seen as a

---

* Was there any other kind?

viable teaching method. Whereas one can't imagine a driving instructor standing on the pavement shouting at a learner passing by 'Drive for goodness' sake, drive!'

Both my parents and my sister being non-swimmers didn't help. Their abject terror of any water above chest height may have affected my ability to relax in the water. I was OK splashing about in the shallows but anything above my waist and I started getting the shakes. If a tsunami had hit West Hendon, our family almost certainly wouldn't have made it.

All of the above does make it odd that Mr Duncan, for reasons only known to him, chose me to race for Weitzman House in the school swimming gala. I suggested to him that perhaps there might be people who could actually swim who were more suitable for the race. But Mr Duncan, like most PE teachers I've met, was not a listener. So it came to pass that I found myself lining up in the middle lane of the school swimming pool for the twenty-five-metre front crawl. Not only could I not swim, I couldn't dive in either. I was, as you can imagine, terrified.

The whistle went, I shut my eyes, belly flopped into the water and started thrashing my way across the pool. Luckily, we started in the shallow end and every so often, I was able to stop thrashing, stand on the bottom of the pool, take a breath and then push off for another five metres of thrash. But at some point, I knew that I'd be in the deep end and putting my feet down wouldn't be an option. About halfway along, I stopped, felt my tip toes hit the bottom, took a big gulp of air and then resolved to thrash until I touched a wall. Which is what I did. It felt like it took forever but I finally felt the comforting edge of the swimming pool. When I came up for air and looked either side of me, I was a bit puzzled to find that none of the other swimmers appeared to have finished. I thought I'd won. I looked up and there was Mr Duncan.

'What the fuck are you doing you fucking idiot?' he said.

I didn't understand the question.

'Why are you over here you moron?' he asked and it was then that I properly looked around and realised that I'd swum in a semi-circle, across all the other lanes and was on the side of the pool. The only good thing was that I was so slow, the other swimmers were well past me by the time I veered across their lane.

'Sorry sir,' I said. I was just glad to be alive.

I wasn't chosen for the swimming team again. But Mr Duncan had to do something with me, so during the next swimming gala, he got me to help out with the timings. I was much happier on the side of the pool watching Miss Honeyman get the kids lined up for the start. I tried not to stare at her legs too much but it was distracting. So much so that I missed the start of the senior boys one hundred metre front crawl final. I only pressed the stopwatch around halfway into the race. Stephen Franks won the race and Mr Duncan came running over holding his clipboard.

'Time?' he barked.

I knew that Stephen had taken longer than twenty eight seconds to swim one hundred metres. I quickly guessed a time.

'Fifty six seconds'.

Mr Duncan duly noted it down. He looked impressed. He had every right to be so. It was only six seconds outside the world record. Slightly surprising for a fourth former at a comprehensive in Camden.

In 1978, a few years after I joined JFS, The Jam released 'David Watts' on what was then known as a double A-side single with '"A" Bomb in Wardour Street'. Aside from being insanely catchy, I also found it funny. I wasn't what you'd call a star pupil and I was under no illusions that I could've been in any way like David Watts. The school team was unlikely to have me as their captain, I wasn't going to pass all my exams and I had no expectation of being made head boy. I didn't know any of the girls in the neighbourhood and even if I had done, none of them would've been the least bit interested in me.

This was another example of The Jam introducing me to other bands. It wasn't like today, where sophisticated algorithms on Spotify or iTunes will see you listening to one band and suggest that you might fancy listening to something similar. In the 1970s, unless you had older siblings or parents who might take an interest, you had to find out for yourself.

I remember buying this single. It had the coolest cover I'd ever seen with arrows pointing in two different directions. When I took the single out and had a look, I wondered 'Who is Ray Davies?' This led me to The Kinks and 'Waterloo Sunset' and 'Apeman' and a hundred other tunes. In turn, they led me to Small Faces and hearing that keyboard intro on 'Tin Soldier' (Paul's favourite track on *Desert Island Discs*). Because of Paul Weller, I've been listening to that song for forty years. It's very much appreciated.

My parents, focused as they were on their own needs and desires, took very little interest in my schooling. My dad left school at fourteen, my mum at fifteen, so they had very few expectations about what education could achieve. My mother got me up and out of the house in the morning, and after that I was on my own. She'd read my school reports, tut at regular intervals and then hand them back to me without a word. As for my dad, I don't think I had a single conversation with him about school. He went to work before I left and came back after I'd got home so he had absolutely no idea what I was up to all day. I think he knew that I went to school but I could've spent my days BASE jumping off tall buildings and he'd have been none the wiser.

If my children were half an hour late in the mornings, we'd get phone calls from the school secretary asking politely about their whereabouts. After an hour, the calls would be less polite. If they missed a whole morning and we hadn't notified them, the authorities would be involved. Whereas if I didn't turn up to school on a Monday, the chances of my parents hearing about it in the same week were minuscule. I think I could've left school at fifteen and it's possible no one would've noticed. I wish I'd tested the theory.

The only time my mother really got involved in my school life was when I was suspended. It happened twice. The first time, I was involved in a fight with a girl in the fifth form. I was in Year Seven (eleven years old) and I was on the small side. She was fifteen and she was the biggest girl in school. She scared the living daylights out of everyone, including the teachers. I was walking down the corridor one afternoon when I saw her coming towards me carrying a big pile of books. I found this surprising. She didn't strike me as a reader. She dropped one of the books and tried, without success, to pick it up without letting go of the others. I tried to make myself as inconspicuous as possible but she caught my eye.

'Oy. Come here. Hold these,' she said. It wasn't a request.

I took hold of the books. She bent down to pick up the other book and I was confronted with the biggest arse I'd ever seen on a living human. It was too tempting. For reasons I still don't entirely understand, I kicked it very hard and she went sprawling across the corridor. There was a boy standing opposite me and I can still remember the look of utter amazement on his face as he watched what I did. I didn't wait around for her to get up. I just dropped the rest of the books, turned and ran.

She moved remarkably quickly for her size and as I scooted round the school, I could hear her pounding down the corridor behind me.

'You're fucking dead.'

I had no reason to doubt that she meant it. I ran across the playground and into the main building. She seemed to be gaining on me; I could hear her breathing. I ran into the boys' toilets, found a free cubicle and locked the door. I was safe. She wouldn't dare cross the threshold and even if she did, she'd be halted by the Fort Knox type security of my cubicle door. She didn't even hesitate. I heard her crash into the boys bogs and two seconds later she broke down the door and beat me up in front of an amazed crowd of boys who, sensibly, did nothing to help me. I put up very little resistance. I just curled up into a ball and waited for it to end. A male teacher appeared shortly afterwards and dragged her off me. We both got suspended for a week for fighting and she got an extra day for breaking the cubicle door. We got on quite well after that. I don't think she could quite believe what I'd done. She thought it was ballsy.

I was always talkative. I enjoyed getting laughs. As an adult, I've built a career on this nonsense but at the time, it got me into serious trouble. I insulted our Hebrew teacher Miss Felberg by loudly proclaiming, when I thought she was out of the room, that learning Hebrew was a complete and utter waste of time. She was in the store cupboard, and came out raging, looking directly at me.

'Did *you* say that?'

Even in my first year, I had something of a reputation. I saw no point in denying it. 'Yeah'.

'Why do you think it's a waste of time?' she asked.

'Because it is,' I said, not giving her much to work with.

'I think you should apologise to me and also to the rest of the class who are all interested,' she said.

I got up and stood at the front of the class. I looked around. I knew for a fact that no one was any more interested than me.

'I'm sorry . . .' I said. A long pause. '. . . that you have to learn Hebrew.'

There was a big laugh from the class. It felt good. Miss Felberg, however, was not laughing and threw a blackboard rubber at me. It swooshed past my head and clattered into the wall behind me. I was watching a lot of cricket at the time and I thought that she had a decent throwing arm. I decided that if it ever came to it, I would not risk a quick single if she was fielding.

'Come with me,' she said 'We're going to see Mrs Abrahams.'

This was not what I was hoping for. Mrs Abrahams had a fearsome reputation. She believed in discipline and God. I had no interest in the first one and I was rapidly losing faith in the second. I was well aware of her temper. I was used to adults shouting, but usually it was at each other. I wasn't looking forward to having her considerable ire directed at me.

We went to her office. Miss Felberg told me to sit down while she informed the secretary what I'd said. The secretary didn't laugh, which made me think that Miss Felberg had told the joke wrong. The secretary took Miss Felberg into Mrs Abrahams' office, and I heard them having a short chat. Miss Felberg emerged and then harrumphed off without giving me a second glance. I waited.

Time passed. I looked around, tried to think about other things. At one point, I started whistling. The secretary stared at me and I stopped. I waited some more. After a time, Mrs Abrahams popped her head out of the door and indicated that I should go in. She was dressed immaculately. She was attractive but in the way that made it perfectly clear that any thoughts in that direction were to be redirected elsewhere. Aside from her face and hands, there wasn't an inch of flesh on display. Her clothes were beautifully made and her hair was perfect. She was shouting as I came in.

'This is a Jewish school'.

She pointed at the mezuzzah (a small scroll attached to doors in Jewish homes and places of work; the person passing through the door is meant to touch it and kiss their hand as a show of devotion to God) on the door. Just in case the fact that the school was called The Jewish Free School and all the men had to have their heads covered and we spent thousands of hours being taught Hebrew and Old Testament religious knowledge were not enough in the way of clues.

'We teach things that will make you better able to contribute to the Jewish community. And one of those things is being able to speak Ivrit [the Hebrew word for Hebrew]. Do you understand?'

I didn't get a chance to answer either way.

'A waste of time?' Her voice got louder. 'Why would you say such a thing to Miss Felberg? How could you say that learning Ivrit is a waste of time? Who are you to decide what is and isn't a waste of time? That is an insult to the other pupils, to the teacher, to me, to the school.' She paused. 'To Israel.'

I suppressed a laugh. I was imagining people in Tel Aviv phoning each other:

'Did you hear what Ian Stone said?'

'No.'

'He said that learning Hebrew is a waste of time.'

'What? The little prick!'

She moved round the desk and came up very close to me. It was like the scene in *Alien* where the monster gets really close to Sigourney Weaver. Apparently, I hadn't completely suppressed the laugh.

'Why are you laughing?'

'I'm not laughing' I said, while sort of laughing.

She was really shouting now.

'Your gross disrespect for our teacher and the language is disgusting'.

'Christ. Keep your hair on,' I said.

★

Later on, when I relayed the conversation to Simon, he started laughing and continued for about a minute and a half.

'You fucking idiot,' he said. 'She was wearing a sheitel.'

'A what?'

'A wig. Religious Jewish women shave their heads and wear a wig.'

'What? Why? How do you know this?'

'My mum told me. A man is not to look upon a woman's hair. It says it in the Torah.'

'Where?'

'I don't know. In the hair section.'

'I don't understand. Why can't they look at a woman's hair?'

'Because it will drive them wild with desire.'

'Hair?'

'Yeah.'

'Fuck off.'

'I'm telling you. She must've hit the roof.'

We were both laughing now. 'She did.'

That was one of the few days at school where I actually learned something. At the time, in Mrs Abrahams' office, I didn't understand any of this. All I could see was her going bright red. I'd never seen anyone go that red. She looked like she wanted to hit me but by the mid-1970s, that sort of schooling was being slowly phased out so she just glared at me for a short time and then took me to see the headmaster.

We trooped over to his office and when he was told, he was, if anything, more apoplectic than her. He ranted for a while and I stopped listening. He was almost always ranting about something, generally to do with not wearing our skull caps. I concentrated on his dandruff. He favoured a black suit with a black cape, so it was always noticeable, but it seemed particularly bad today. As he spoke, I could see it falling off his head like a moderately heavy snow shower. Like it might settle. It piled up on top of the dandruff already there. His shoulders looked like a ski resort. He told me to go home and he would speak to my mother in due course.

And so it was that I had a week off school. It was incredibly boring. Today, with all the different TV channels and Xboxes and the like, I could've kept myself busy. Back then, there was nothing to do. One of the only things stopping us bunking off more than we did was the almost complete lack of entertainment available at home during work hours.

I watched *Pebble Mill at One*. This was a magazine show broadcast at, would you believe, one o'clock in the afternoon. It was broadcast live from Birmingham during the week and was very popular with students, the elderly, the bedridden and people who were snowed in. The audience was entirely made up of old people. The women all had white hair, most of the men were bald.*

---

* Twenty-five years later as a fledgling stand-up comedian, I was offered a slot on the show. Because it was live, daytime TV, the producers required a full script of the act you were going to do so as not to offend the delicate sensibilities of the daytime crowd pottering about at home. I faxed (!) the script over and an assistant called me straight back.

'You can't say arse.'

'Can I not?' I had a joke where the punchline was 'right on the arse' and I was hoping I could get away with it. Apparently not.

'No.'

'Oh. How about bum?'

'Hang on a minute.'

He put the phone down on the desk and I hear a muffled shout across the office. 'Can he say bum?' There's a pause. I don't hear the reply. The assistant comes back on the line.

'Bum is out.'

'Oh. Bottom?'

'Hang on.' We go round the same routine again.

My mother was really upset with me because she had to take a week off work. I didn't take a lot of looking after but without her, I wouldn't have eaten. She made me food, knocked on my bedroom door to tell me it was ready and told me to turn the music down. It was like having the angriest room service ever.

The following Monday, she had to come in and sit with me in the head's office while he laid into me again for what felt like a week. He was shouting and spitting. One small bit of spittle landed on my mother's bag. All three of us saw it happen but no one said anything. As we were leaving, he made it very clear that if I ever said anything else grossly insulting to the Jewish faith, I'd be expelled. Did I understand? I did. I almost said something grossly insulting there and then, just to get it over with.

'We'd rather you didn't.'

'Bottom? Really?' And I want to say, 'Who's watching this show? Nuns?' but I refrain.

The assistant has an idea. 'You couldn't say rear end could you?'

'Rear end?'

'Yeah, rear end.'

I think about it. The punchline 'right on the rear end' does have a certain alliterative quality.

'Alright then.'

I imagine a rubber stamp bashing down on the script. Approved!

A first class return ticket to Birmingham arrived on my doorstep and I travelled up on the day. The audience was not really my target demographic. 'Right on the rear end' was met with complete indifference as was everything else I said. It was the worst death I've ever had on or off TV. The old people stared at me for my allotted five minutes and the only solace I can find is that they're all long dead by now. When it was over, the presenter said 'one more time for Ian Stone' and got absolutely nothing from them. I still think 'Arse' would have got a laugh.

Things We Didn't Have in the 1970s

Part Three

Part Three: Male Grooming

Take a walk around the average chemist in 2020. There's usually a section devoted to male grooming, often an entire aisle. Hundreds of different types of shaving cream, shaving oil, aftershave, forty-eight-hour deodorants (presumably for those men who have only got time to wash every other day), moisturisers, four- and five-blade razors with swivel heads, nose and ear hair trimmers and hundreds of 'Just for Men' shampoos, conditioners and shower gels. Back in the 1970s, because men were expected to be 'men', they didn't groom. Men bathed once a week. The rest of the time, they shaved, threw some aftershave on and put Brylcreem in their hair. That was it for male grooming. Cats did more grooming than men.

Chapter Four
True Inseparables

Paul Weller wrote 'I Got By in Time' in his early twenties. I have no idea how he knew all this stuff at such a young age. From my teenage perspective, he seemed to have lived an entire lifetime. There was such beauty in the idea of not recognising a girl that he used to know because he was looking at his own face. The irony being that it would've completely passed me by because I was too busy looking at my own face to see if my nose looked smaller from ANY angle (I positioned mirrors in the bathroom so I could get a 360 degree view – it didn't). I certainly didn't spend a lot of time deep in thought, being much more like my dad than I cared to admit. Thinking deeply wasn't a Stone family character trait.

I never tire of listening to this song. Going out with girls, falling in love, thinking that she was my world and that I'd never live without her but getting by in time. I know all this now but it was a revelation at fourteen. This sounded exactly like the sort of stuff that adults would be doing, although not the adults I knew. My parents were not ones for letting time heal their wounds. If anything, they were getting angrier. Even if I had somehow managed to persuade a girl to go out with me, I don't think I'd have introduced her to my mum and dad. And even if I had, I wouldn't have asked for their approval. They were hardly people to look up to in the matter of relationship advice. It didn't matter anyway; it would be another couple of years before I would get anywhere near a girl. As I discovered, desperation is not an attractive trait in a potential partner.

'What do you want in a man?'

'I want a cripplingly lonely man child who looks like he's never had sex before.'

'I've got just the boy for you.'

As for friendships, Paul's observations were just as acute. The idea of running into a guy that he used to know and how it seemed to hurt him to say hello, I absolutely adored that. I still do. To me, and I imagine the other young boys and girls hanging on Paul's words, this sounded like wisdom way beyond his tender years. I know people develop at different speeds and at different times in their lives. Paul seemed a very old twenty. I was a very young fourteen year old.

I always felt I had so much to learn. Just over a year before this song came out, I'd had my Bar Mitzvah, the Jewish coming of age ceremony. These coming of age rituals are very common across the world, but they vary from place to place. In some countries, they happen when the boy is a bit older and involve more physical tests. There may be some courage required, some display of fortitude. Luckily, rather than wrestle a wolf, I just had to read some Hebrew in front of the congregation in the synagogue. It's harder than you think, particularly if you don't speak a word of Hebrew.

Ostensibly, once I'd done that, I'd made the leap into manhood. But I only had to take a look at myself in the mirror, a slightly podgy boy with bum fluff, squished into a brown velvet suit, to realise that this was not in fact the case. In truth, I was still light years away from manhood. Sometimes, I think I still am.

Boys struggle with this stuff more than girls. It may be a gross generalisation but girls seem to manage growing up better than boys, mainly it seems because they communicate with each other about how they feel. From primary school onwards, they're chatting away. The process may be drawn out but it's ongoing.

Whereas with boys, we might talk about football or sex or music or football, but we never talk about the sort of things that Paul Weller sang about. Simon and I may have listened to a song like 'I Got By in Time' on a loop, but we never talked about what it meant. It's only now I see that Paul's writing helped me and a lot of other young men grow up. It helped us understand ourselves better. For boys particularly, having a strong male role model who isn't the same age as your dad can make all the difference. Showing us how we might fit in, how we might be useful. I think that was a big part of the appeal for me. It felt like having a cooler, older brother to look up to.

When Paul sang that he supposed that none of it means anything, I loved that 'I suppose'. So conversational and so grown up. Young people rarely suppose anything. They (think they) *know* stuff. Even back then, I knew that the friendships I made as a child may not last. It had already happened to me. As a kid, you're still growing up, still developing and finding your way. You move from primary to secondary school, make new friends. Sex becomes a factor (although not in my case). Any number of things can get in the way.

But as an adult, I always imagine that the friendships I make will be for life and I still find it disappointing when I realise that I no longer have the need to see certain people. Although not as disappointing as when I realise that people no longer seem to have the need to see me. I don't deal well with situations like that. I didn't then and I'm still not much better at it now, age fifty-seven. I'm getting there but it's a slow process. I'm hoping that just before I die, I'll have a fleeting moment when I think 'I can live with this'.

I know that things change. Even though I didn't fully understand the implications, I knew when I first heard this song. Through my life, I've gradually lost touch with so many people that I thought I'd know until either they died or I did. People that I got monumentally stoned with. People I spent Christmas and New Year with. People I shared flats with. People who helped celebrate my thirtieth birthday and who were no longer around for my fortieth. People whose weddings I went to. But as the man said, that's the way that it goes.

Things We Didn't Have in the 1970s

Part Four

Fashion Sense

The 1970s has been described as the decade that fashion forgot. But who could possibly forget multi-coloured tank tops? Or gold lamé hot pants. Or flares. Flares had high waists with loads of buttons and enormous bell bottoms that quite often dragged along the floor. Colours were loud and garish. Yellows and oranges and pinks and purples. The patterns were psychedelic. I'm amazed that people left the house, although there were often power cuts, so at least they could still be seen in the dark. Aside from the Milk Tray Man in the advert, no one wore black (The Milk Tray Man was a man dressed all in black who used to break in to women's bedrooms late at night and leave a box of chocolates on the bedside table; not creepy at all). If you see pictures of Elton John in the 1970s, the reason he looked so outlandish is because he was trying to outdo what everyone else was wearing on a daily basis.

Chapter Five

Reality's so hard

The campaign to go and see a Jam gig live continued throughout 1977 without success. I bitched and moaned to my mother but she wasn't having it. To punish her for not letting me get my way, I behaved so badly and had so many tantrums that I almost certainly proved her point about being too young. I wasn't rebellious enough to disobey her and just go anyway. I preferred to stay in and be moody. I was feeling very sorry for myself and I must have been horrible to be with. When I wasn't glowering at her or monosyllabically grunting in her general direction I retreated to my room, turned up the first album to maximum volume and played the songs over and over again just to annoy her. She must have known them almost as well as I did. I figured I might wear her down. I suppose I did in the end.

Music for me back then was about getting a quick fix of energy, a three-minute hit of adrenalin that would temporarily distract me from the humdrum reality of life. There were songs on *In The City* about love and dancing and being young; they always hit the spot. I loved the finality of 'I've Changed my Address' and Rick's drumming on the *Batman* theme. I bopped about to 'Art School'. The whole thing felt so alive.

51

But the title track was a new experience for me. Later on in life I heard Elvis Costello and Bob Dylan and Billy Bragg singing political songs, but at fourteen hearing a song which talked about social change turned on a light in my head. I knew that Paul was political and I'm sure a lot of working-class kids got their first insight into politics listening to this album.

The lyrics on 'Away from the Numbers' explored the idea of breaking away and taking control and freeing your mind and soul. I was well up for that but how I was going to make that happen, I had not the first clue. I had a terrible haircut, a big nose, no independent financial means and very little in the way of social skills. Who was going to let me break away and have control of anything?

Paul seemed to have such fierce individualism; I had nowhere near that level of conviction in anything. I wouldn't go as far as to say that I was an idiot, but I had very few in the way of independent thoughts. My world revolved around needs or emotions. Hungry, angry, miserable, tired, that sort of thing. Other than that, I had vague notions and ideas which, with careful nurturing, might have turned into solid opinions, but they were subject to change at the merest hint of argument on the part of someone who knew better. Or even someone who didn't. It would've been comforting to know that everyone I hung out with was feeling much the same way that I did.

I realise now that becoming a fan of Paul Weller and The Jam was my first real attempt to try and define myself. To consciously distance myself from my parents. To say, 'This is who I am and this is what I believe in.' The fact that all I really believed in was what Paul Weller told me to believe in was neither here nor there. Before The Jam, I tagged along with this and that group or fad but aside from Arsenal, nothing really captured my imagination. Now I had something to hold on to. Something that my parents couldn't understand and actively disliked. Something that wasn't nice. I knew as soon as I heard the first album that it was what I'd been waiting for. Someone not much older than me who seemed to have got their act together. There was hope after all.

But only after I got out of the house. Home was chaotic at best and toxic at worst. I was living with my parents Ken and Helena, and my sister Beverley. My parents hated each other and stayed out of each other's way whenever possible. Beverley was six-and-a-half years younger than me. Being a teenage boy, I had very little in common with her. My mum stayed in the bedroom, my father in the lounge, Beverley in her room and me in mine. We were four strangers living in the same house. (I read recently that Paul Weller had a sister and there was a similar age gap and he didn't have much to do with her. I felt a little frisson of kinship when I heard that.)

I kept away as much as I could. I even stayed later at school just so I wouldn't have to go home. I tried to get detentions so I could have an extra hour away.

'I think that's enough, Stone'.

'We haven't done the full hour, Sir'.

My mother can be a funny woman although this became less apparent the more time she spent with Ken. She once went into a shop that sold nuts and asked them if the raisin shop was nearby. She had a nice line in sarcasm. As the marriage deteriorated, we saw less of this side of her.

I understand why my mother got married. She came from a religious family, so it was expected she'd get hitched as soon as possible. She said she was frightened of being left on the shelf although, as she was nineteen-years-old, she may have had a few more years before she withered away. She said that she was concerned that being the last of her siblings to get married, she may well be left with the task of looking after her elderly parents. These are all perfectly valid reasons to get married. Just not to my father.

Ken was born a baby, graduated to early childhood and decided that, emotionally, that was far enough. His thinking was along the lines of 'I have control of my bowels, what else does one need?' He was assisted in this first of all by my grandmother Cissie who indulged his every whim and thought the sun shined out of his arse. Although it's difficult to know how she could tell seeing as he never got off it. And then by my mother, who was too fearful of being alone to tell him to grow up and maybe help around the house once in a blue moon. With their assistance (and one or two other female members of the Stone family), he's managed to go through his entire life without ever doing anything that he didn't want to do. He's never cooked a meal, never cleaned up, never done any DIY. He changed one nappy and he still talks about it to this day. 'Your sister's done a packet,' he regularly says (often at dinner when Beverley is sitting at the table), referring to an occasion almost fifty years ago when my sister had filled a nappy. 'An absolute packet,' he'd stress just so we knew how much shit he'd actually had to deal with. My mother had, for the only time in Beverley's early childhood, left Ken with the responsibility of looking after her and it traumatised him for life. He's eighty-seven this year and is the singularly most useless adult I've ever known. Beverley described him as a great dad and a terrible father and husband. Everyone else thinks he's a legend. They never had to live with him, or needed him to do anything for them.

My parents got married in November 1958 and went to Bournemouth for their honeymoon. On the Friday night, my dad turned to my mum. 'I've got something for you,' he said. 'It's a surprise.' I guess any newly married bride would like to hear a sentence like that from their husband. She may have imagined new clothes or perhaps even tickets to a big show. What she almost certainly did not imagine was that on the Saturday afternoon, my father, as a surprise that, let's face it, would endear him to any woman, produced two tickets for Bournemouth versus Brentford at Dean Court in the English fourth division. I imagine it was a pretty big surprise. According to historical weather data, it was a very cold but mercifully dry day. I'd like to think that as they were on honeymoon, my dad splashed out on a couple of seats, but it's perfectly possible that three days after she got married, my mother found herself standing on an open terrace in the freezing cold watching two teams she'd never heard of playing a game she hated. And that may well have been the high point of the relationship.

My mother is no angel. She has been known to be demanding. But only by people who've met her. Being demanding is a fairly typical* character trait when it comes to Jewish mothers and it's accepted in lieu of other more positive attributes. But it's not useful when you're married to a man as inured and impervious to demands as my father. My mother demanded, my father completely ignored her. There were a lot of arguments and very few laughs.

My mum felt trapped. By 1977, she was smoking way more than she used to and possibly drinking as well. I knew things weren't going well in the marriage. One only had to listen to the way my parents spoke to each other to realise that any love they may have felt for each other had long gone. Living with my father cannot have been easy. My mum was working a full time job and doing *all* the household chores whilst her partner got in from work, sat down on his arse, and demanded dinner. This might have caused some simmering feelings of resentment.

My mother started talking about divorce. The volume and frequency of the arguments had increased and it felt, to her at least, like the only way forward. My dad was having none of it. Aside from being regularly screamed at, he was living a cushy life. He

---

* Universal

would sit in his chair reading the paper while my mum cleaned around him. At dinner time, she'd bring his meals to him. He never offered to help, never thanked her, never even looked at her.

He used to nervously pull his lip. I don't know what he had to be nervous about. Possibly the fact that one evening, my mum would down tools, never cook for him again and he'd slowly starve to death. My mother hated him pulling his lip. She started to fixate on it.

'Don't pull your lip,' she'd scream at him. He'd stop pulling his lip for a short while and then do it again. She'd leave the table in disgust.

By the end, they weren't communicating at all. My mum would see him in his favourite chair and call him.

'Oy.'

He wouldn't respond.

'Oy,' she'd say again, only louder.

He'd look up.

'I need you over here.'

'I'm doing something,' he'd say. He wasn't doing anything. He was reading the paper.

'But I need you over here.'

He'd reluctantly move his backside and come over.

'What is it?' he'd say

'Fuck off!'

He looked like he was going to hit her. 'No, you fuck off!'

He'd go back to his chair and she'd laugh bitterly.

That was how they spoke to each other most of the time. As far back as I could recall, I'd never heard them use each other's first names. I was at a family party when I was eighteen and someone called my mother from across the room.

'Helena.'

I remember thinking, 'Oh yes, that's right . . . it's Helena.'

★

In the end it all got too much at home and my mother took an overdose of tablets and tried to commit suicide. I knew my mum was taking tablets 'for her nerves'. Everything got 'on them'. My father obviously. My grandmother when she took his side (so, every time). Me when I argued with her, or when I played The Jam too loudly. She was forever popping pills. I just thought that's what adults did. I guess she just cracked one afternoon. I was in my room listening to music when I heard a commotion in the hall. I came out and saw a blue light flashing outside. Two men emerged from my mother's room guiding a bed on wheels through the front door. My mother was on the bed. She was out cold. One of the men saw me as he went past and gave me a look of pity. I can still see it now.

Nowadays, if a trauma like that befell a family, one would hope that a wide range of health care professionals would get involved. Social workers and mental health practitioners and perhaps drug dependency counsellors would swing into action and provide all manner of assistance and support. Back then, while my mum may well have got some help at the hospital she was taken to, no one said anything to me. I probably could've used a chat about the whole episode but I didn't know how to bring it up or even whether I should. My dad never mentioned it and I went back to school the next morning.

It was thought best that I should go and live with my Aunt Irene in Redbridge in Essex for a couple of weeks. I certainly wasn't capable of looking after myself and if it had been left to my dad to feed me, I'd have starved to death. I'm not sure who was looking after Beverley but I think she was shipped off somewhere as well. I have no idea who looked after my father. He was less capable of looking after himself than my sister and she was only seven.

My aunt Irene also never talked about what had happened. The adults in my family seemed to think that my mother's attempted suicide was best dealt with by not acknowledging it at all. In truth, I didn't mind being in Irene's house. It was very neat and tidy and it smelt clean. There was a baby grand piano in the lounge and a lot of books. Irene was married to a gentle and very sweet Canadian guy called Alvin. He told me jokes to try and cheer me up. They might have been funny in Canada. My cousins, David and Barry, were a little older than me but I got on with both of them. It was an OK place to hang out for a few weeks. No one was shouting at anyone else and the food was great. My aunt made amazing chicken soup. She kept asking me if I was fine. I was fine. I liked chicken soup. The journey to school took a bit longer but I didn't care. I'd have been happy to move in indefinitely but at some point, adults decided that it was time for me to go back to West Hendon.

Home was a more subdued place when I got back. No one spoke about what my mother had tried to do but there was a little less shouting and screaming, at least for a few months. I now realise that my mother was monumentally stoned on anti-depressants. I also now realise that I could've used a few myself.

Things didn't improve. The arguments slowly got going again. My dad was incredibly angry that my mother had tried to kill herself. Mainly, he was angry with the fact that for once, he wasn't the centre of attention. This changed soon after. At the time, he was working at the Post Office sorting depot at Mount Pleasant in King's Cross. One afternoon, he didn't fancy going back in after lunch. Most people would've gone to their boss, told them they were sick and taken the rest of the day off. My father went to a phone box and, in a Northern Irish accent which to this day he point blank refuses to do in front of me no matter how much I beg, called in a bomb threat. This was in the days when phoned-in bomb threats were the IRA's preferred method of warning the public. They had to be taken seriously, even if, as in this case, the supposed IRA bombers accent was the most suspect thing about him. Thirty thousand workers spilled onto the street and a major search took place. Nothing was found of course. I guess it's difficult to locate a dodgy looking parcel in a sorting office. My dad got the afternoon off.

The first we knew about all this was late one night when my mum and I were sitting at home watching the film *Gyspy* on TV. We were starting to wonder where my dad had got to when there was a knock at the front door.

I was despatched. 'Could you see who that is, luv?'

Standing in the doorway, filling it really, was a massive policeman. I thought about the poster in my room.

'Is your mother in, son?' he asked.

'Yeah. What's going on? Is it my dad?'

'Just get your mother,' he said.

The way he said it, I honestly thought my dad was dead. The policeman must have seen something on my face.

'He's fine, son. Just get your mother'.

I went to get my mum and she went to the front door. I heard snatches of the conversation.

'He's what?' and 'For fuck's sake.'

Two minutes later, she came back into the living room.

'Your father's been arrested,' said my Mother. This was one of the more surprising moments of my life. Ken was a difficult man, and for my mother a nightmare to live with, but I'd never envisaged him as a criminal. He was a child trapped in a man's body.

'What for?'

'Terrorism offences,' said my mother and I couldn't have been more astonished if she'd said that he'd be trying to foment a revolution in Latin America. Che Kenneth. I went to ask for more details but my mother held up her hand as if to say, 'I can't talk about it anymore'. There wasn't much we could do at that point so we watched the rest of the film.*

Over the years, I tried to speak to him about it but he always changed the subject. Even to someone as preternaturally immune to shame as my father, this episode was a bit embarrassing. But as time has passed and it's been established that this was a minor blip in an otherwise crime-free life, he's been more willing to open up.

'You were really unlucky to get caught the first time you did it,' I said to him recently.

'Oh no, it wasn't the first time,' he said laughing. 'I did it ten or twelve times. And I wasn't the only one.' (To this day, I'm not sure if he was joking). No wonder Britain was struggling in the late 1970s. The threat of terrorism was real enough without idiots phoning in non-existent bomb scares just to get the afternoon off. If you had trouble receiving your post around that time, this may have been a factor. In fact, I think it's fair to say that my father and his workshy mates were a small part of the reason why Margaret Thatcher got elected. I can only apologise.

He told me that he had a bomb threat routine. I guess when you do something as often as my dad phoned in bomb threats, it becomes routine. He'd work in the morning in his normal fashion. At least as normally as anyone who was planning an act of terrorism can do. He'd then go off for his lunch, find a phone box, phone the office and say there was a bomb planted somewhere in the building and they had fifteen minutes to get out. I asked him why he did it.

'I wanted to spend more time with your mother and sister,' he said.

---

* I went to see a West End revival of *Gypsy*. They sang 'You've gotta have a gimmick' and I was instantly transported back to that night.

I seriously doubted this. Beverley was at school and even if he did want to spend more time with my mother, she certainly didn't want to spend any more time with him.

'Did you go home then?' I asked him.

'Sometimes,' he said. 'But on a Friday, I'd go to the pub. They had strippers on.'

This was news to me. Up to this point, I never knew that my mum and sister were stripping. I mentioned this to him. He didn't laugh.

'I was under a lot of pressure,' he said.

He told me that he got caught because the Post Office, annoyed at the disruption and cost of thirty-thousand people spilling onto the streets twice a week while they looked for non-existent suspect packages, decided to act. They suspected that it might be employees trying to skive off work, so they posted lookouts around the local phone boxes, and put two and two together. He was nabbed after one phone call, marched back to the office and arrested. He confessed without much of a struggle.

'I was sacked on the spot as well,' he said sounding somewhat surprised.

While he was on bail, the atmosphere at home got even worse. He didn't have a job so he was contributing basically nothing to the household. My mum couldn't even look at him. He went up in court a couple of months later and, with the help of my auntie Irene acting as a character witness, somehow got away with a suspended sentence. I think my mum was disappointed he wasn't sentenced to death by firing squad.

Things We Didn't Have in the 1970s

Part Five

Reality TV

I'm glad about this one. With all the reality I was getting at home, I didn't need any more on my TV screen. There were one or two shows that did actually feature real people. The *Up* series, which followed school kids through their lives at seven year intervals, could be classed as reality television but it was really more of an anthropological study. What we didn't have was beautiful but talentless wannabees cluttering up our TV screens on *Love Island* and *Big Brother*. Sometimes, it really was better in the old days.

Chapter Six

You can smell the fear and hate, generated by all around

The line 'you can smell the fear and hate, generated by all around' is from 'The Combine', an album track from *This is The Modern World*. It's nowhere near my favourite song, not even the best song on an album that The Jam themselves said was rushed out. But it stayed with me. It was an idea that Paul revisited with '"A" Bomb in Wardour Street', where 'fear and hate lingered in the air'.

Whatever fear and hate it was that Paul was sensing, a lot of us sensed it too. It's hard to comprehend from our oasis of liberality (Donald Trump and Brexit notwithstanding) in the third decade of the PC twenty-first century but racism was *very* popular in the 1970s. The Irish were 'Paddies' or 'Micks' and were considered fair game for jokes about their perceived stupidity. The Chinese were 'Chinkys' (as in, 'Do you fancy a Chinky takeaway tonight?'), people who came from any of the countries on the Indian sub-continent were 'Pakis', black people were 'coloureds' or 'sambos' or 'wogs' or 'coons' or 'darkies'. A black friend of mine told me that when he was ten years old, he was walking down Fulham Broadway and a taxi driver slowed down to tell him he was a black bastard. When he was ten! People would often claim that some of their best friends were black and that they weren't 'a racialist'. They generally were.*

Mainstream TV did not help. It was only up until the year before that BBC1 had broadcast *The Black and White Minstrel Show* on Saturday nights. A white male voice choir would black up and be wheeled out to sing the hits of the day. This was what passed for entertainment; over ten million people used to watch it. Not that there was a lot of choice.

'What's on telly?'

'There's a quiz on ITV or there's a racist singalong on BBC1.'

'I hate quizzes. Let's go for the singalong.'

Meanwhile, a sitcom called *Love Thy Neighbour* featured a white man expressing surprise that he was having difficulty getting on with his new black neighbour. The fact that he regularly referred to him as a 'nig-nog' may have had something to do with their strained relationship. It's amazing they haven't brought that back.

I was at football most weeks and that was a particular breeding ground for all sorts of abhorrent views. The National Front used to sell their newspaper outside Chelsea and there were plenty of willing buyers. Certain clubs would not pick black players

---

* Sometimes though, it's difficult to tell. Years later, I went with Rosie, my missus, to a local fish shop. The guy who worked there was a cockney geezer. I used to get more cockney when I spoke to him.

'Alright mate, how's it going?'

'Not bad mate. Cor blimey, guvnor.'

That sort of nonsense. Rosie would give me a look and whisper in my ear, 'Why are you talking like that?'

I'd whisper back, 'I'm just trying to fit in and get cheaper fish.' It was the method I adopted with car mechanics, people who came to fix things in the house and most of the shopkeepers in the local area.

The fishmonger wanted to talk about Arsenal.

'I like your team,' he said.

'Yeah, they're playing well at the moment.'

although at West Bromwich Albion, their larger than life manager 'Big' Ron Atkinson played Laurie Cunningham, Cyrille Regis and Brendon Batson in the same team. He dubbed them The Three Degrees and got the actual Three Degrees to pose for a picture with them. It was casual racism, meant affectionately. Ron later got exposed as a less casual racist when, in 2004, long after these attitudes were meant to be a thing of the past and thinking that the microphones were switched off, said that the French footballer Marcel Desailly was 'A fucking lazy thick nigger', possibly the worst sentence I've ever heard.

It was thought that black players could only play well in nice weather. Also, black players would never be picked to play in areas of the pitch requiring a more cerebral approach. There were no black central midfield players. Black men were chosen purely for their physical attributes of speed and strength. Although apparently, they were unable to display those attributes if the temperature dropped below a certain point. It was only late in 1978 that Viv Anderson became the first black player to play for England. For a time, Everton only had white players and during a Merseyside derby, Everton fans shouted 'Niggerpool' and 'Everton are White'.

He continued to fillet the fish I'd asked for. 'Yeah. That darkie up the front is a good player.'

I felt Rosie stiffen beside me. We bought the fish and left. When we got outside of the shop, she turned to me.

'I never want to use that fish shop ever again,' she said.

'I understand,' I said. 'That was an appalling and horrible thing to say.' I paused. 'But the fish is lovely.'

We then got into a discussion about how racist he would have to be before we'd stop buying his fish.

I went in there the week after. The fishmonger was serving. There was a black man also working there. They were cracking on together and were obviously mates. I was confused.

Inside the grounds, there were people shouting the most awful abuse and no one lifted a finger to stop it. The stewards were terrified of them and felt that it wasn't their job to stop racists shouting abuse. Mainly because it was so normal that even if they did, it would just start up again somewhere else. And also because some of them would've wanted to join in. The added disincentive, for the stewards and also those of us who felt sick hearing monkey noises and might have asked them to stop, was that the people shouting this abuse were enormous violent thugs who would think nothing of thumping anyone who did. I've found that liberals are rarely built for physical confrontation. We just had to put up with sitting near white men making monkey noises at black men as they ran past. The irony of them accusing black men of being like monkeys while actually behaving like animals from further down the evolutionary scale was lost on the thugs. Fathers, sat next to their sons, would racially abuse players. Prejudice was being passed from generation to generation. Wingers got it the worst. Playing down the centre of the pitch, I'm told that one could almost imagine it wasn't happening. But people who played most of their game on the touchline were under no illusion. Taking a throw in or corner would result in fearsome abuse. It was grim.

Then there was the fruit. One racist wag thought it would be funny to throw bananas at the black men; it started happening all over the country. Even within this horror, there were rules. Black players who played for the home team would be cheered at the same time that bananas would be thrown at the black men playing for the opposition. It was bizzare. It must've been great for greengrocers. One of the gang must've been charged with paying a visit to their local shop on the way to the game. Sales of bananas must have rocketed.

This abuse wasn't confined solely to black players. Tottenham had a large Jewish following – Arsenal fans used to sing songs about gassing Jews and how Spurs were on their way to Auschwitz. It was awful. I fucking hated that fans of my club would sing songs like that. I knew that people didn't like Jews. I could see it every lunchtime in the playground at school. There was also the odd comment about being tight that I overheard as I walked to synagogue when I was younger. And my grandparents made sure to remind me not to trust 'the goyim' (slang term for non-Jews).

I saw this prejudice up close one weekend. I'd got a Sunday morning job with my friend Robert, working for two Jewish brothers called Maurice and Leo Greenberg in their shop on Petticoat Lane, East London. The late 1970s was the tail end of the Jewish schmutter trade in the East End (schmutter – Yiddish slang for cheap clothes) and one could get all sorts of keenly priced gear. There was a shop called Goldrange that sold sheepskin and leather jackets and coats from their discount centre in, as the advert said, the big red building in Petticoat Lane. According to Paolo Hewitt's *The Jam: A Beat Concerto*, Paul Weller bought his first Crombie coat up there.

The shop used to sell Marks & Spencer clothes that had a small fault and had been rejected. There were cotton/polyester trousers for seven pounds a pair. They came in either beige or brown. Personally, I would've rejected them for that reason alone. We sold shirts for a fiver. There were also Safari suits for twenty quid. I thought they were only worn by Roger Moore in James Bond movies, but they turned out to be very popular with the large number of Nigerians who came to the shop. I remember wondering whether they actually used them on safaris. I didn't know exactly what happened on a safari but I figured the large number of pockets would perhaps come into their own. I tried one on once but I looked ridiculous.

There were also five or six rails of clothes out front. This area was looked after by an old Jewish guy called Jack. He'd stand out front shouting 'Come and have a look inside' to try and entice people into the shop. It rarely worked, possibly because he used to put his hand down his trousers and adjust himself on almost a minute-by-minute basis.

'Quiet day,' he'd say, not realising that an old man constantly feeling himself up was hardly encouraging for passing trade. I never wanted to know what was going on down there, but he'd let me know anyway.

'Oh, they've gone again,' he'd say before stuffing his hand down his trousers and hauling his bollocks back up to where there were meant to sit. I never understood this when I was fifteen, but I do now.

There was also a small workroom upstairs where they did wig fitting. Robert and I were never allowed up there but it wasn't difficult to spot the men wearing them. For one thing, there's always something odd about a man who turns up bald and an hour later leaves with a full head of hair. That tends to be a bit of a giveaway. There was also something very wig-like about the wigs. They were made from real human hair but they just looked wrong. The men all looked like they had seventy-year-old faces and twenty-five-year-old hair. I'm sure there have been improvements in fitting and style since then but in the late 1970s, men wearing wigs might as well have been wearing a sandwich board that said, 'This is a wig. Please feel free to take the piss', with an arrow pointing upwards.

Petticoat Lane had quite an illicit feel back then. There were a lot of petty criminals wandering about. People who looked like Private Walker, the spiv character in *Dad's Army*. They'd suddenly appear with a tray full of knocked off perfumes and pitch on any available bit of pavement. It was entirely illegal.

'Come on, girls. Got some of your favourites here. Paco Rabanne, Chanel, Opium, all sorts.'

A small crowd would gather and brisk cash sales were made before a policeman would be spotted, a signal given, the tray would be folded up double quick and the crowd would melt away clutching their now entirely legitimate goods. One afternoon, Maurice told me to shout ''Ave em up Arry'. I didn't know what he meant but I shouted it anyway and the illegal perfume seller ran off down the street. He came back ten minutes later. He had to be restrained when he found out it was me.

There were also more opportunistic thieves who targeted the shops. There was a period when we were robbed almost every week. Why anyone would've wanted to steal what we were selling was beyond me, but it drove Leo crazy. I think he counted the trousers at the end of most weeks so he knew when it had happened. The shop's entire stock must have been worth ten grand at the most but after repeated robberies, Leo installed an alarm system that cost twice that amount. The robbers would've been better off nicking that.

Maurice and Leo were the first people I'd ever met who were politically active. I'd heard Paul Weller singing about political issues and societal problems but I'd never spoken to anyone about anything like this. Maurice and Leo hated right wing politics and the National Front and with good reason. Leo was more religious than Maurice and wore a skull cap and a prayer shawl where the tassels hung over his trousers. He was very visibly Jewish. National Front skinheads would abuse him as they wandered past the shop and it fascinated me to see him take them on.

I remember one thug stopping outside the shop. He was looking at the rails of clothes but there was something not quite right about him. For a start, he was wearing a Crombie coat, a checked shirt, tight jeans and sixteen hole Doctor Marten boots. We'd recently started selling Harrington jackets so he may have been after them but he certainly didn't seem the type to buy beige or brown polyester cotton mix trousers with a slight fault, even for the bargain price of seven pounds. Leo was serving another customer. I was watching from the doorway of the shop. I was absolutely not going to go out and serve the thug.

'Oy, Jewboy,' the thug said, looking at Leo. I winced. I'd been called Jewboy more than once; it was never a friendly greeting. If the thug wanted help with trouser measurements, he had a funny way of asking for it. I could only see Leo from behind and he continued to serve the other customer but there was something very tense about his back.

'Oy, Jewboy,' he said again, slower this time. More deliberate. Leo looked up. The thug then started making a hissing sound. I knew what he was doing. It was the noise of gas escaping. Cunt. I guess that in his twisted ideology, he'd calculated that the Jewish man may not have been pleased about the Holocaust reference coming his way but being money obsessed, wouldn't have broken off from the customer for fear of losing the sale. He calculated incorrectly. Leo lunged towards him with alarming speed. He was a big guy and in that moment, he looked very dangerous. The thug, with a slightly surprised look on his stupid face, ran for his life with Leo following close behind. The customer and I stood there silently watching them disappear down the road. There was very little to say. Leo didn't seem to be coming back any time soon. After a while, I asked the customer if he wanted to buy the pair of trousers he was holding. It took him a moment to regain his composure and then he looked down at the trousers and nodded. I think he thought it was probably the least he could do, but I'm fairly certain shopped elsewhere from that point onwards.

Leo came back eventually. He looked agitated and no one said anything for a few hours. I spoke to Maurice, who said that Leo would be fine but we should leave him alone for a bit. I wasn't about to start a conversation with him even though I was desperate to know if he'd caught the thug and, if he had, what he'd done with him. I was also keen for him to know that I'd completed the sale. I hoped he'd let me have the commission.

I was surprised at Leo being up for physical confrontation. People didn't expect a guy wearing a skull cap and a religious shawl to be up for a fight, but Maurice told me that a few years previously, Leo and he used to find out where the National Front were holding political meetings, turn up with other young Jewish men, and crack some heads. I thought this was great. Maurice told me that it was very effective in putting off all but the most ideologically committed Nazis; it was only when the police intervened that the National Front started being able to organise properly. I could see why. It's all very well meeting up with other like- (and also feeble-) minded right wingers but if you're banging on about being part of the master race and you keep getting the living daylights beaten out of you, you might start to have some doubts.

Following their example, I was very enthusiastic about the concept of direct action, although with the size of the skinheads abusing us I was loath to get personally involved. For years afterwards though, I would argue that a skinhead caught defacing Jewish graves with swastikas should be roundly beaten until he agreed never to do it again. I've since realised that education and debate might also play a part, but I guess all that Old Testament 'eye for an eye' stuff that I was taught at school left a lasting impression.

With Maurice and Leo's help, I was fuelled with a sense of injustice and a certain feeling of solidarity with other oppressed minorities. So when I heard that the Anti-Nazi League had organised a Rock Against Racism march from Trafalgar Square to Hackney followed by a concert, I decided to go. I was a big fan of The Clash anyway but more than that I felt like this was possibly the first thing in my life, aside from Liam Brady's passing ability, that I actually believed in.

The Anti-Nazi League were very active around this time; there was a lot to be active about. Shortly before Margaret Thatcher was elected, the National Front decided to hold an election rally in Southall in West London, an area with a large Asian population. For some inexplicable reason, this was not considered a provocative act by the authorities. The Anti-Nazi League took a different view and organised a counter demonstration. In the ensuing riot, an anti-racism activist teacher named Blair Peach sustained head injuries (possibly at the hands of a Special Patrol Group policeman) and died.

So it was that in April 1978, two months after my fifteenth birthday, I went with Simon to Trafalgar Square and we readied ourselves to walk the six miles from central London to Victoria Park in Hackney. I'm not sure parents nowadays would permit their fifteen-year-old kids to go unaccompanied to an enormous political march, but these were different times. It's also possible that I didn't tell my mother where I was going.

When we arrived, there were already thousands of people there. It felt great. (I always loved being part of a big crowd, I still do. Whether it's at football or at a gig, I love that feeling of being part of something bigger than oneself. I don't know if this was partly a factor of insecurity. If you've got a terrible haircut and a big nose, people are less likely to notice if you're one of thousands.) Straightaway we joined in the chant 'The National Front is a Nazi Front, smash the National Front'. I really felt like I belonged. A bearded man offered me a placard which said 'Down with Nazis' and 'SWP'. I agreed with the sentiment about Nazis but I didn't know what SWP stood for, so I declined. I also didn't fancy carrying a placard for six miles. We set off. We found ourselves following The Clash who were playing on the back of a flatbed truck as it slowly made its way to the gig. At one point I actually sat on the truck, but I got down after a short distance.

Mainly because it didn't seem like sitting down and listening to music brought much to the fight against racism but also, I was right up against Topper Headon's drum kit and my ears were starting to ring.

We were abused as we walked through parts of East London. There were one or two Nazi salutes from skinheads watching us go past. I was a little concerned. They were massive and looked like they hated us, but there were way more of us so I figured I'd be fine. I was also angry. My parents grew up around here. Who the fuck were these morons with their tattoos and their shaved heads and their beer guts going on about the Master Race? If they were a master race, you'd have thought they'd have looked more evolved. Should a fight have started at this point, while I wouldn't have joined in, I would've been very encouraging and supportive to the anti-fascists who did. We were less than half a mile from Cable Street, a place where, forty years earlier, Oswald Mosley (a Hitleresque figure who tried to get fascism up and running over here) and his blackshirts had marched. And where my grandfather, along with every other Jewish man who'd been demonstrating against the march, claimed to have been the one who'd thrown the brick that had hit Mosley on the head and forced him to fall down into his car. I felt like I was with him. Some coins and a few other missiles were thrown. A bread roll narrowly missed my head, and I realised it was quite some time since I'd had breakfast. The marchers responded with catcalls and someone tried to hit one of the skinheads with a placard. A policeman firmly told him to stop it.

When we got to Victoria Park, we waited. They didn't want to start the gig until most of the marchers had got there. This was going to take more time than had been allowed, the organisers having underestimated how much anti-Nazi sentiment there was. Simon and I got a burger and stood about feeling pleased with ourselves. If 100,000 teenagers marching six miles, eating a burger and then watching a concert couldn't stop the Nazis, nothing could.

This was the first gig/political rally I'd ever been to. It was encouraging to know how many people felt the same way that I did. When the bands finally started coming on, it was very exciting even though the sound was terrible. The line-up was The Tom Robinson Band, X-Ray Spex (I was never a fan but I used to play their hit 'Oh Bondage Up Yours!' at home just to wind up my mum), Aswad (before they were a household name), The Clash, Steel Pulse, Generation X, The Ruts and Sham 69. Sham were possibly the strangest choice, as most of their fan base seemed to be the same National Front skinheads that had been abusing us on the way down here, but their lead singer Jimmy Pursey seemed sincere in his leftie political convictions. As Tom Robinson belted out 'Sing if you're glad to be gay, sing if you're happy that way' and we all enthusiastically sang along even though the majority of us weren't, it felt like change could really happen. A year later, Margaret Thatcher was Prime Minister; not the change we'd envisaged or hoped for.

Things We Didn't Have in the 1970s

Part Six

Quite as Much Foreign Food

There was a lot of overt racism, so it's no surprise that foreigners were less inclined to open eating establishments. There were Italian restaurants dotted around and there was a curry house on most high roads but there wasn't much else. People ate out less, and food experimentation was only for the most adventurous. We ate what we knew. We had full English breakfasts in caffs. We had baked beans or eggs on toasted white bread. We had Welsh Rarebit. We'd go for fish and chip suppers and at the seaside, we'd have Knickerbocker Glories for dessert. We'd eat hot dogs and burgers at football from mobile food stands that were essentially grease on wheels.

People were wary of spices. There may have been one or two middle class homes where there was a well-stocked and used spice rack, where thyme jostled for space with tarragon and oregano. Where people said, 'Darling, we've almost run out of rosemary'. In our house, salt and pepper were the only acceptable condiments. As long as it didn't induce toxic shock, we would use as much of the former as possible. If that really wasn't enough, there was ketchup, brown sauce (either Daddies or HP) or salad cream. That was it. Mayonnaise was considered impossibly sophisticated. As for chilli, my father would have no more eaten something spicy than joined the Ku Klux Klan.

Chapter Seven

Truly out on the floor

'Non-Stop Dancing' was a lot more soulful than anything else on *In The City*. It was still recognisably a Jam tune but it was the subject matter of the song that really appealed to me. Unlike the rest of the album, 'Non-Stop Dancing' was about everything just being cool because he was dancing with his girl by his side. This sounded great, and was definitely on my to do list. It was something I'd yet to experience.

I loved dancing, though. I think I got it from Cissie, my paternal grandmother. She'd wanted to be a dancer when she was much younger and in her flat, there were pictures of her in the 1920s. She looked quite the young flapper. Then she'd met my grandfather and he'd put a stop to that. He was a tailor and he felt that it would be unbecoming for him to have a dancer for a wife. It's a shame really because he could've knocked up some lovely costumes for her. I don't think she ever quite forgave him.*

---

* After this disappointment, she used to indulge her passion vicariously through others. When I was eight, my gran, like every other Jew on the planet, went to see *Fiddler on The Roof* at the cinema. She brought the album back home and I played it constantly. I entertained the family one night with my rendition of Tevye singing 'If I Were a Rich Man'. I really looked the part with the skull cap and prayer shawl. It was the most Jewish I've ever been. Cissie could not have looked happier.

I used to go to discos at the Maccabi club in West Hampstead with Simon. It was torture. Waterboarding may have been less painful. I would cruise round the room looking for girls who might be amenable to a dance. If I saw one, I'd lurk in their general vicinity. I did a lot of lurking. Once in a while, when 'Eye to Eye Contact' by Edwin Starr, 'Cuba' by the Gibson Brothers or 'You Make Me Feel' by Sylvester came on, I'd get out on the dance floor and try and wow the girls with my dance moves. With experience, I've learnt that young Jewish men may have many assets but the ability to wow young women with their dance moves is not one of them.

Every so often, they'd play a slow song. 'Wishing on a Star' by Rose Royce was a particular favourite of the DJ at the Maccabi club, and one that I dreaded. (I only discovered in my forties that it wasn't by a woman called Rolls Royce. They'd sung a song called 'Car Wash' so I'd made the connection.) At that point, you'd either have to stand at the side of the dance floor and muster as much insouciance as a fourteen-year-old boy can manage. Or, if you were feeling lucky, you could sidle up to a girl of your choice and pluck up the courage to ask her to dance. I had varying degrees of success. By that, I mean they always said no, but some of them said it quite nicely. One time, I spied a girl I liked the look of, took a deep breath and went over to her. 'Would you like to dance?'

She looked at my face and then her eyes scanned slowly up and down at my specially chosen 'pulling' ensemble. She looked like someone had offered her a plate of vomit and shook her head emphatically. I now realise that I must have given off an air of desperation that couldn't be any more obvious if I prostrated myself at her feet, but the emotional scarring from that rejection ran very deep. I hope her life didn't work out the way she would've wanted.

It was surprising to hear a Jam song that referenced James Brown; I was only just beginning to join the dots with Paul. Yes, he was an angry young man, outraged at inequality and violence and right wing politics and lack of decent housing. Because of him, so was I. I was all for shouting along with songs about police brutality or the government not giving a fuck. But it turned out that Paul had a gentler, more soulful side as well. No other band of that era were namechecking James Brown or doing covers of 'Midnight Hour'. As I hadn't been to a live gig as yet, I was unaware of how deep the soul connection went. It was just nice to know that Paul, like the rest of us had other preoccupations as well.

Paul certainly helped my soul music education but my love of disco had already pushed me in that direction. I remember seeing Legs & Co dance to Harold Melvin & the Bluenotes singing 'Don't Leave Me This Way' on *Top of the Pops*. There's also a great performance of the same song by Thelma Houston. Hearing Donna Summer sing 'I Feel Love' made a big impression. From there, I'd graduated to Sam Cook, Marvin Gaye and Aretha Franklin; I wasn't completely musically illiterate.

A lot of these tunes would be played at parties. There were a lot of parties around this time. Word would go round the school that a party was happening at the weekend, and it would take two or three days for everyone to find out. There was a fair bit of jeopardy involved. You'd go up to a mate in the playground.

'You going to Shelley's party Saturday?'

The answer you wanted was 'Yeah, you?' and not 'What party?' That was embarrassing for all concerned. I'd been on both sides of this conversation and neither was pleasant.

I was invited most of the time. Or if I wasn't, the other kids were very good at not letting me know; I wasn't a complete social leper. We had a few of those. There was one kid, a strange and solitary boy, who was an absolute wizard with maths and electronics and he built radios out of old electrical equipment. I'd like to think he's a multi-millionaire now with his own hi-tech firm. Although it's possible he's serving a long prison sentence for making a homemade bomb and threatening to blow something up. I'm not sure I ever saw anyone talk to him for the entire five years I was at that school. This may have been because his levels of personal hygiene were variable. I stood next to him once in assembly and the odour was overpowering.

He also had the most crooked teeth I've ever seen. We nicknamed him Uncle Fester. We were sensitive like that. A private orthodontist would have been able to retire on the contents of his mouth. There seemed to be teeth everywhere but none where they should be. In order for him to breathe in and out through his mouth, the air had to take a number of diversions. He was the noisiest breather in history. Without holding his breath, it would've been impossible for him to sneak up on anyone. I hope he's had his teeth fixed. I hope he's happy. I hope he's had a wash.

Because girls would be at the party, getting dressed up was a big deal. I see my son going off for parties nowadays sometimes wearing a suit and looking *so* cool and grown up and I'm jealous. Wearing a suit at a party was not the done thing back then. The choice of clothes I had was limited, and I didn't have an extensive wardrobe, but these things were important nonetheless. Paul had taught us that. I had a couple of bits that I liked and I did the best I could. I flat out refused to wear *anything* my father wore. Ken could've been the most prominent style guru of the 1970s, he could've dressed like Jason King, but he was still Ken. I never even liked to admit we were related, so I was hardly going to wear his clobber. I had a couple of shirts. For one period during the mid-1970s, I was down to one because I'd recently bought a shirt from a catalogue and when it arrived, it was to all intents and purposes a pyjama top. I put it on and stood there in front of my mother. We both knew. She made all the right noises because it had cost four pounds fifty.

'It's nice,' she said.

I never wore it again.

The parties were all at the houses of kids from school, so they were always in North London. We'd get a bus or train to the party and pile in. Everyone had a bigger house than I did although I never factored in the possibility that those of us with small houses that smelt of cat pee may not have hosted parties. These house all had open plan kitchens, dining tables and front and back gardens. Some had driveways. One had a gate where you had to ring a buzzer. One of the parties was catered. I wanted to move in.

If you've got this far in the book, you may have surmised that I was not the life and soul of the party. An excited 'Ian's here' was not a cry that went up when I arrived. It's not as if I was drinking, so I couldn't knock back a beer and launch myself on the throng when I felt pissed enough to not give a shit. I still headed for the kitchen. At least I could busy myself getting some juice while no one talked to me. I tried to look confident. I'd even do some washing up if there were no glasses available.

I didn't really know where to put myself so I'd wander aimlessly from room to room. Sometimes you'd open the door on a couple snogging. I know people have discovered infidelity this way but not having a girlfriend, that wasn't a worry I had.* I tended to avoid the rooms where people were sitting around cross-legged. (Years later, when dope appeared, those were my favourite rooms but I didn't like them back then.) If there was dancing, I might stay for a bit. Sometimes, I'd join in. When I was with my mates, we'd try and shout over the music and watch the girls dancing. It wasn't the worst thing in the world.

---

* Years later, I 'pulled' a woman at a party and we were snogging in a bedroom when some mates came in and started making rude comments about her. My feelings were hurt but probably not as much as hers. We were basically being heckled. I wasn't quite so quick with the put-downs back then.

Sometimes, you'd have to queue for the toilet. If you were lucky, there might be a girl you liked in the queue with you. There was the possibility of talking to them. It felt less pressurised. You both had something else to do but you were thrown together. I used to go to the loo even if I didn't need to, just on the off chance.

I got invited to a party by a guy I knew from school called Danny. He was a good footballer and we hung out after school. I went round his house once. He had four of the biggest Alsatian dogs I've ever encountered. His dad had to lock them in a side room before I could come in. I could hear them straining to get through the door and attack me as I walked down his corridor. I never went round there again. Danny was popular with girls. I used to like going to parties with him just because I thought I might get his cast-offs. I never did. I think the girls liked the fact that he shaved. He was one of those boys who had started shaving before anyone else. He'd come into school in the morning having shaved and by eleven, he needed to shave again. By the middle of the afternoon, he looked like George Michael. He was also the first person I knew, aside from my mother, who smoked. He used to smoke Benson & Hedges. He'd buy packets of ten from an accommodating newsagent on Camden High Road. On warm days, when we left school, he'd put his blazer in his bag, roll up the sleeves on his shirt and light up a cigarette as soon as we were outside the gates. With his five o'clock shadow, he looked like a grown man. It was as if my uncle had picked me up from school.

On the way to the party, I got a bit of a tummy ache. When we got there, I left Danny to his harem and found the loo. It was mercifully empty. I was there a while but finally I flushed. I felt like I'd dodged a bullet. The room smelt bad so I used about half a can of air freshener. I opened the door and Danny and three women were waiting. They recoiled as the smell hit them. It was like someone had taken a giant shit in a pine forest.

★

I loved 'Non-Stop Dancing' because of the joy of it. I didn't have a lot of joy in my life and it was nice not to fixate on the negative. Most of the time, I was just looking for fun and this song captured that feeling. That unbridled, hedonistic feeling of abandon that Paul sang about, how he was truly out of his head. That sounded fine to me. Later on, after The Jam had split up, I spent a good proportion of my twenties being out of my head. I had a great time.

When Paul sang about getting the feeling that you belonged, that was all that any of us ever wanted. I got it from Arsenal and then I got it from The Jam. I was just another suburban kid, alienated, angry and disillusioned with my life and worried for my future. The Jam seemed to point the way. And later on, when I turned up at gigs and there were other kids there who felt the same way I did and the records were number one, it felt good to know you weren't alone.*

---

* I'm fifty-seven and I still go dancing nowadays. This year, on New Year's Day, I went to The Egg, a club in King's Cross. Me and five mates met up for brunch and then wandered down to the club for four in the afternoon. They have a regular trance gig and we spent four hours dancing. I was the oldest of our group but only just. For the older raver, I cannot recommend afternoon clubbing highly enough. There is nothing quite as satisfying as four hours of dancing and still being home in time for the ten o'clock news.

Things We Didn't Have in the 1970s

Part Seven

Mobile Phones

People used landlines (if you're under twenty-five, ask your parents). If someone rang after seven at night, the person receiving the call would always say, 'Who could that be at this time of night?' Not having mobile phones wasn't a bad thing. We actually used to look at each other and our surroundings rather than check our emails every ten minutes. We'd still ignore each other in restaurants but there was no screen to look at so we just stared into the middle distance and contemplated the emptiness of our lives and how bad the food was. When we were walking about, we looked where we were going. It didn't stop me treading in dogshit but it wasn't because I was looking at a mobile phone. (Dogshit was everywhere by the way. This was before the time when people were expected to clean up after their dogs. They just left it in the street for the rain to wash away. In 1976, it didn't rain for four months.)

But there was a downside. Meeting up required speaking to each other from your home phones and making an arrangement. Once you were out of the house, if you were running late, the other person waited without any idea where you were or whether anything had happened to you. At some point, you had to make an executive decision about how long to wait before you gave up. There were phone boxes liberally placed around the city and if you could find one that a) worked and b) didn't smell too much of urine, and you had the correct change and the coin slot worked, you could make a call. The trouble was of course that if you were trying to get hold of the person who you were meeting, that wasn't possible because they'd already left the house. As you can imagine, it was a tense time.

Chapter Eight

Say you'll stay make my day

When I first heard 'I Need You', it might as well have been written in another language. It was so far from my experience at that time. There's no reason why a fourteen-year-old would understand a song like this but hearing it gave me a different perspective. It was not just the fact that Paul needed this woman to keep him straight, it was the fact that he was asking her to do so. To slap his wrists and send him home and to tell him he couldn't come again.

Needing a woman to keep me in line was a concept I was nowhere near comprehending. That came much later. I loved the idea though; that vulnerability, again. It's amazing to me that a twenty-year-old wrote a song about love that was way more grown up in its attitudes to relationships than the vast majority of men twice his age. The fact that Paul was saying he needed looking after. I was definitely not grown up enough to admit anything like that and I don't think most of the boys at Jam gigs were either.

I sometimes wondered what girls got from The Jam, but I'm sure songs like this would've helped. A guy telling a girl how much he needed her. It must have been refreshing for girls to hear a song like this and think that there were guys out there who didn't want to get involved in the macho bullshit knocking around back then.

And there was a lot of it knocking around. Most men might have been supporters of women's liberation and the burning of bras but only because it left breasts unfettered. They had a particularly simplistic view of women. If they didn't fancy them, they patronised them. If they did fancy them they still patronised them but there were also pats on the bottom and hugs that went on far too long and entire conversations conducted with a woman's chest. There was, 'Go and make us a cup of tea love' and 'I'd definitely shag her' as soon as she was out of earshot and sometimes when she could still hear. There were wolf whistles every time a woman walked past a building site. Women put up with this shit. What else could they do?

Every day, on page three of *The Sun*, there was a woman with no top on. On a Sunday, the *News of The World* and *The Sunday People* had topless women on every page. Television featured comedians like Benny Hill, an older man perving after busty, much younger, women in their underwear; situation 'comedies' like *On the Buses* where older men perved after a succession of busty, much younger women and the *Carry On* films where, you guessed it, older men perved after younger busty women. It was everywhere.

There were a lot of men who exposed themselves to women. Nowadays, you can take a high resolution photo of your penis and send it to whoever you want. When he invented the world wide web, I'm not sure Sir Tim Berners-Lee envisaged that it would be used to send pictures of penises instantly around the world. Personally, I've never been too keen on any of my passport photos, so goodness only knows how I'd be about taking a picture of my penis and emailing it to women I thought might like to see it.

Back then, however, men didn't have that outlet so they would walk around in parks and other public places wearing an overcoat with nothing underneath. It must have been draughty. When an attractive woman approached, they would throw open their coat to reveal an erection underneath. Pretty much every woman I know was flashed back then. I'm not sure what reaction these men were hoping to provoke. Some of the women got angry, some moved away as quickly as possible. One of my friends chased the man out of the park. It can't be easy to run with an erection although it probably disappeared fairly quickly.

Like most boys of my age, my interest in girls was on a very superficial level. Paul Weller might have needed a girl, but I just wanted one. It wasn't even completely about sex (only 95%), although if they were willing to give it a go, I was game. Not that it happened and, looking back now, I can see that it was never going to. Girls were a total mystery to me. I could talk to them but, like most of my immediate circle, I had not the first clue what I would do if I ever found myself in some sort of romantic entanglement with one. I'd first kissed a girl when I was eleven. I was away on a school trip somewhere near Horsham and a girl in my class let me stick my tongue down her throat. It was pleasant enough even though neither of us knew what we were doing. Plus, her nose was almost as sizeable as mine so there was an awkward moment prior to the kiss when we clashed and parried like two Olympic fencers trying to find an opening.

For a couple of years after that, very little happened. It was probably for the best. Reliable information on how it all worked was hard to come by. *The Joy of Sex* was published earlier in the decade and someone at school managed to get hold of a copy. We crowded round and looked at the illustrations. Some of the pages were stuck together. I didn't understand why. The man in the book had a beard. I thought about growing a beard.

There was no one I could turn to for advice. Certainly not my parents, although I would never have asked them anyway, even at gunpoint. My father would have been no more capable of offering advice on sexual relations than he would on quantum mechanics. He would've told me to ask my mum and my mum would've told me to get out of the kitchen. Plus, it's entirely possible that they had only had sex twice more than me (to produce me and my sister) so it hardly qualified them as experts.

Sex education was almost non-existent. There were no well written and beautifully illustrated children's books on sex education. At school, we had one lesson, taught by my biology teacher, Mr Shah, which concentrated totally on the mechanics. This goes in here, you move up and down, stuff comes out. Unusually for me, I paid attention and at the end, I knew the basic moves. How one persuaded a girl to let you do something like that to her however, I had no idea. It's not really stuff they can teach you at school.

Aside from that, I got my sexual education from two sources. When we weren't talking about football or music, my mates and I talked about sex quite a lot of the time. We weren't what you would call well informed. My friends may have talked the talk but they'd almost certainly never walked the walk. Not that I knew for sure. They sounded convincing but the truth was, they could've told me anything.

'And then you put the penis in her ear.'

'What?'

'Yeah, they really like that.'

'But how does it fit in?'

'The ear expands when they're excited. Have you ever seen a girl with really big ears?'

'No'.

'That's because you haven't got one excited yet.'

The other source of sex education were pornographic magazines, and I admit that education wasn't the primary reason I looked at them. They weren't easy to get hold of. The entire top shelf of the newsagents was taken up with them but they wouldn't sell them to anyone my age. Luckily my dad had a collection. It was just a case of locating them. My dad kept his in the cupboard under some shoeboxes. They were originally kept in his bedside cabinet, but I'd borrowed them once and put them back in the wrong drawer so he'd moved them.

Each page would bring a new woman happily posing with their legs wide open presumably ready for action. Page after page of vaginas; they were essentially vagina catalogues.

You like this one? No? Well how about this one? No? What about this two for one offer?

All I really learnt from them is what a vagina looks like. I saw a lot of vaginas. There were marked differences between individual vaginas but I felt fairly certain that if I ever got the chance, I would recognise one when I saw one.

Penises were a whole different thing. Back then, erections were not allowed to be shown in pornographic magazines. I assume this was because the man looking at the pictures would have an erection of his own to peruse and a second erection would've been distracting. The foreskin was another complication. Like all Jewish boys, I'd been circumcised when I was eight days old. This was before I understood what was going on, because if I had understood, I'd have put up more of a fight. I went to two Jewish schools, so any changing room contained exclusively circumcised cocks. There might have been size issues[*] but they all looked roughly the same.

But at some point, I saw, in a magazine, my first uncircumcised penis. I was in the toilet at home having one of the many

---

[*]   That's for another book.

wanks I would have that week when I saw a man with something markedly different between his legs. I stopped masturbating and started comparing. What the fuck? What is that? What is this? I was staring at it for quite a long time.

I didn't know who to turn to. As I mentioned, my parents were a non-starter. If I'd have asked my mates, they would still be taking the piss now. There was no helpline. There was no internet. No helpful sites I could go on. No www.comparethepenis.com. I was on my own. It was a traumatic few weeks but I found out in the end. Someone at school had managed to obtain some hard-core magazines showing actual people having actual sex and through the photo storyline, I could follow a flaccid penis transforming into something erect that looked (except in length and width) very much like my own. It was a huge relief.

I had a friend from primary school that I saw once in a while. Ivor Baddiel had access to an extensive collection of pornography. He didn't need to go and forage about, he just had to go next door to his dad's bedroom. One afternoon, I was sitting in Ivor's room and we were listening to music, talking about football and idly browsing through vagina catalogues. I was in a chair, he was sitting on the bed.

'Look at this one,' I'd say and pass him the magazine. He'd nod appreciatively. 'What about hers?' he'd say and pass another magazine back over.

A convivial silence settled over the room.

'Who have you got this weekend?'

'Man City away. What about you?'

'Spurs at the Bridge?'

And so the afternoon passed.

'Come and sit over here,' he said at one point. He patted the bed. I was a bit taken aback. 'What?'

He patted the bed again. 'Come and sit over here,' he said. 'On the bed. Next to me.'

I was very disturbed. One minute we were talking about football and looking at vaginas and now, he wanted me to sit next to him. Was Ivor making a pass at me? We were good friends but I'd never thought of him in that way. I'd never had those sort of feelings around Ivor, or anyone male. Until now, I was sure he felt the same way. I reluctantly sat on the end of the bed, as far away as it's possible to be when you're sitting on the same bed.

'No, not over there,' he said. He seemed irritated. 'Over here. I want to show you something.'

I wasn't in the least bit bothered whether Ivor was gay or not. He was a good mate so I'd have loved him whatever (not that I would've expressed it in those terms). I wasn't even totally sure that I wasn't gay. If I was going to have to wait much longer to have sex, I might even have considered it just to double my chances. All I knew for certain at that moment was that I didn't fancy him. But by this point, I was getting irritated as well. If he was going to try and kiss me or make a grab for my cock, we might as well get it over with. I plonked myself down next to him and awaited his next move. A large fart noise resonated through the room. There was a whoopee cushion under the blanket. We both laughed, him because he was an idiot who thought fart noises were funny, and me also for that reason, but also from relief.

When I was thirteen, I'd taken the afternoon off school and went to see *Death Race 2000*. There was a special promotion that week; the car from the film was parked outside the cinema. It was some sort of sports car but it had fake teeth on the radiator and a couple of horns with fake blood where it had supposedly impaled victims. It looked as impressive as it sounds.

The film was an X certificate meaning that it was only meant to be seen by people eighteen years old or over. I figured if I wasn't wearing my school uniform I might get away with it. I removed my tie, rolled up my blazer and put them both in my school bag.

'Could I have one for *Death Race 2000* please.' My voice had just about broken by then. I hoped that might be enough.

The lady in the box office looked at me over her glasses. 'How old are you?'

'Eighteen,' I said. I hadn't shaved for a week to prepare for this moment.

There then ensued the longest silence I can ever recall. (Except for one time after I did a corporate gig for some garden equipment manufacturers and opened with 'If Snoop Doggy Dog did some gardening, would he use a hoe?')

'Is that right?' she eventually said, after so long that I might well have been eighteen by then.

'Yes.' I tried not to look her in the eye.

She was smiling. 'When were you born?'

I'd rehearsed this moment. '1957. February.'

'Have you got any ID on you?' She wasn't going to make this easy for me.

I searched about in my pockets. Surprisingly, I didn't.

'No, sorry.'

She looked at me some more. She probably thought that if I wanted to damage my developing brain with ultra-violence, it was up to me. 'Go on then.' She printed off a ticket.

'Thank you,' I said, thinking I'd fooled her. I bought some popcorn, took my seat in the virtually empty cinema and watched the Pearl & Dean adverts.

Pah pa pa pa pa pa pa pa pa pa pa, pa pa pa pa pa pa pa, yup.

There were adverts where men with deep voices would say, 'I'd love a Babycham.' There were also adverts for very strong cigarettes that featured rugged-looking men and cool-looking women although no one coughing up blood and dying at fifty-two. Some of the ads were funny. There was a series of ads for

Martini with Leonard Rossiter and Joan Collins where she kept getting drinks spilled over her. There was an advert for the local curry house.

'After the film, how about a trip to the Raj Curry House. 255 Brent Street, Hendon.'

This accompanied by sitar music and still pictures of Indian food. Every local cinema in the 1970s had these adverts.

I was waiting for the film trailers when a man smelling of cigarettes and aftershave sat down next to me. I was irritated. There was a whole cinema to choose from and he'd sat down right beside me. I carried on eating my popcorn. I then felt a hand on my knee. It wasn't my hand. I stared straight ahead, barely breathing. His breathing on the other hand was quite laboured. The feeling of his hand on my knee wasn't disagreeable as such, it was more that I was bemused. Why did this man have his hand on my leg? Did he want some of my popcorn? Surely it couldn't be what I thought it was. Not one girl had shown the slightest interest in touching my leg and yet *he* wants to? The hand slowly crept upwards. I guess he took the fact that I hadn't objected as some sort of encouragement. When his hand reached the vicinity of my crotch, I realised it was exactly what I thought it was. I took his hand and removed it and then moved seats. When I left, I looked at the woman in the ticket booth accusingly. She looked back at me as if to say, 'Well, it's your own fault for going to see an X.'

I absolutely could not tell my parents what had happened. In my house, sex was never discussed. Anything outside the narrow boundaries of straight sex in the missionary position was not something my parents wanted to think about. Gender fluidity was not considered 'normal' in my house. If I'd turned up one afternoon wearing eyeliner or in fact anything that was considered feminine, my mum might have been OK with it but my dad would've freaked out.

As for the possibility of me being gay, I think it would've been too much for my parents to take in. It should be remembered that homosexuality had been legal for less than ten years in 1977. We had no gay relatives, at least none that had come out. Any homosexuals on TV were extremely camp. They wore bright colours and had exaggerated gestures and fancied any man that they met. That was just how they were, all the time. It must've been incredibly tiring. There was very little understanding of what 'gay' was. My mother announced one evening that Freddie Mercury was 'flamboyant'. We all agreed that he was. The idea that he was gay wouldn't have occurred to us. Even though he had a big moustache and was the lead singer of a band called Queen.*

---

* Years later, I was sitting with my dad, watching *Top of the Pops*, when Culture Club were introduced. My dad watched open-mouthed.

'What is that?' he said.

'It's Boy George, Dad,' I said.

'Is that a bloke or a woman?'

'He's called Boy George, Dad. He's a bloke,' I said even though he looked less like a bloke than any man I'd ever seen.

'Well, why's he dressed like that?'

I had no idea. It was certainly an unusual outfit.

'He's exploring the boundaries of his sexuality, Dad.' I'd recently had a discussion with someone at work and this was a phrase she used.

'Well, why does he have to do it on *Top of the Pops*?' my dad said.

Things We Didn't Have in the 1970s

Part Eight

A Nuanced View of Sexuality

When it came to sexuality, things were much less complicated in the 1970s. You were either straight or gay, and if you were gay, we'd rather you weren't. As for any of the others, it was beyond most people's comprehension. David Bowie shook things up a bit but he was allowed to because he was a pop star. Very few people would've walked down their local high road dressed like Aladdin Sane. They wouldn't have made it to the end. For comparison, nowadays, the current acronym covering non hetero/cis sexuality is LGBTQIAPK+. This stands for Lesbian, Gay, Bisexual, Transgender, Queer, Intersex, Asexual, Pansexual and Kink.* How does one choose? Is it in fact a choice? Do you join a group and then look around and think, 'These people are *nothing* like me.' The + is there just in case more types will be added. I have no doubt that more will be.

---

* I have issues with the K, which stands for 'Kink'. It seems to me that we've all got our preferences. Some of them are kinky, some aren't. I'd imagine there are intersex people who are not kinky at all and straight people who are off the scale kinky. I'd say kink could be all of us or none of us.

Chapter Nine

Please welcome the best fucking band in the world

I'm told that, like my mother, I have unreasonably high expectations. I get very excited about things I'm about to do, see or try for the first time. I guess that when I was younger, you could call it the triumph of hope over experience, but I'm still the same now even though I have some experience. Don't get me wrong, I quite like being this way. I get an enormous amount of enjoyment from the anticipation of something being brilliant. I've been known to be overexcited for weeks before an event. Even if it turns out to be a massive disappointment and like an eight-year-old child, I'm completely and utterly distraught when it all goes tits up, at least I've had the fun of imagining how good it might have been. It's probably not healthy.

I know that other grown-ups live life in a more adult way. My partner, for example, feels that if she doesn't get too excited about anything, she won't be in the least bit let down when things go wrong, as they often do; she'll be pleasantly surprised when things go well. I always felt that she was overly pessimistic, but she would describe it as realistic. And also not deluded. (For any England football fans, I would recommend her method, not mine.)

In late 1978, after a relentless eighteen-month campaign of alternate sulking and shouting, my mother finally relented and gave her permission for me to go to see The Jam live. In the end, she was so sick of the barrage of misery and complaint coming her way that I think she agreed just to shut me up. This was a lesson I noted for future events. For her, it was a win-win. If I was murdered on the mean streets of London or got home safely, either way she wouldn't have to listen to it any more.

I told Simon I'd been given permission to go and he bought tickets for me, him and Robert. I remember the rush I got when he showed them to me. I thought the top of my head was going to come off. This would be my first proper gig. I'd seen Rock Against Racism in Victoria Park, but this was The Jam, at night, in a proper venue. I counted down the days.

As the date approached, it would be safe to say that my excitement levels were on the high side. Aside from the build-up to losing my virginity, which was still in its early stages at this point and would be for some time, this was the most excited I'd been about anything. In the weeks leading up to the gig, I thought of little else. If it was possible, I ignored my parents even more than usual. My concentration at school, never acute at the best of times, hit a new low. I spent weeks sitting at the back of lessons looking into the distance and humming Jam tunes to myself. I read reviews of past gigs they'd done, looked at photos of them performing live. I could not wait.

The big day arrived. School was breaking up for the Christmas holidays that day, so we were bouncing off the walls anyway. I'm not sure a school day has ever passed so slowly but, finally, it was over. It felt wrong to go home rather than walk the half a mile to the venue but staying in our school uniforms may have made it more difficult to get served at the bar so home we went to get into the correct gear. Simon and Robert were both going to wear Paul Weller suits. They'd been to a shop in Carnaby Street called

The Carnaby Cavern that stocked them. They had three buttons, side vents and thin collars and they came in light grey. With a white shirt, black tie and black winkle picker shoes with white flashings on the toes from Shelleys, the total cost was around eighty pounds.

Robert, whose parents were quite well-off, supplemented the look by spending another twenty quid on a green parka. It had Jam and Who patches on the front and a large target on the back. (Later on, he sold it to an Israeli kid that we knew and the first time he wore it, he got chased down the Camden Road by some boys from Holloway school one afternoon. He was outraged. 'Why did they chase me?'

'I don't know. Perhaps it's because of the giant target sewn onto the back of your parka.')

My parents certainly couldn't run to a hundred pounds just to keep me fashionably attired. I'm not sure they spent a hundred pounds on clothes throughout my childhood and they certainly weren't going to splash out that sort of money just so I could look like 'that bloke out of The Jam'. I just did the best I could. I cobbled together a look and became what I thought was a mod. There was a Fred Perry top and a Harrington jacket that I loved.*

The gig took place at the Music Machine in Mornington Crescent in London on 21 December 1978. It was a late-night gig but it had been arranged that Simon's mum Carole would pick us up afterwards. Rock and fucking roll! We got down there

---

* I've since met and become very good friends with a real mod and I realise that I was at best playing at the whole thing. My friend lives the lifestyle 24/7. For him, it's less about the music and more about the look. I've never seen him not perfectly turned out. It's way more effort than I'm prepared to make. He lives in the country and has animals to look after but he always looks immaculate. He owns a cape although since a comment about Darth Vader, he's lost a bit of confidence in wearing it. And if there's one thing you need when wearing a cape, it's confidence.

quite early, but there were already hundreds of fans milling about outside. We were fifteen but weren't even close to being the youngest kids there, which tells you something about how young fans of the band were, and also about attitudes to parental care back then. We went straight into the venue. Robert was way taller than either myself or Simon, so we got him to go to the bar. He bought three halves of lager; licensing laws were seen as more of a general guide at this time. We piled into the main hall and looked around. It was louder and darker than I expected. I took a sip of beer. It was, I think, the first beer I ever had and I was instantly intoxicated by both the beer and the atmosphere. The first support band were on stage. They were a rock/reggae band called Jab Jab. I liked them although I didn't know any of the tunes. The bass drum sounded great through the speakers particularly when I put my head right next to one. Neither Simon or Robert mentioned the danger of hearing loss. Even if they had, I wouldn't have been able to hear them.

Jab Jab were followed by The Nipple Erectors although they were currently in the process of changing their name to Pogue Mahone. Simon told me this meant 'kiss my arse' in Gaelic. After half a lager, I found this incredibly funny. Pogue Mahone (later, The Pogues) featured a very young lead singer called Shane Mac-Gowan. Shane was dressed in a tutu and Doc Martens boots and danced about like he'd had a quite a few. I had no idea what he was singing about. It's possible he didn't either. 'Fairytale of New York' was, at this time, just a twinkle in Shane's very glazed eyes.

After them came a punk/new wave band called Gang of Four. The political references completely passed me by. They were a bit plodding for my liking and they went on for what seemed like a week but, finally, they said their goodbyes, the houselights came up slightly and the roadies got to work. They cleared away all sorts of shit from the stage until it was just two microphones and one drumkit with a large number of amps behind them. And then, very late in the evening, after they'd played some old soul tunes including 'Hard to Handle' by Otis Redding, 'Hold on I'm Coming' by Sam and Dave and most memorably 'Land of a Thousand Dances' by Wilson Pickett, the lights went down and a silver haired man who turned out to be Paul Weller's dad walked onto the stage and in a forty-Marlboro-a-day voice said, 'Please welcome the best fucking band in the world, The Jam'.

The band walked out to a huge roar and launched into 'It's Too Bad'. I was ten feet away from the front of the stage and everyone started jumping up and down. It was, and remains, the most exhilarating moment of my life. Paul Weller attacked the guitar like it had personally insulted his mum and spat out the lyrics to his songs with venom, Bruce Foxton sang harmonies and leapt about and Rick Buckler sat at his drum kit in dark glasses looking like the coolest fucker on the planet. The noise that three guys could make was insane. For the next hour and a half, they played a blistering set of some of the best pop tunes ever written. I knew every word of every song. I still do.

Things We Didn't Have in the 1970s

Part Nine

Electronic Gadgets

Our house had one TV, a couple of radios, a stereo, a fridge freezer, an oven and a kettle. We didn't even own the TV. We hired it from Radio Rentals for two pounds a week. I think my mum had a hairdryer. We might also have had a vacuum cleaner and an iron, though I never personally used either of them so I can't completely vouch for their existence. As I look around my gadget-strewn home of the twenty-first century, I wonder what we spent our spare money on back then. Except, I've realised that we didn't have any.

Chapter Ten

Didn't we have a nice time

For those parents who diligently attend church/synagogue/ mosque/religious temple of your choice for a year, just so you can get your precious offspring into a 'good' school, I know you do it for the right reasons. But you should be aware that although they may well get good grades and move on to university and a marginally less uncomfortable life, you're subjecting them to the misery of compulsory religious knowledge lessons for five long years. The Jewish Free School was no different in that regard to any other religious school, but we only studied the Old Testament. There was absolutely no mention of any other religion. Or Jesus. He was the one that got away. It was all about how the Israelites had smitten the Amalakites or the Sammurites or the Sadducites. There was a lot of vengeance and eye for an eye stuff. This was our legacy. If we were wronged, take revenge. Easier said than done. The Israelites never had to deal with the Holloway boys or the tramps around Camden Town station.

Mr Goldberg, our Religious Knowledge teacher, was a lovely fella. He was so old, we felt there was a chance he'd experienced some of the biblical stories first hand.

'What was Moses actually like, Sir?'

'Shut up, Stone.' He was laughing though. He wasn't much of a teacher but we weren't the greatest pupils. He must've known that no one had even the slightest interest in anything he ever taught but he ploughed on regardless. I often wonder how he felt at three in the morning when he contemplated his life of being ignored. Kathy Wilton once spent an entire RK lesson hiding behind a curtain wearing a gas mask and asking muffled questions. We were all in hysterics. Mr Goldberg must have thought everyone was in a particularly good mood that day.

I just couldn't take it seriously. I wore the skullcap and the prayer shawl under my shirt although I removed them the moment I stepped out of the gates. I went to synagogue most weekends but my heart wasn't in it. I tried to be a good Jewish boy; I'd had my Bar Mitzvah when I was thirteen, but if my coming of age meant anything, it was the dawning realisation that I was not going to be a good Jewish man. I stopped going shortly after that, and me and God rapidly drifted apart. I couldn't see how a god could exist that would allow my parents to ever get married. I knew about free will but I thought that in such an obvious case, even God wouldn't have stood by. And the fact that he hadn't stepped in made me doubt he was up there watching.

Plus I was getting bullied about my nose and I figured that if there was a God, he either wouldn't have let it happen or he didn't give a fuck about me. Whichever it was, I didn't want anything to do with Him. The bullying caused me no end of pain and anguish. I had a big nose. It was my destiny. My parents both have big noses, my grandfathers both had big noses and no doubt their mothers or fathers also had big noses.* At some point in the dim and distant

---

* Years later, I was at my uncle Phil's funeral and it was the most nose-heavy do I've ever been at. A festival of noses. A nasal extravaganza. I said this to my mum.

'Look at all these noses. What a freaky looking family we are.'

'Stop it,' she said.

'Honestly, Mum. It's like two hundred male and female versions of me.'

past, it's possible that one of my ancestors had a little button nose like the woman from the TV show *Bewitched*. But by the time I turned up, the noses had grown to impressive proportions.

I cursed my parents. How could they do this to me? What were they thinking? With their outsize profiles, hadn't they considered the consequences of having children? I couldn't watch the film *Pinocchio*. Seeing a boy with a nose that grew was distressing. (When *Monty Python's Life of Brian* came out a few years later, I loved all of it except for the Sermon on the Mount Big Nose scene. It was pathetic really.) Boys from school would snigger when I walked past, and I knew why. I got to the point where I would cross the road if I saw they were ahead of me. Or if that wasn't possible, I got very good at turning my head at just the right moment, as if momentarily distracted, so that they wouldn't see my face.

As for girls, the nose was too much for them, or so I figured. If it was, I can't blame them. I was impossibly shy and odd-looking. Most of them would look away. Some were nasty. One girl mercilessly teased me about it. She called me Concorde (a long nosed supersonic passenger plane that operated in the 1970s) every time she saw me.

'Alright Concorde,' she'd shout across the corridor. Hundreds of kids would turn to see who she was shouting at. Most looked at me with pity, one or two with sympathy.

'Shut up,' I'd say without much conviction.

'Coming into land are we?' If I hadn't been the butt of the joke, I'd probably have found it quite funny.

She'd do an impression of an air hostess. 'Concorde on final approach,' she'd say. 'Fasten seat belts everybody.' I fucking hated her and I hated that plane.*

I'm not sure why she singled me out. It was a Jewish school, I

---

* When it crashed in Paris years later, the loss of life was of course terrible but there was a tiny bit of me that was pleased.

wasn't the only one with an outsized hooter. Normal size noses were the exception rather than the rule. But every time she saw me, she'd make some comment. It was *so* unfair. I never said anything about her, even though she was a little dumpy girl who looked like a baby had overnight become thirteen, but retained all her baby features. I was acutely aware of how painful these sorts of comments were so I refrained. Even writing this now, I feel slightly guilty but if she hasn't lost the puppy fat by now, I imagine she's made her peace.

I was so miserable, I nagged my mother into making a doctor's appointment so I could discuss the possibility of corrective surgery. She looked sceptical but I kept at it. In the end, she relented and we went to see Dr Collins. She waited outside the surgery while I went in. He regarded me with some sympathy.

'So what seems to be the problem Ian?'

'It's my nose.'

'OK.' He looked at my nose. 'What's wrong with it?'

'It's too big,' I said. 'I'd like it to be smaller.'

'Hmm,' he said, looking at it from a number of angles.

'Well, it is on the big side but you'll grow into it,' he said. Like I'd been given an adult nose while still a child.

'But I've heard that noses and ears get bigger as you get older.'

'That's true but not until much later in life.'

I imagined myself at fifty looking like a Jewish anteater. Unable to hold my head up because of the weight.

'Would it not be possible to have plastic surgery?' I asked him.

'Rhinoplasty?' he said.

'Pardon?'

'Rhinoplasty. Corrective surgery on the nose.'

The fact that it was called rhinoplasty did not do much for my already low self-esteem. Apparently, I looked like a rhino.

'Are you sure that's what you want?'

'I think so,' I said, but I wasn't sure at all. I just wanted the dumpy baby-faced girl to stop taking the piss out of me. If there was corrective surgery to make her go away, I'd have opted for that.

'Well. I could put you on a waiting list but it could take over a year.'

'Let me think about it,' I said, knowing full well that I wasn't going to go on a waiting list and think about it. The only thing I was thinking about were ways to kill dumpy baby-faced girl.

'Or you could go private.'

I thought that for a family that still rented their television for two pounds a week, private surgery was unlikely.

I never got round to it. Now, I think the time has passed.

As I stride confidently through my sixth decade on earth, I've come to terms with it. It is an outsize nose but it's mine. Some women actually like it. It's probably helped with the comedy. I used to walk on and mention it first, just to get it out of the way. One could almost say I needed to deal with the elephant in the room but that would be way too literal. People hardly ever point it out any more and if they do, I'm amused. Most of the time.*

---

* Even now, I still have to put up with abuse once in a while. One time, I was queueing up to get into Arsenal when a man behind me started talking loudly to his girlfriend.

'Look at the size of that fucking hooter.'

She started laughing. I was hoping he wasn't talking about me, but I knew that he was. The queue inched slowly forward. I was going to have to put up with this for a while.

'Fuck me. That is a fucking honker and a half.'

More laughs from her. I really didn't want to turn around.

'I'm surprised he can stand up with a nose like that.'

She laughed some more. I sneaked a quick look at them. He was a very fat man. She was way more attractive than him but just as rude. As he chuntered on, I weighed up my options. I could say something about his weight but I knew that pretty much anything I said would probably raise the stakes and end in a fight that I was unsure I would win. Or I could just stand there quietly seething, hoping that an enormous rabbi would magically appear and threaten him with harm. Which, on a Saturday afternoon, was unlikely. So I just took the abuse until we

The physical abuse was harder to deal with. This was in the days before parents and teachers used to get actively involved in preventing this sort of thing. I never told my parents and, even if I had, there was not much they could do. They wouldn't have considered talking to the headmaster. He'd have shrugged his dandruff covered shoulders. Essentially, no one cared. It could've been *Lord of the Flies* out there, and frequently it was, but as long as the teachers weren't being bullied and no one died, they felt that was as good as it was going to get.

I was not one to fight back, particularly in the early years. I don't remember a single piece of advice my father ever gave me but if he ever told me to stand up to bullies, I never listened. Consequently, I was preyed on by a succession of vindictive

---

got inside the ground at which point I could move away from him and pray that he wasn't sitting near me. Which he wasn't.

After that, every time I went to Arsenal, until we moved to the new stadium, I used to scan the crowd for the man. I never saw him again but it played on my mind. So much so that a year later, I was on the way to do a gig in Portsmouth and I spent the entire train journey going through the conversation and the things I would've said to him if I'd been calmer and there was less chance of physical confrontation. Even as I thought about it, it seemed crazy to still be bothered a year after it happened but these scars ran deep.

The Portsmouth venue was notorious for rowdy crowds and this night was no exception. I was introduced.

'Please welcome Ian Stone.'

I walked on to a round of applause.

'Fuck me. Look at that nose' before I'd even got to the mic. I looked down. There was a tremendously fat man sitting at the very front. Not the same one unfortunately but at this point, it hardly mattered. I'd never before spent an entire train journey or indeed the previous year practising for a response to a heckle. This poor deluded idiot had no idea of the can of worms he'd opened.

All the insults I'd been over raced through my head. I opted for simplicity.

'You're in no position to make rude comments about people's physical appearance, you fat cunt.'

It perhaps lacked the panache of Oscar Wilde, but it certainly worked for a Christmas gig in Portsmouth.

young men who no doubt spent their weekends tying fireworks to dogs and probably ended up as very successful city traders. One was much stronger than me and he regularly wrestled me to the ground, pinned my arms down with his knees and gleefully spat in my face. He used to produce the spit and let it hover over me before sucking it back up. But sooner or later, he couldn't control it and it would plop into my eyes or on my nose or into my mouth. He'd then hawk up another bit of phlegm and repeat the process. It was grim. I wanted to kill him and myself.

There was another slightly podgy boy, a year above me. He had very straight, very white teeth which I sort of held against him. I wasn't particularly scared of him but he used to hang around with a couple of bigger boys who properly terrified me, including one big blond kid who was taller than Robert. The podgy one and his mates would drag me over to the long jump pit in the playground and push me about. One time, it amused them to shove my face in the sand and make me eat it. I actually did fight that one, but there were three of them. It was the one time when I wished I was beneath the boy who spat in my face.*

---

* Unlikely as it may seem, I didn't keep in touch with either the boy who spat in my face or the podgy boy after I left school. I wasn't sure we had that much in common and I never developed a taste for sand. Thirty years later, I was just about to go on stage at Camden Jongleurs in front of five hundred people when Podge sidled up to me with a big grin on his face.

'Hi,' he said. 'I don't know if you remember me.'

I remembered him straight away. It was the teeth. What I wanted to say to him was, 'Of course I remember you, you cunt. You made me eat sand. Now fuck off!' But I didn't say that. I was so astounded that he had the front to just walk up to me as if nothing had happened, I didn't say anything. I looked at him for a second and then the compere said, 'Please welcome Ian Stone.' I walked on stage and did my gig but my mind was in a sandpit in Camden. There was a large part of me that wanted to tell the audience who he was and what he'd done to me and shame him to the point where he burst into tears and begged my forgiveness. But I wasn't sure there were too many laughs in that strategy. I just did the gig and fucked off as soon as I was done.

★

As I moved through the early secondary school years, the only thing that kept me going was Arsenal. I worshipped at Highbury, that made way more sense to me than going to synagogue. If I was going to believe in anything, it might as well be eleven men playing a game I loved to watch. Liam Brady regularly performed miracles in front of my eyes. My faith might have wavered from time to time but just when I thought my prayers would never be answered, we'd beat Spurs or stick four past Manchester United and I could leave Highbury exultant.

Shortly afterwards, The Jam appeared and Paul Weller took centre stage in my affections. He was the one I idolised. I obsessed about him. The look, the music, it felt like he'd rummaged around in my head, taken my hopes and dreams and turned them into stories in his songs. Who wouldn't like to be a famous footballer or a rock singer or a big film star? As I sat listening to Mr Goldberg tell us some fairy story about how some bloke lived to be nine hundred and fifty years old, built an ark, somehow persuaded two of every animal to get on board, made sure that the bigger animals did not eat the smaller ones and then survived a storm that consumed every other living thing, I used to think that if I was a famous footballer or a rock singer or a big film star, I wouldn't have to listen to this drivel. Sadly, I was none of these things so for the moment, I was trapped in a Noah Wonderland.

When I considered my options, film stardom seemed like a non-starter. I didn't take drama at school. No one in my family or indeed anyone I ever grew up with had been blessed with what you'd call film star good looks and I hadn't yet heard of the phrase 'character actor'. The thought of stepping on a stage terrified me; it's weird how things turn out.

Famous footballer was more of a possibility, at least in my head. In the real world, I knew early on that I didn't have the necessary skills to make the grade. The best footballer in our school, by miles, was a kid called Bruce. He was small, tough, had a lovely first touch and he could turn in very tight spaces. In the playground, no one could get near him. With him in the side, the school team did very well for a while. But as far as I'm aware he didn't even get close to a professional contract. Very few Jewish footballers ever did. It was as if the scouts had taken a decision that Jews are not athletically gifted, based purely on the evidence of what they could see with their own eyes.*

As for being a rock singer, my prospects were not quite as bleak. There were loads of Jewish rock stars. Marc Bolan, Leonard Cohen, Neil Diamond, Bob Dylan and plenty more where they came from. It was a veritable feast of Jewish talent to look up to. Debbie Harry might have been the most non-Jewish lead singer of all time but she was living with the guitarist Chris Stein. And on top of all that, there were a number of artists out there at the time who did not conform to the rock star stereotype looks. Ian Dury was a short, grizzled looking man, Pete Townshend had a nose almost as big as mine.

---

* I continued to have football related dreams for years afterwards. They generally involved falling two goals behind to some sloppy defending before the stirring comeback where I'd score two goals to get us level, the game would seesaw this way and that and it would then culminate in me making a lung busting run up the field to get on the end of a cross and score a last minute winner to complete my hat trick. Always in front of my adoring home fans. And often after I'd cleared off the line not a minute before to save an almost certain winner for them. I was nothing if not a glory hunter. But there had to be some pain first. Interestingly enough, I have friends who dream about their team winning 7-0 with them scoring five of them. That was too easy for me. Even in my dreams, I needed to suffer.

I abruptly stopped having football dreams one night in my forties. I made my now customary long run upfield in the last minute of a game and as I was about to head the winner, I stopped and thought, 'This is ridiculous. I couldn't even run that far in the first minute let alone the last. I'd have a heart attack.' That was it for my fantasy career.

The problem I had was a complete lack of musical ability. There were no musical instruments in our house. If there was a guitar, my mother would've removed the strings and stretched them across the hallway in the hope of decapitating my dad when he came in from work. Music was something to be listened to quietly, as background. The music I liked was always 'Too Loud!'. At school, I had one music lesson in twelve years. Mr Hampson was my music teacher and he could not have looked more miserable. His whole demeanour screamed 'What am I doing here with these people?' When I was at home, I knew exactly how he felt.

I suppose that if I'd walked into the class, sat down at the piano and played Grieg's *Piano Concerto*, he might have taken an interest. But it wasn't going to happen. Not only could I not play piano, I didn't know who Grieg was. I was told to sit quietly in one corner of the class while other, more gifted pupils played pieces and were then criticised by Mr Hampson. He was brutal.

'What the bloody hell was that?' he said to one girl after she'd played a Bach piece rather beautifully, I thought.

'The first part was too fast, the timing was all over the place generally and it was too loud. Try to stroke the keys rather than hit them like you're trying to get ketchup out of a bottle.'

She looked like she was about to cry. She was the most hard-working pupil in the entire school; she probably practised for weeks to get it right. I decided there and then that I would try to stay on the right side of Mr Hampson, mainly by not going to any more of his classes. This was fine by him. And me.

Even through the years when I didn't listen to The Jam that much, the years immediately after they broke up, I still listened to 'To Be Someone'. I think it's such a perfect pop song. It has such a beautiful wistful quality to the opening, almost dreamlike. And the 'Yes, I think I would like that' always makes me smile. (I have the same feelings now when I'm idly musing on what I'd do if I won the lottery – yes, I think I would like that.) Of course, like all the great Jam songs, there was a savage twist and the song descended rapidly into drug taking with people he didn't like.

But that opening, well, we could all dream couldn't we. For the kids who would go to The Jam shows, kids from council estates and rundown towns and cities, and sing along to songs about how unfair the world was and how it was going to change when we got our hands on it, dreaming was all we had. In real life, our options felt extremely limited. But to be someone who had a dull admin job in a regional office on the outskirts of London wouldn't have had the same allure to it.

The bitterness when Paul sang about having a nice time, and the way he delivered the lines, left one in no doubt. He hadn't had a nice time at all. There was that dark underside again. Everything going along quite nicely and then we're hit by some hatred or vitriol or disgust. I know that when the song was released, Paul's career was still on the up so I knew it wasn't particularly autobiographical. Even if he was taking drugs, I can't imagine he was snorting brown chalk instead of cocaine. But he doubtless would've seen some casualties. People whose money ran out and then they were out on their arse with the rest of the clowns. We all knew what that felt like. We were those clowns.

In our final year, some idiot bought three or four cans of shaving foam into one of Mr Goldberg's lessons. It might have been me. Simon got a small blob on his hand and, as if by way of a greeting patted Mr Goldberg on his back. From then on, every time he turned round to write something on the blackboard, we all found it very funny. But then things got a tiny bit out of hand. Simon sprayed me with shaving foam, I grabbed the canister and sprayed him with shaving foam. And before anyone knew what was happening, all thirty pupils in Mr Goldberg's fifth form Religious Knowledge class were absolutely covered in shaving foam. He tried to restore order but it was a losing battle.

At one point, Simon and I were wrestling over the last of the foam, crashed through the door into the corridor and collided with another teacher. She took one look at us and stormed off towards the headmaster's office. This was not a healthy development. We ran back into the classroom and relayed the news that our deranged headmaster was on his way. There then followed a manic two minutes where we all tried to remove all traces of shaving foam from the room. At the end of the two minutes, we looked relatively normal but the room absolutely stank of shaving foam. If our headmaster had suffered a terrible accident where he'd lost all sense of smell, we might have got away with it. Sadly, as soon as he burst into the room, it became apparent that his nose was working fine. He shouted at us for what felt like an hour. Our behaviour was disgraceful. Simon and I were identified and told to go home. We were suspended for the rest of the week.

Things We Didn't Have in the 1970s

Part Ten

Debt

Part of the reason we didn't have any spare cash is because no one would lend us any. Being in debt is completely normal now. In fact if you're not, people are suspicious. Debt was much rarer forty years ago. The vast majority of working people in this country weren't trusted to borrow money and pay it back sensibly. Looking at the mountain of debt we now find ourselves owing, whoever decided these things may have been right. There were credit cards but they hadn't got to our bit of West Hendon. There were some mortgages but to get one, you needed to have known the bank manager personally for twenty years or have some sort of family connection. Surprisingly, even though the Jewish people have supposedly been running a global banking conspiracy for quite some time, no one in my family knew the bank manager personally and the only connections our family had were with other members of our family. So we spent only what we earnt. I know. Weird.

Chapter Eleven

The teachers who said I'd be nothing

'Modern World' is great. Of all Jam songs, it's the one that instantly transports me back to when I was fifteen, but without the attendant feelings of inadequacy and rampant virginity. It was great live. I can clearly see Paul playing his guitar like this might be the last gig he ever does, attacking the strings with that intensity that he had. Bruce jumping up in the air and Rick working away furiously but seemingly without effort behind them. It had such energy and the lyrics were so *angry*. It felt like the biggest 'fuck off' to everyone who wasn't at the gig. I loved it.

'What kind of fool do you think I am?' is, I think, my favourite line of any Jam song. It's the sort of thing you ask when you fancy having a row. Most of the time, I steered clear of confrontation. I'd heard more than enough rows at home to last me a lifetime. This was different. This was Paul pushing back against our so called betters, being incredibly dismissive. The combative nature of the question thrilled me. The confidence to ask it. It was brilliant. I would never have asked a question like that, but Paul was not one for meek submission.

As for learning to live by hate and pain and it being his inspiration drive, well, fucking hell! This was heady stuff. It knocked me sideways when I first heard it. I'd seen plenty of hate and pain at home, but I'd just retreated into my room. To be driven and inspired by it was an incredible concept for me to think about back then. I hadn't cottoned on at this point that one could turn a negative into a positive; it was an eye-opener.

When he sang about how even at school he felt quite sure, Paul seemed to be saying that he felt destined to be in this position. I didn't feel I was destined for anything except a life that was, I hoped, slightly less drab than the one my parents were living. He used to bark out the line about teachers who said he'd be nothing and he'd really sound the G at the end. It got me every time. Like he *hated* them.

Even though Paul was young, he genuinely seemed not to care what other people thought. It was very impressive for someone his age, or any age. I still wonder how he could be so confident and where that self-assurance came from although from what I've read, his home life seemed very stable. I guess it helps to have parents who are paying attention. When they played the song live, instead of 'I don't give a damn about your review', he used to sing 'I don't give two fucks about your review'.

I cared what other people thought all the time. I'm less bothered now but I still have my moments and I'm fifty-seven. I never felt sure about anything at school except that I didn't want to be there. 1970s schooling was a lottery of birth. If you came from a rich family and could afford the fees of an independent school, or you could move to the right area so you could send your precious offspring to Camden School for Girls or its male equivalent, things might turn out OK. The rest of us had to take our chances with the comprehensive system. You might get lucky and end up in a well-run village school with polite children and kindly teachers. Or you could end up in some sort of Darwinian experiment with the feral kids at Holloway Boys.

JFS was halfway between the two. It was an inner city school but, notwithstanding some bullying incidents, it wasn't violent in the way that Holloway Boys' School most definitely was. Being a Jewish school, most of the pupils would no more get involved in physical confrontation than join Hamas. But it wasn't what you'd call exclusive. There were fifteen hundred kids at JFS, and it was hard to stand out. If you were in the top 10% and had some understanding of what was going on, you got some attention. If you were in the bottom 10% and you were so badly behaved that you needed attending to as a matter of urgency, you got some attention. Everyone else, including me, was ignored (except for once when I played a great game of football at lunchtime and arrived back in class so sweaty and stinking of body odour that I was to all intents and purposes unignorable). I was indifferent to school and school was indifferent to me. There were a couple of exceptions. I enjoyed physics because I was good at it and the teacher Mr Sutcliffe liked me. And I enjoyed English because of Mr (call me Clive) Lawton who also happened to be my form tutor. Other than that, academically, it was a complete waste of time. I spent the vast majority of the five and a bit years I was at JFS staring out of the window at the buses passing on Camden Road. I got quite good at predicting when the next one was due.

How we did in our exams was of no consequence to anyone. There were no tutors and no after school enrichment either unless one counted stealing from the local newsagents.* There were no past papers or revision timetables. There were no school league tables to compare results, so no one gave a fuck. We were

---

* After a highly lucrative two-year career stealing bars of chocolate, I got caught trying to steal a two-litre bottle of R Whites lemonade. I thought the owner was going to call the police but he just threw me out. I learnt my lesson. I never stole from his shop again.

given the date of the exam and told to be ready. If we turned up, it was a bonus. If we did well, good for us. We could go to university and possibly have a shot at a decent career and life. If we did badly, hard luck, now go and get a menial job and don't bother us again.

My O level studies did not go well. I tried to revise, but I found it hard to summon up the motivation, and it was difficult to find a quiet place to work. My home life was not conducive to concentrated learning. Studies have shown that it's hard to retain much information about the geographical features of a glacier when, in the background, you can hear your mum threatening to stab your dad with a bread knife. Somehow, I managed to get three O levels (two Bs and a C if you're wondering) and, incredibly, this was enough to get me into the sixth form. They must have been undersubscribed that year.

I took English Literature. I wasn't thinking clearly but I probably had some idea that it would give me a veneer of sophistication. My reading to this point had been limited to the Richard Allen *Skinhead* and *Suedehead* books, James Herbert's *The Rats* series, the James Herriot books about a vet in rural Yorkshire (I have no idea why, I just found them funny), and the thousands of football programmes that were kept in a cupboard in my room, so I was not prepared for the Bronte sisters or William Wordsworth. The class was full of kids I'd had nothing to do with for the first five years and was taught by a tall, balding, but very well kept man who had a florid complexion and dressed immaculately in roll neck sweaters and a checked jacket. He hated me on sight and the feeling was mutual. He thought I was uncouth and had no business in his class. I thought he was a condescending prick. We were both right. He liked us to analyse poetry which, if you didn't count 'Four and Twenty Virgins', was not something that I'd taken much of an interest in. We were reading 'Ode to

Autumn' and he asked why Keats may have given it that name. No one answered. It was very quiet. I put my hand up.

'Is it because it was written in October?' I suggested.

The entire class laughed at my joke even though I hadn't actually been joking. I just figured that if you were staring out of a window at a clear blue sky, you were unlikely to write 'I wandered lonely as a cloud'. I was quite a literal boy. Mr Condescending Prick looked at me like I'd just taken a dump in his tea. I don't think I attended another of his lessons. Shortly afterwards, I was asked to leave school for persistent gambling. Our head had caught us playing poker in the sixth form common room. He'd tried to tear the cards in half. He struggled and strained for a while and I was genuinely worried for his health. He sent me home from school and during half term, my mother received a letter requesting that she didn't send me back.

'You'll have to get a job,' she said.

'Fine by me.'

Aside from the physical attributes, I was no more grown up when I left school than when I arrived. Unlike Paul in 'Modern World', I still had no idea who I was or where I wanted to be. Whether I wanted to fit in, whether I wanted to be different. School didn't help me with that at all. I don't think my experience of school was untypical. Not terrible, not brilliant, just ordinary and essentially pointless. Schools were places where children were safely stored so that our parents could go out to work secure in the knowledge that we were at least partially supervised; or so they thought. I suffered a bit of lasting psychological damage from the bullying, but nothing that ten years of therapy and a career in stand-up comedy couldn't cure. The main purpose of the school seemed to be about teaching us not to do serious damage to ourselves or each other. It was about leading us towards being, if not good citizens, at least citizens who wouldn't go on to commit serious criminal offences. Mediocrity and the ability to conform were acceptable. Almost desirable.

One thing they didn't want too much of was independent thinking. And while being one of tens of thousands of fans hanging on the every word of a singer could hardly be described as independent thought, the things that Paul Weller was singing about definitely were. Being part of what felt like an anti-establishment youth movement was the nearest most of us would ever get to rebellion.

Things We Didn't Have in the 1970s

Part Eleven

Any Restrictions on Smoking

Smoking was permitted almost anywhere. In pubs, obviously, although sometimes it got a bit much. One could walk into a pub and visibility could be down to a couple of yards. You'd have to feel the facial features of friends to make sure it was them. You could smoke in offices. If you were a non-smoker and you worked next to a smoker, you were also a smoker. You could smoke in cinemas and theatres and playgrounds whilst waiting to pick up the kids from school. You could smoke in hospitals. You could puff away in a waiting room right up to the point that you developed lung cancer. Then they'd just wheel you into the next room and start the treatment. You could smoke on buses, but you had to go upstairs. There was nothing more alluring to some school children than puffing on a fag at the back of the bus. On tube trains, there was a smoking carriage at the back. It was the one place that during the rush hour, you were almost guaranteed a seat mainly because it absolutely reeked of cigarettes. Even smokers thought it smelled awful and they couldn't smell anything. If I think hard enough, I can still smell it now.

On aeroplanes, there were designated smoking seats at the rear. Nervous flyers could puff happily away as long as they were sat in rows 55 to 60. If you were a non-smoker, row 54 was a nightmare. With all the smoking, there was a small chance of starting a fire but luckily we were still allowed to carry liquids so they could be easily put out.

Chapter Twelve

It's blown up the West End, now it's spreading through the City

I started to spend quite a lot of time 'up West' as my Dad called it. I was a Londoner and I wanted to explore. When I was bit younger, we had the odd family outing to one of the big cinemas in town to see the latest Disney film; that stopped after I threw a large bucket of popcorn in the air. It just felt like the right thing to do at the time. Later on, when I'd developed a taste for eating popcorn instead of throwing it, we saw mainly biblical epics. *Ben Hur*, *The Ten Commandments*, stuff like that. Films where my distant ancestors were pictured wandering the desert for forty years. The films were so long, they felt like real-time documentaries.

On hot days, we'd get ice cream and watch the people go by. I'd get a Fab, a sort of rocket shaped lolly with three different flavours and hundreds and thousands sprinkled on the top. My dad would have a cone and my mum liked a Mivvi which was ice cream covered in flavoured ice. My father insisted that we go and look at the clock outside the Swiss Centre in Leicester Square. Every hour on the hour, the cowbells would start ringing and we'd watch the models of cows and milkmaids appear from the clock. They still do. And even with the advent of any number of other distractions, tourists still watch it. They must have a very low threshold for what they find entertaining.

There were some strange people in the centre of London. Sometimes, we saw the man with the sign which said 'Less lust by less protein: meat fish bird: egg cheese: peas beans lentils and sitting. Protein Wisdom Booklet 5p'. Who wouldn't want a booklet of protein wisdom for five pence. My dad as it turned out, who thought the man was unhinged. Which was a bit 'pot and black kettle' if you ask me. And anyone who was against sitting was never going to be popular with my dad. Personally, I didn't mind the idea of less peas, beans and lentils, but even as a child the poor grammar and the lack of punctuation bothered me.

We went and gawped at Big Ben and the Houses of Parliament. We went to Trafalgar Square and fed the pigeons. You could buy little pots of pigeon food (a mixture of cigarette butts and old bits of newspaper) and hold them at arm's length and the birds would come flocking. My dad made me do it once; it was disgusting. I'm thankful for bird flu scares so children don't get put through that nonsense any more.

I don't think my dad ever took me to Soho. Even he knew it wasn't a place for kids. There were a lot of dodgy people hanging around. People who were 'characters'. People who looked like they rarely saw daylight. People who, if you saw them nowadays, would still pay cash for everything. When I first went up there on my own, I couldn't believe how friendly the women were. I soon caught on.

'Fancy a quickie love?'

I was fifteen. I wanted to explain that I'd never had sex before and it was liable to be quicker than any quickie she'd ever experienced but I just carried on walking past.* The whole place felt

---

* The prostitutes are still there. A few years ago, I had the most ridiculous conversation with a woman one weekday afternoon.

'Hello, sir,' she said. 'Would you like a girl?'

illicit and a bit criminal. When I was a teenager, I thought it was great.

Aside from the dodgy characters and the women offering actual sex, there were also a number of sex shops. They were hidden behind plain doors with signs that said 'adult store'. Nowadays, the sex industry has gone mainstream. Sex toys are advertised on TV and couples go into sex shops together to look for bits and pieces they might find mutually agreeable. Back then, the only visitors were men, often wearing raincoats. They were known as the 'dirty mac brigade'. Everybody looked furtive. Being a store detective in Soho back then must have been a nightmare.

There were peep shows. Men would go in for a short period and come out ready to face the day. One never knew exactly what went on in there. Years later, I was having a wander around Soho with a fellow comic. We were between shows at The Comedy Store. We saw a sign that said 'erotic dancing show' so we decided

---

I always feel massively affronted when I get asked whether I want a woman. Do I look like the sort of man who needs female company? Apparently, yes. Interestingly, I started getting asked whether I wanted women at around the same time I stopped being asked whether I wanted to go clubbing. I still get asked whether I want drugs and, pathetically, this makes me feel good about the way I look.

'No thank you,' I said. I was always polite, even to people involved in the global trade in sex trafficking. And then, feeling like I should give a reason for my declining her offer, said, 'Sorry, I have to go and pick up the kids from school.'

This didn't seem to put her off. In her mind, the kids could wait while Dad was given some 'relief' from the stresses and strains of daily life. Yes, I might be slightly late for the school run, but how much happier would I be when I actually got there.

('You seem in a good mood Daddy'.

'Yes, I've just been wanked off by a stranger'.)

'Don't go,' she called after me. 'I've got twelve girls, they're all shapes and sizes.'

What I wanted to say at this point was, 'All shapes and sizes? Twelve? Surely that doesn't cover all shapes and sizes. Have you got an octagonal one?'

But I didn't say that. I just apologised again and walked away a bit quicker.

to go into one and find out. What happened was that you sat in a (for obvious reasons) soundproofed booth, put fifty pence in a slot and a letterbox-sized hole would appear in the wall. I put my fifty pence in and the letterbox opened up. Inside the room, women in their underwear were gyrating in a desultory fashion. One was sat in the corner having a cigarette and reading the paper. It was about as erotic as a fish-and-chip supper on a wet Sunday evening. When the women saw an opening appear, they'd dance towards it and on request, remove their remaining clothes so you could get a closer look. It was like the doctor had come round to do a gynae-cological examination and even though the woman was locked inside the house, she'd decided to go ahead with it anyway. The post boxes were opening up very regularly. There were obviously a lot of men in Soho who had a bit of spare cash and fancied star-ing at a vagina for a few minutes. The woman on a break put her cigarette out, folded the newspaper and got back to work. I saw my mate's letterbox open up. Our eyes met for a short while before a woman's backside blocked the view. After a criminally short period of time, my letterbox shut. I decided against invest-ing any more money. I met the other comic outside. I think he'd had another fifty pence worth.

There was also a cinema on Piccadilly Circus that showed por-nographic films. It features in the film *An American Werewolf in London*. It actually started out as a cartoon cinema. My dad took me to see some Daffy Duck cartoons when I was around seven or eight. As its clientele grew up, I guess they wanted to offer some-thing to keep them coming, as it were. One hopes that there was a suitable gap between the cartoon cinema closing down and the porn cinema opening up. It would've been unfortunate to see an expectant family turn up hoping to see some Looney Tunes and being confronted with something quite a bit more racy.

★

Even if it started with the streets being paved with blood, with cataclysmic overtones and ended with Dr Marten's apocalypse, I loved the fact that '"A" Bomb in Wardour Street' was about London. This was my city. That hook gets me every time. Also, it was one of the most violent songs I'd ever heard. I knew it wasn't actually about a nuclear attack but the title may well have worried my parents' generation. The Cuban Missile Crisis was only fifteen years in the past and people were still jumpy. The major world powers had huge amounts of nuclear weapons pointing at each other, the Berlin Wall was still standing and the Soviet Union was still seen as the evil empire. I knew all this but I didn't walk to school every day fearful of a nuclear holocaust. The Holloway boys were a far more pressing concern. The death and destruction caused by a nuclear attack would definitely have been a downer but on the plus side, it would've saved me having to learn any more religious knowledge. The one thing it wouldn't have done would be to stop my parents arguing, although it's possible my mum would've blamed my dad for the fallout.*

At that time, Wardour Street was not as trendy as it has since become. There were cafes and menswear shops and some of the film companies had offices there but it was all a bit run down. It did have the Marquee club, one of the best small music venues in London. Everybody played that venue. The Jam did it quite a few times early on in their career. They also played a secret gig there as John's Boys. A lot of bands did secret gigs. One snowy evening in London, when they were one of the biggest bands in the world, The Police played there. Because of the weather, most of the people invited never made it and someone was stationed outside to try and get people in. The story went that as people were

---

* Five years later, I spent an afternoon watching *Threads*, a film about Britain before, during and after a nuclear attack. I was depressed for weeks.

rushing past, this poor young man was standing in the freezing cold.

'Fancy coming in? The Police are playing a free gig.'

'Yeah, right mate.'

I saw a lot of gigs there. I saw Hazel O'Connor and The Damned. Not together obviously. I saw John Coghlan's Diesel Band. I'm not sure my hearing has ever totally recovered. I saw The Skids.* I saw Eddie and The Hot Rods sing 'Do Anything You Wanna Do'. Just for a moment, we all felt like it might be possible. Simon and I went to see a band called The Photos one evening. They had an attractive lead singer called Wendy Wu and a great single called 'Irene'; support that evening were a little known Irish band called U2. It was one of those venues that had atmosphere dripping off the walls. Or it could have been mould. It was hard to tell. But to be in a packed club while your heroes did their thing on stage not five feet from where you were jumping around was just fantastic. It was the sweatiest venue in music history. I used to come out of there looking like I'd been caught in a monsoon.

I'd started going to comedy in town as well. In early 1980, I got a phone call from Simon.

'I've been to this brilliant place in the West End. It's called The Comedy Store. I'm going next Saturday. Do you want to come?'

Since Simon had essentially changed my life by introducing me to The Jam, I was more than happy to go along with his suggestions.

Growing up, I loved comedy. I'd spent thousands of hours of

---

* When I was in my early twenties, I started playing in a regular five-a-side game at Jubilee Halls in Covent Garden. Richard Jobson, the lead singer of The Skids, used to play with us. I put him through with a nicely weighted pass, he finished with aplomb and he turned round and gave me the thumbs up. It was a thrilling moment to give an assist to a pop star.

my childhood watching *Laurel and Hardy* repeats on BBC2. I watched one called *Blotto* hundreds of times. Stan Laurel's laugh used to make me howl. I'd seen a lot of *Monty Python's Flying Circus* as well although at that time, it was a little sophisticated for my tastes and I didn't understand some of the references. I'd also loved the Spike Milligan Q shows, but they could also be hit and miss.

Comedy in the 1970s was a mixed bag. Some of it was really good. I loved watching *M*A*S*H*, an American sitcom about a medical unit during the Korean war. It was a very funny and one of the characters, Corporal Klinger, had a bigger nose than me. *Fawlty Towers* and *The Two Ronnies* were great; I can still watch them now. *Porridge* was, and remains, my favourite sitcom; the timing was immaculate. Morecambe and Wise were loved by just about everyone. Even my parents would call a temporary cessation in hostilities to watch Eric and Ernie over the festive season. A Christmas truce. Like the First World War, except the fighting was more vicious at home.

Some of the comedy back then could be sexist, racist and homophobic but then so could real life. *On the Buses* was on ITV and getting audiences of ten million viewers. (I watched a rerun of *On the Buses* recently and it's just shit. For a country that also produced *Monty Python* to come up with that is beyond comprehension. Perhaps that's what Jung meant when he talked about the duality of man.) Meanwhile on the BBC, *Terry and June* had been running for what felt like a thousand years, per episode. Looking back, it was possibly the worst sitcom ever broadcast. I was nine when it first appeared, and even then I could see it was awful. It was set in a middle class household so, instantly, it looked unlike anything I'd ever experienced. The family sat round a table for dinner. Sometimes, they didn't have the TV on at all. Terry Scott blundered and blustered about, and June Whitfield was his long-suffering wife; although not as long-suffering as the audience.

There was also plenty of stand-up comedy on TV. I was a big fan of the TV show *The Comedians*. The comics wore the standard comic's uniform of velvet jackets and frilly shirts, and the jokes were mostly of the 'these two fellas walk into a bar' variety. There were a lot of jokes about mothers-in-law. This was a pure stand-up comedy show where men (until Marti Caine, it was always men) delivered jokes straight to camera. It featured most of the famous comedians of the day including Bernard Manning and Charlie Williams. Another of the regulars was a guy called Ken Goodwin. When I was eight, I found him hilarious. He used to tell a joke and when people laughed, he'd say, 'Settle down now.' I nagged my mother into letting me join the Ken Goodwin fan club. She resisted for a while. Perhaps she was just reluctant to have another Ken in the house. After a few weeks, she gave up, sent off the joining fee and a few weeks later, a large envelope arrived with a thank you letter signed personally by Ken and a membership pack containing a badge, some photos and all sorts of hitherto unknown (to me anyway) Ken Goodwin details.

At some point, *The Comedians* morphed into *The Wheeltappers and Shunters Social Club*. It was essentially the same show but once in a while, it featured an 'exotic dancer'. It was introduced by a lugubrious chap called Colin Crompton who used to ring a bell to quieten the audience down. There are occasions when I'm on stage and I wish he was there with the bell. There was also *The Good Old Days* on BBC2, a weekly show where the audience dressed up as if they were at a Victorian music hall evening. A lot of the jokes came from the same era. There was a moustachioed MC who would jolly the whole thing along and there were singers and variety acts, but it also featured Les Dawson and Ken Dodd. I thought they were great.

I loved Dave Allen. His attitude to religion was brilliantly irreverent although when I first saw him, I never made the connection between the ridiculousness of the Catholic Church and some of the silliness that my lot (the Jews) got up to. It was also my introduction to storytelling stand-up – it was a revelation to me. The idea that a man could sit there, drinking and smoking and be so cool and funny. Oddly, I never appreciated Ronnie Corbett doing pretty much the same thing until I was much older. I remember the first time I saw Billy Connolly on Michael Parkinson's show. He was already pretty famous in Scotland, but hadn't reached a national audience until that night. He told a joke about a man whose wife had died and he'd buried her in the back garden but left her bum sticking out of the ground.

'Why have you left her bum sticking out?' asked his mate.

'I want somewhere to park my bike.'

I watched that with my dad and he was laughing so hard, I thought he might choke to death. My mother looked hopeful.

Simon had recently passed his driving test and bought a Triumph Herald, so I knew I'd get a lift into town. He'd already almost killed me with it. I was walking to a party in Edgware one evening when he pulled up. He was also going to the party. The house was about four hundred yards along the street.

I looked inside the car.

'Can I have a lift?' I said hopefully.

There were already five in there. 'I'm full up,' he said. 'But you can have a lift on the bonnet.'

Now as a grown man with a partner and children and friends who love me and some sense of mortality, I would of course say, 'Don't be ridiculous'. But as a seventeen-year-old, I thought, 'That seems like an excellent idea.'

'Yeah go on then,' I said. 'You won't drive too fast will you.'

He shook his head. Of *course* he wouldn't. I got on the bonnet and he took off like a shot. I suddenly felt that this was a very bad move on my part. I turned to look at him and his laughing face will stay with me for as long as I live. I don't know if you've ever travelled on the bonnet of a car but there's very little to hold onto; almost as if one would be better off inside the car. I grabbed hold of the windscreen wipers and Simon, being the man he is, put them on fast. He kept telling me to put my head down because he couldn't see where he was going. I suppose I should've appreciated his commitment to safety. I don't know what speed he reached before he hit the brakes but I do know I rolled a fair distance up the road and narrowly missed a lamppost. It's amazing I reached my twenties intact.

On the following Saturday, he picked me up in West Hendon. He wound down the window.

'Do you want to go on the bonnet again, or would you prefer inside the car?'

'Fuck off.'

We drove into the West End. Unlike today, with its residents' parking and quick off the mark traffic wardens, back then you could park pretty much wherever you wanted. Simon couldn't drink of course, but it didn't stop the rest of us, and I think everyone would agree that there is nothing more appealing than a gang of seventeen-year-olds who've had too much to drink. The Comedy Store was situated in a strip club on Meard Street opposite some rather shabby flats, all with red lights in the windows.* You got into the club by going up in a lift for four people. At midnight, after the strippers had got dressed and gone home, the comedy started.

By the time I got down to the Comedy Store, Alexei Sayle had been replaced as resident MC by Tony Allen. The bill was a mixture of half-decent acts, some of whom would go on to become household names (Rik Mayall and Ade Edmondson used

---

* The current property value is around £1m for a two bedroom flat. The prostitutes have moved on and been replaced by whoever can afford a million quid for a pokey flat in central London.

to do an act called The Dangerous Brothers) and people with serious mental health issues. The people with mental health issues were often funnier. There were cabaret singers, impressionists and a lot of men banging on about left wing politics. There was a Scottish Jewish comedian called Arnold Brown who provided a welcome change of pace from the rest of the evening.

'My name is Arnold Brown. I have a cult following. The cult following me at the moment is the Hare Krishna movement. I wish they'd leave me alone.'

A few years later, there was a lot of telling Margaret Thatcher to fuck off, although she was Prime Minister for another eleven years so I'm not sure the message reached her. I thought it was great. I wanted to tell her to fuck off myself. It felt like we were watching the beginnings of an unofficial opposition. We weren't of course, we were just watching men and women shouting and quite a lot of them weren't that funny but it was all we had at the time. There was a *lot* of swearing. Steve Jones would definitely have approved. Heckling was also encouraged. I don't remember anyone being thrown out for spoiling the show. Although one or two of the acts should've been.

At the end of the evening, after the main show had finished, members of the audience would get up on stage and try their hand at stand-up comedy. The audience spots, as they were known, would normally start around two-thirty in the morning and sometimes go on till four. Everybody was outrageously drunk, including the acts. It was carnage.

I watched as Tony Allen wrapped up the main show and portentously announced that it was time for our turn. There was a buzz in the room. This was what most people came for. He then produced a list from his pocket and introduced some poor sap who died on his arse. Another few came and went. They might have been brilliant but to us, the audience, they were just sacrificial lambs put up for us to devour. When the booing and catcalling got too much, Tony Allen would bang a gong at the side of the stage and that was that. Everybody would cheer. I was having a great time until I heard the words, 'Please welcome the next of our intrepid audience members, Ian Stone.'

Simon and our other friends started laughing and I realised that he'd put my name on the list. This came as a shock to me. I'd been drinking steadily through the evening. I was inexperienced when it came to booze and by this time of the morning, I was pretty pissed. What I should've done of course was turn to them and say, 'There is no way on earth that I'm going up there. And also, after this evening, I'm going to get some new friends.' But, being seventeen and drunk meant that my critical faculties were not working quite as well as they might. I thought that as my name had been read out, I had no choice in the matter and I stepped unsteadily onto the stage.

'Hello,' I said.

No one said hello back. The lights were very bright. I peered out into the darkness. I couldn't see a thing. The silence was palpable. My mouth felt terribly dry. I took the microphone out of the stand. The lead was all tangled up. I couldn't get it to untangle. In the end, I just left it as it was. My left hand was shaking and I put it in my pocket to try and stop it. It didn't help. It just caused the entire left side of my body to shake.

As my eyes adjusted to the light, I could see some of the audience. *Everyone* seemed to be looking at me. For some reason, I found this surprising. I racked my brains for something funny to say. Normally, you couldn't shut me up but now, with one hundred and fifty pairs of eyes on me and when I needed inspiration the most, none was forthcoming. The silence continued. But not for long.

'Tell us a joke,' yelled someone from the darkness. It might've been Simon. The bastard.

The Jam at The Marquee. According to my mother, this was too dangerous for a fourteen year old. Even though it's entirely possible that the majority of the heads you can see watching the band are younger than fourteen.

Simon, Warren and me on the Northern line. We're on our way to catch the overnight train to Glasgow for the Loch Lomond Festival. I'd say we're a little underdressed for Scotland, even in June. I used to pose a lot like this in photos back then. I think I was trying to make my nose look smaller.

Warren and me in the tent with the Dundee Boys. If you're reading this, thank you for not letting your fellow countrymen kill and burn us.

Paul Weller after a gig at the Rainbow 1979. Taken by my mate Robert who asked neither me, Simon or Warren to be in the picture.

Aside from Woking, I went to all of these. Thanks to Warren for his obsessive collecting and filing.

Two different Jam gigs around 1979/1980 that Robert, Simon and I attended. (I'm fairly sure that Paul didn't have costume changes.) We obviously liked this particular position in the crowd. I couldn't say where they are for certain although the top one might be The Rainbow.

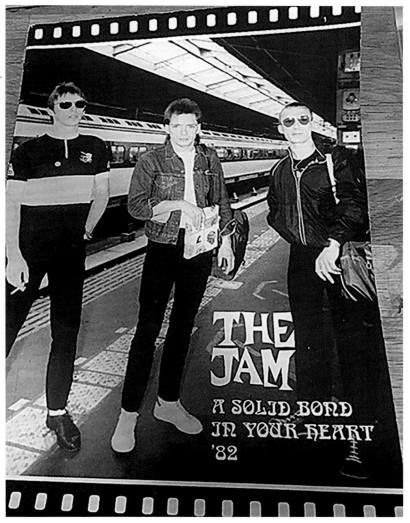

The Jam on tour. The programme revealed a very eclectic mix of venues. Leeds, Liverpool and Brighton but also Genk and Poperinge in Belgium.

The class of 1977. I'm second from left, top row. This wasn't even close to my worst hairstyle. Front centre is our tutor Clive Lawton. He changed his clogs for sensible shoes just before this photo was taken.

'Hold on,' I said, a phrase I've found rarely works with pumped up audiences at two in the morning. They were getting restless. Through the haze of alcohol, I concentrated hard and a joke popped into my head.

'Here's one. Two lepers walking down the street. One says "How are you?" and the other one says "Mustn't crumble".'

The booing and heckling started pretty much straight away.

'Fuck off.'

'Next.'

Taking his cue from the audience, Tony Allen rang the gong next to the stage.

'That's quite enough of that shit,' he said, and I could only agree.*

We went almost every week for six months. We saw so many acts. We saw Clive Anderson when he had hair. The whole thing was a thrill. I watched Simon like a hawk.

'Where are you going? Do *not* put my name down for an open spot.'

'I'm just going to the toilet.'

We heard that there was another club starting at the Raymond Revuebar, another strip club in the centre of town. This was known as The Comic Strip, and a lot of the acts who would later go on to fame started here. The compere was Alexei Sayle. As well as Ade and Rick, Nigel Planer and Peter Richardson had a

---

* Twelve years later, I went back to The Comedy Store, this time with a view to actually starting a comedy career. I did my five-minute spot and when I came off, Don Ward the owner came over to me.

'You've been here before,' he said.

'Yes, I've watched a lot of shows over the years,' I replied.

'No,' he said, 'you've performed here before.'

I was a bit taken aback. 'Well, yes . . . I did an open spot twelve years ago. It wasn't very good. How on earth did you remember?'

'The nose.'

double act called 20th Century Coyote, French and Saunders started out here, as did Rowan Atkinson. We saw Lenny Henry, Keith Allen did a spot and we saw Angus Deayton as part of a parody musical group called The Hee Bee Gee Bees. Mick Jagger and Jerry Hall came down one night to see what all the fuss was about. Finally, I was part of the in-crowd.*

---

* This is a joke by the way. I've never been part of the in-crowd. I've worked in showbusiness for the last twenty-five years and I've been in its vicinity once or twice but that's as close as I've got. If I was considered part of the in-crowd, I'd start to wonder whether it was actually that 'in'. I'm not totally sure what the in-crowd would look like but I've always imagined it would include Bryan Ferry and Marie Helvin.

Things We Didn't Have in the 1970s

Part Twelve

Raw Vegetables

I think we may have had salad once at home but it didn't go well. It was lettuce, tomato, cucumber and a bit of radish with a dollop of salad cream. It wasn't well received and we never spoke of salad again. After that, vegetables were cooked. The basic rule for the cooking of vegetables was to boil them until they were begging for their lives. And then boil them some more. I don't know if it's possible for food to have a negative nutritional value but some of the carrots and cabbage we had must have come close. A couple more minutes and they would have been puree.

Chapter Thirteen

They smelt of pubs and Wormwood Scrubs

I went to Our Price Records in Golders Green and bought 'Down in The Tube Station at Midnight' on the day it came out. The picture of the boys on a tube platform in the city I was brought up in was thrilling for me. I remember running back home from Hendon Central so I could listen to it. I think it might be my favourite opening of any song ever. Even before the lyrics started, there was the sound of the tube train and *that* bassline. And then the beauty of a distant echo of faraway voices boarding faraway trains taking them home to those that they love and who love them forever. I love the romance and the optimism of these lines. Paul may, to a certain extent, have been taking the piss, but it didn't matter. Maybe there were people who actually lived like that. I knew full well that my dad was not going home to a house where someone who loved him forever was waiting for him. But 'To take them home to the ones who they hate and who'll hate them forever and frankly would rather they never came home again' might have made you wonder why he didn't just stay out.*

---

* I still think of this song when I'm on the tube now, forty years later. Music

157

*

As often happened with Paul Weller tunes for The Jam, things took a downward turn very quickly. There are glazed, dirty steps and litter and grim newspaper headlines about Mr Jones getting run down and a madman on the rampage. The lyricism of this song was so vivid to me. Paul said that our hero fumbled for change and pulled out a Queen and she was 'smiling, beguiling'. I never had him down as a royalist but it was a beautiful image nonetheless. I read that this may have had some connection with The Beatles' 'in his pocket is a portrait of the Queen' from Penny Lane. I hoped that was true. And then Paul sang about putting in the money and pulling out a plum, a reference I assumed to our hero managing to get something out of one of the old style vending machines that used to be on station platforms (which would've been a miracle worthy of a religious shrine and regular pilgrimages to the station). Those machines were unreliable to say the least. There was a phone number one could call if you lost your money and wanted a refund. It must have been constantly engaged. Late in the evening, drunk people regularly attacked them because they'd been unable to obtain their chocolate peanuts. I once saw a man take a running kick at one, a tactic that I've found rarely works on vending machines.

The meat of this song is about some poor bloke on the underground late at night. He's got a takeaway curry and he's on the way home to his wife when he's beaten up by some thugs. Personally, I thought it was quite late to be bringing a takeaway curry home. I never liked to eat that late. Plus, who gets a takeaway and then gets on the tube? Surely there's a local curry place nearer his house.

---

has this ability to transport you. By the same token, if I ever take a ride on the New York Subway, I'll definitely have the theme tune from the original *Taking of Pelham 123* running around my head

Paul said that 'Tube Station' was about the violence at that time. We all understood that; it was dangerous out there. I'm not quite sure why, but the 1970s seems like the most dangerous period (aside from the world wars) in modern history. In the 1950s and at least some of the 1960s, there was still a deference to authority. National service played its part as well. But by the 1970s, young men with very little respect for anyone and no prospects to speak of were lashing out. When I think back, I'm stunned by the amount of low level violence. It was relentless. There were very few stabbings and even fewer shootings (an acid attack would've caused public outrage and calls for the reintro-duction of capital punishment – I'm aware this happens now but it would've been more mainstream back then) but it was differ-ently violent. More immediately violent. There were places that people of delicate sensibilities just didn't venture into. Estates where you just didn't go after a certain time of the day. Whole swathes of London where taxi drivers refused to go.

'You're takin' your life in yer 'ands if you go down there.'

'Down there' included pretty much anywhere south of the river. It also included any area with poor people or black people. I know this. I'd been brought up in Harlesden, an area with both. Not that I ever got taxis there but that was what they said appar-ently.

I saw all sorts of violent incidents. I saw one guy get thrown off a bridge ten foot into a stream below. He got up but he looked in considerable pain. I saw a number of running battles between skinheads and punks. If you were identifiable as a member of one youth culture, you were vulnerable to attack from people who belonged to another one.

There would be no way anyone would describe me as 'handy' in a fight. On the street, I was regularly pushed about by bigger kids. So was almost everyone of my age; it was just what you had to put up with. Overgrown fifteen-year-olds who'd started shaving before secondary school would throw their weight around and you had to deal with it. Sometimes, you'd get spat on, sometimes a slap or a punch and you were shoved against a wall. Occasionally, you'd be knocked down and kicked a few times. Nothing serious but it was still damaging to one's ego and confidence.

You had to keep your wits about you. In this, I've developed an instinct which has proved very useful (including a couple of times in comedy clubs when it's late at night and the drink has taken hold). I seem to be able to sense when things are about to go pear-shaped. That's why I always felt quite safe in the centre of London. There were lots of people about for one thing, and I'd grown up there so things felt familiar. Also, in town there were less marauding gangs of overgrown schoolboys. And if it did kick off, I did have one thing in my favour. As I was officially the eighth fastest schoolboy in the London Borough of Camden, I had legs that could take me far away very quickly. My strategy of running from trouble at almost every opportunity had served me well in the past and I was happy to employ it whenever it was needed.*

Youth culture was strongly demarcated and very tribal. There were mods and punks and rockers and they didn't like each other because of the way they dressed and the music they listened to. There were skinheads and suedeheads as well but I couldn't really tell the difference. We learned to live with the possibility of getting beaten up by any of the members of the myriad youth cultures roaming the streets. And they liked to roam, mainly because there was nothing to do indoors. People might bemoan our youth staying on their sofas playing *Call of Duty* but at least the ones who are doing that are not out stabbing people.

---

* I still am. The reaction time is the same but the movement takes a little longer.

There were even different Jewish gangs. We once went over to Epping Forest Country Club for a disco and Robert ended up having a fight with the Fairlop Boys. I'm not sure how it started but before I knew what was happening, Robert was fighting with a boy over the pool table. I watched on in horror. It was over almost before it started.

'Thanks for helping,' Rob said to me.

'That's alright,' I said, before I realised he was being sarcastic.

As if I didn't have enough violence in my life, I went to see a lot of football as well. I saw most of England's matches around this time.* I used to go to the home internationals at Wembley. These were played between England, Scotland, Northern Ireland and Wales and, as can be imagined, they were fiercely contested both on and off the pitch. Through trial and error, I realised that if you managed to get to the front of the upper tier at Wembley Stadium, there was a ten foot drop to the lower level so you could have an unimpeded view of the pitch and also any scraps happening in the lower tier. There was a tremendous amount of fighting in the crowd. I once watched in wonder but also complete safety as the most amazing punch-up between England and

---

* The England football team had fallen a long way from their World Cup-winning peak twelve years earlier. I often wonder whether the FA missed a pivotal moment in British history, every bit as important as the Magna Carta or the reformation, when they failed to make Brian Clough the manager. I think that with Brian Clough at the helm, England would've qualified and gone on to do quite well at the World Cup of 1978. If they could've somehow knocked Argentina out, politics in that country would've taken a very different turn. Without a World Cup Final victory, General Galtieri would not have been emboldened to invade the Falkland Islands. There would've been no taskforce sailing to the South Atlantic, no monumental turnaround in the polls for the 1983 election for Margaret Thatcher and Michael Foot would've been Prime Minister. Admittedly, these predictions get a little hazy but the point is, in not appointing Brian Clough the FA have a lot to answer for. Depending on your politics, you may want to thank them personally for saving us from Michael Foot.

Wales fans unfolded directly beneath where I was standing. A man was punched in the face. It was like they'd arranged a fight just for my entertainment.*

I got the football bug when I was seven years old. As much as this is a book about The Jam, Arsenal were my first love. There were a few years in the 1980s when I lost interest and there have of course been ups and downs and a few moments where I've almost called it a day. But after all this time, me and Arsenal have come to the realisation that we're stuck with each other. It's like I'm in a long term and somewhat co-dependent relationship with Arsenal, although I need them way more than they need me. Whereas with The Jam, they appeared in the late 1970s and I was instantly and completely smitten. By 1982, they were gone. We had an intense five-year affair, and the effects have rippled down the years.

Liam Brady was my hero. A skinny Irish kid, he'd joined Arsenal as a fifteen-year-old and come up through the ranks. He was our boy. He scored a fantastic goal away at Spurs. He glided over the turf and he had a wand of a left foot. There's something about left-footed players and I'm very glad I got to see him in the flesh. And I got to see him a lot. I got a Saturday morning job in the local Co-Op when I was thirteen and, with the money, every weekend through the winter months when I could make it, I'd travel the length and breadth of the country watching Arsenal. It was fun but incredibly dangerous. I can't believe my mother let me go on my own. I guess she figured I might actually be safer without my dad.

---

* I'm ashamed to say this but I used to quite enjoy watching the fights. There were never weapons involved so it never got too heavy. I often thought that when there's a scrap, I could happily get into a cage and have it lowered into the centre so I could watch in safety. A bit like what people do when they want to look at sharks up close.

'Have a nice day,' she'd say as I'd venture north to Coventry or Stoke or Derby or Liverpool or anywhere that hated Londoners. These towns all looked poor and dispirited, probably because they were. I'm sure there were nice parts but town planners didn't often build stadiums in upmarket areas. To the people in those places, I was just some 'flash cockney bastard' who came from somewhere posh like London. Even though most of them, if they ever saw Harlesden or West Hendon, would very likely have stopped trying to hurt me and organised a benefit gig for me and my family.

On matchday, a huge mob of Arsenal fans would meet at whichever railway station we were leaving from. Even though it was early in the morning, people would be drinking. Regular travellers and young families on a day trip hurried past looking horrified to be sharing a station concourse at nine in the morning with hundreds of drunk, abusive men. Often there would be fans of other teams milling about waiting to travel. There would be skirmishes. There were no colours so it was difficult to know who was who.

I travelled by myself but there were always familiar faces to nod hello to. It was very similar later on at Jam gigs but with much more of a possibility of violence at the football. At some point, we'd pile onto the football special and we'd be whisked (well, rarely whisked, trundled perhaps, or limped) to our destination. Sadly, the word 'special' denoted the fact that the train was not part of the regular timetable rather than signifying a high level of on-board facilities. There were very little in the way of comforts. Most of the lightbulbs didn't work. The toilet facilities were basic. There was never a buffet car. Sometimes, someone would come round with a big bag of white bread rolls, either cheese or ham. I was still vaguely trying to eat only kosher food at this time so I always opted for cheese until one afternoon when they only had ham left. I was starving so I guiltily nibbled on my first ever ham roll. I figured that if there was anytime I might get away with it, it would be on the Sabbath, when God may well be otherwise disposed. It was very nice and I've never looked back.*

Most people bought alcohol onto the train and would sit and drink, smoke and play cards. Once in a while, a fight would break out. It was seen as practice for later in the day. There was a lot of singing and swearing. When we arrived at our destination, waiting for us at the end of the platform would be a large number of the biggest coppers available locally. They'd be wearing high visibility jackets and they'd make it very clear that we were not welcome. At that time, the relationship between police and football fans was at an all-time low. We'd sing songs about how shit their town was. We weren't often wrong, but that was hardly the point. We'd also do pig impressions. We used to sing 'Harry Roberts is our friend, he kills coppers'† to wind them up.

They looked like they wanted to kill us; I can't say I blamed them. Some of them had big Alsatian dogs who also looked like they wanted to kill us. I once had a police dog sink his teeth into the arm of my jacket.

'Get him off. He's got my jacket,' I said to the handler.

The handler looked at me with utter contempt. 'Fuck off back to London you little cockney cunt.'

His fellow coppers started laughing. So did some of my fellow fans.

---

* I once took an epic trip to Bolton away. There was a derailment ahead of us on the way up, we arrived half an hour late and missed the only two goals in a 1-1 draw. On the way back, there was another derailment ahead of us and we stopped at Nuneaton station for two and a half hours (with nothing to eat. I appreciated the irony. No-one else seemed to). I got back home around four in the morning. The next day, I overslept, missed the start of *The Big Match* and missed the goals again. I've never seen them.

† A notorious murderer serving a life sentence for killing three policemen.

'I'm going to report you,' I should've said but didn't. I had to hide the jacket from my mother for weeks.

Often, there would be a large mob of the home fans waiting and hoping for a chance to attack a few of us. The police would've been more than happy for them to do so, but their job was to escort us through the town centre towards the football ground and stop us from starting a full scale riot. We'd kick over a few bins and even smash the odd window but really, there was very little damage we could do to, to choose three towns at random, Derby or Stoke or West Bromwich that would make them look any worse than they already did. It felt thrilling to see the look of terror on the faces of Saturday afternoon shoppers as we marched through the shopping precinct. Having said that, I'm under no illusion that the locals were looking at this mob of football hooligans and thinking, 'Do you know who really scares me out of that lot? The little Jewish looking one in the middle.' It was like a criminal gang had bought a trainee accountant on a day out.

Once inside the ground we were relatively safe aside from a few coins that were thrown at us. The cages that kept our hooligans in also kept their hooligans out. We'd sing some more songs. I got quite adept at starting the songs although it was a risky business. I once shouted very loudly, 'Give us an "A"' at the wrong time, and no one did. It was very embarrassing. If we were up north, our fans would wave ten pound notes at the home crowd.

'Buy yourself a house, you northern cunts!' I can't fathom why they didn't like us.

I thought that would be fun, so the next time we were playing up north, I asked my mum if I could borrow a tenner.

'I can't afford it,' she said.

'I'll bring it back,' I said. 'I just want to wave it at northerners. So I can highlight the economic disparity.' I might not have said the second bit. My mother reluctantly handed over the money.

I'm sure my mother saw news reports of football violence and worried about my safety. But not enough to stop me going. I think if it would have been after the Hillsborough disaster, she might have objected more strongly but at that time, aside from a match at Ibrox Park in Scotland where sixty-six people died in a crush at an Old Firm game and which may well have completely passed her by, people didn't die at football matches. As for my dad, he saw all sorts of running battles and general mayhem, but I guess he thought I could handle myself.

It was dangerous. At Ashton Gate in Bristol, I got involved in a near riot in a park and got knocked over by a police horse. At Sheffield Wednesday, we were herded down the very same tunnel that Liverpool fans died in some years later. In Liverpool, I got chased three miles back to the train station by youths who wanted to steal my sheepskin coat (I must have lost around half a stone in sweat staying ahead of them). If my parents saw any of that, they may have thought twice about letting me go to football. Luckily, they didn't. There was just a vague 'Be careful' from my mother as I left on a Saturday morning. She still says that now.

I only got beaten up once. In Wolverhampton, I got separated from the main herd of Arsenal fans making our way back to the coaches. As I said, it's not like I had any mates to look out for me. I nipped down an alley for a piss and by the time I came out, the bulk of the fans had turned a corner and disappeared. The Wolves fans who had been following fairly close behind spotted me and the chase was on. They caught me on a piece of waste ground. It was as grim as it sounds. I was like a young zebra, alone on the plains in Africa being cornered by a group of hyenas.

SCENE

A David Attenborough wildlife programme. We see a fifteen-year-old with a big nose walking alone through a Wolverhampton housing estate. There is a sense of foreboding.

ATTENBOROUGH (Voiceover)

Here in Wolverhampton, the young, big nosed cockney male finds himself alone. He only went into a paper shop for some chewing gum and when he came out, the rest of his mates had disappeared. He now finds himself lost and vulnerable and awaits his inevitable fate at the hands of his natural predator Wolverhamptonus Hooliganus.

Before I knew what was happening, I was surrounded. They pushed me around. I have no idea why but I took a swing at one. I figured I had nothing to lose but it may have been a mistake.

'Fookin 'it the cockney bastard,' said the leader. I'd never heard as broad a Black Country accent as that before; I thought it was ridiculous. I started laughing. That probably didn't help either. They piled in.

'Why's 'e laughing?' said the leader as he punched me in the head.

'Listen to yourselves,' I wanted to say. But I just curled up in a ball and waited for it to end. After a while, they got bored and ran off. I picked myself up, wandered back to the station and got on the train home. Having fought for the honour of the team, I was expecting some sort of hero's welcome, perhaps a round of applause but I got nothing.

The one place where I almost never encountered any violence was when The Jam were playing. Others have a different experience. Not least the band, who definitely saw some punch-ups. But for me and my mates, Jam gigs were more of a celebration of the music and the community. There was also something about having the lead singer's dad in charge that seemed to calm everyone down. John Weller looked like the sort of guy not to be fucked with. He may have been nice to the fans and made us tea and provided us with tickets for gigs but we could see there was another side to him and none of us wanted to be in his bad books. He'd had to deal with record company executives for one thing although it's unlikely they would've met anyone like him. It was like we'd come to a party at Paul's parents' house and we all had to mind the furniture and each other while we were there. It was more about youthful energy and exuberance. Paul and the boys seemed to channel any violent thoughts into the lyrics and the songs. However angry we might feel, Paul was angrier. No one could've attacked another member of the audience as violently as Paul attacked his own guitar.

Punk gigs were marginally more dangerous, the dancing in the mosh pits was more violent. But the main danger was being spat on. There was *a lot* of spitting.* I used to get home and find bits of spit in my hair. It was disgusting. I got the idea that punk was about upsetting the social mores of the time, and there was nothing more upsetting to polite society than spitting. But I still can't understand how, when the first person spat at a band during a punk gig, the band didn't just instantly stop playing and make an announcement. Something along the lines of, 'Look, I don't know who just spat at me, but it's disgusting. If anyone else does that, we'll stop the gig straight away and I will jump off stage and punch the spitter in his drool filled mouth. We might all be punks and I'm all for bringing down the system but I won't be much help if I catch a communicable disease.' That would've nipped that in the bud there and then.

Skinheads were still the number one danger. Even though Paul had not been specific about who the thugs were in 'Tube Station', there were enough hints through the song that the men who'd administered the beating were a gang of skins. Men who smelt of pubs and Wormwood Scrubs and too many right wing meetings.

---

* Robert once upset Sting when he spat at him at an early Police gig. Robert is now a very successful business- and family-man.

That was one of my favourite lyrics. The idea that the smell of right wing meetings could linger. If that wasn't enough of a clue, there was also 'the smell of brown leather'. Unless the poor man was being beaten up by particularly thuggish right wing business-men wearing recently polished brown brogues, this could only be skinheads. I've since learned that proper skinheads were not like that at all. That they listened to ska music and hung out with black people. Which was great but, from where I was standing in 1978, it was hard to tell the difference.

The most important thing was to keep your eyes open. If you saw more than two shaven heads moving in your direction and you weren't a doctor specialising in the treatment of cancer, the easiest thing was to get away as quickly as possible. I was quick for my age and skinheads were weighed down by their massive boots. It was definitely not a good idea, having heard the song, to sidle up to them and try to have a surreptitious sniff to see what pubs and Wormwood Scrubs and right wing meetings might smell like. As it turned out, aftershave, leather polish, and aggres-sion caused by a crisis in their masculinity.

One time, me and Simon went to see Bad Manners at the Electric Ballroom in Camden. Like all ska bands, they had a large skinhead following but we figured that if we kept ourselves to ourselves and just skanked for an hour, we'd be fine. It was quite dangerous on the way there. England had beaten Scotland 2-0 earlier that day at the football at Wembley and London was teem-ing with men in kilts drunkenly singing songs and growling at the locals so there was very little chance for public gloating. One man tried to poke me with a Scotland flag. I ducked at the last moment.

When we got inside the venue, I felt, incorrectly as it trans-pired, on safer ground.

'Great result today,' I said. Simon grunted his agreement but I don't think he was listening. I pressed on.

'I'm glad we beat them. I hate those Scottish bastards,' I said even though if I thought about it, I didn't hate them at all. Indeed, I had a lot of respect for the Scots. They'd invented television and penicillin. I appreciated that. And their commitment to football was admirable. These were people who saved up all their money to trek all the way to London to watch their team humiliated on a biennial basis. Some of them went all the way to Argentina for the World Cup. It was rumoured that one or two of them had never come back. In my opinion, these were people who had their priorities correctly ordered.

Simon grunted again. He was watching the support band. A large skinhead suddenly appeared in front of me. I moved to one side so I could once again see the stage but the skinhead moved with me. I looked up. This bloke was not much taller than me but he was much, much wider.

'Excuse me mate,' I said in as cockney an accent as I could manage. I always found that people responded better if I affected to be more working class than I actually was. It didn't produce the required response.

'What was that you said?' he said to me. 'About the Scots?'

'Nothing,' I said.

'Cos I'm Scottish,' he said. It was odd. He clearly wasn't Scottish. He couldn't have sounded less Scottish. For one thing, I could understand what he said. He sounded very cockney. He sounded like the last ten generations of his family had been born and brought up in East London. He sounded like an extra from *Oliver!*. The only correct response would've been to laugh in his face and say, 'Don't be ridiculous, you sound like Arthur Mullard'* but I'm not sure he'd have taken it that well. So I mumbled some apology about not meaning to offend his Scottish ancestry.

---

* A character actor in the 1970s who specialised in cockney geezers. He had a chart hit with Barbara Windsor and appeared in *Chitty Chitty Bang Bang*.

He shoved me in the chest and I fell against a wall behind me. He sneered at me and wandered off, no doubt feeling proud to have avenged William Wallace and given the effete English bastard a piece of his mind.

When 'Tube Station' was released in late 1978, it was banned from airplay by the BBC due to its 'disturbing nature'. Which goes to show you how out of touch the bosses at the BBC were at that point. Not least as we now know that what was going on in the BBC studios was so much worse. I think enabling Jimmy Savile to sexually abuse children on the premises was a whole other level of disturbing compared to a song about violence on the tube.

There was a rumour that the Radio1 DJ Tony Blackburn had complained about the song. 'It's disgusting the way punks sing about violence. Why can't they sing about trees and flowers?' he'd possibly said. Even if he hadn't said it, it sounded exactly like the sort of thing Tony Blackburn would say. I had nothing against songs about trees and flowers. I loved 'California Dreamin'' by The Mamas and the Papas. But I didn't go to Jam gigs to listen to songs about nature. Most of the kids who worshipped Paul Weller lived in poor neighbourhoods. We barely saw trees and flowers and even if we did, we didn't spend too much time admiring them because we were on the lookout for marauding gangs of skinheads.

I recently asked my parents what they remembered of that time and whether they were concerned for my safety. My dad said he wasn't worried at all. I was slightly put out, but I guess that by that time, he'd managed to get to his forties unscathed and on some unconscious level, I think he understood that if someone like him, someone with no common sense whatsoever, could make it, anyone could.

My mother felt very differently. She said she worried almost constantly. She had every reason to do so. I'm sure there would have been evenings when, even with all the sleeping pills she was necking, she still would've had trouble sleeping. When I'd been to Bolton or Liverpool or Derby and the train had been delayed because there'd been a riot at the train station and I still wasn't home by eleven. And there were no mobile phones to let her know I was still alive and most of the phone boxes had been vandalised and someone had taken a shit in the only one that worked. But I'd always walked through the door at some point so I guess she came to some sort of acceptance that even though I was unreachable* I was probably OK.

As a parent of two teenage boys, I can't begin to imagine letting them put themselves in the sort of danger that my parents allowed me to flirt with. Things are very different now. We're much more aware of the possibilities. Kids rarely play outside any more, at least not unsupervised. What with all the pretty much constant media stories about paedophiles lurking on every corner, what parent would risk it? The same goes for a giant political demonstration against the Nazis. I might agree with the sentiment but if there's a reasonable chance that racists will attack the march, I'd think twice before letting my boys attend. And as for allowing them to go and watch Sham 69, a band with a huge right wing skinhead following, I might ask whether they could find safer ways to fill their evenings. Like painting graffiti on motorway bridges or surfing on overground trains.

Most of us survived of course. There was the odd death at football or on protest marches. One or two kids got run over by drunk drivers and somebody probably got decapitated leaning out of a train window. But even with all the playing outside from eight in the morning until it was dark and the lack of seatbelts

---

* Which I was, both in and out of the house.

and smoke alarms and the drug experimentation and the pervy bloke at number 45 that we were all told to avoid, most of us got through to adulthood. On some deep level, even my mother must have figured everything would probably be alright. She'd lived through the war so danger was a relative concept.

Things We Didn't Have in the 1970s

Part Thirteen

Endless Football on the Telly

It's amazing to think that back then, we were only allowed to see a maximum of eight hours of televised football per year. Now they show more than that on any given Sunday. The only live game shown on TV, on both the major channels, was the FA Cup Final. My dad and I would settle down at nine in the morning and, except for toilet breaks, not move until late afternoon. We'd flick between the two channels although that required getting up so we'd only do that when things got really dull. Snacks would be provided, I have no idea who by. There being nothing of interest for her, my mum would take Beverley out for the day.

The whole broadcast would start with the viewers being introduced to the teams at their respective hotels. We would then be 'treated' to a cup final version of *It's a Knockout* where representatives of the two competing teams would play stupid games involving them falling in large pools of water. This would be commentated on by 'the voice of rugby league', Eddie Waring. Stuart Hall used to do the voiceover and laugh when people fell in the water.* Once we'd got that out of the way, we'd join the teams on the bus for the drive up Wembley Way. At three, we'd get to watch the game. Usually, it was a massive disappointment.

---

* Although I imagined he was laughing less when, like so many other BBC presenters of the day, he was convicted of indecent assault and multiple sexual offences.

Chapter Fourteen

And if I get the chance
I'll fuck up your life, Mr Clean

I bought the *All Mod Cons* album the day it came out in November 1978. Waiting for a new Jam album or single became part of the ritual of being a fan and we'd heard months before that something was in the pipeline. When a release date was announced, we'd mark it on the calendar. There's very little nowadays that I have the same feelings for. Perhaps when I was waiting for the latest episodes of *Breaking Bad* to download during the last series, but not much else.

Once I had it in my possession, my mother would see very little of me for the next three months. I'd just drive her mad playing it really loudly on a loop. The more pissed off she got, the louder I played it. In between telling my father not to do any one of the approximately five thousand things he did that irritated her, she'd bang on the door and yell at me to 'Turn that noise down.' (Beverley would be sitting in her room. She told me that she heard the songs so often, she knew when the guitar would kick in and she could tell the exact moment when my mum would yell at me.) Whatever my mother said, I completely ignored her. I'd long ago stopped listening to anything she, or indeed my father, said to me and having a new Jam album could only help. It gave me something to focus on for a few months. Something to help tune out the shit happening inside and outside my house.

My parents were twenty years into a loveless relationship. It had started badly, gone downhill from there and things were definitely coming to a head. My father's arrest and suspended sentence had been the final straw; the loathing was now out in the open. I caught my mum glaring hatefully at my dad one time and she looked like she wanted to vaporise him there and then. As much they both got on my nerves, I didn't want to see that, so most of the time I stayed in my room.

Sometimes, against my better judgement, I got involved. My parents were standing in the hall screaming at each other one evening. I have no idea how the argument had started. By this point, I'm not sure they did either.

'You never do anything around the house,' said my mother, not without some basis in fact.

She turned to me for support even though I just happened to be passing. 'He never does any stuff around the house.'

It was true but I shrugged my shoulders as if to say, 'You married him.' I'd lived with my father long enough to know that doing stuff around the house wasn't his thing. Anything that didn't involve pleasure for Ken Stone wasn't his thing.

'I'm always doing stuff around the house,' said my dad, with no basis in fact whatsoever. He may well have even believed this, as if lifting his feet to let my mother hoover underneath constituted 'stuff'. Even I looked sceptical. He tried not to look at me.

'Shut up,' screamed my mother getting very emotional. 'Shut up!'

'Shut up, shut up, shut up!' repeated my dad. 'That's all you've got in your vocal berry.'

We all stopped for a second. Vocal berry? What the hell is that?

My mother worked it out first. 'Vocabulary, you fool,' she said, laughing bitterly.

I laughed at this as well. My dad didn't and stormed off, no doubt to do more stuff around the house.

All Mod Cons was, I think, the best Jam album to date. From the first chord of the title track, it felt like a massive step forward. 'The Place I Love' had some beautiful, poetic imagery. 'Neon lighting controlled by lightning' was a favourite. 'Billy Hunt' was about a boy dreaming of a better life. There was a great line about not being pushed around by anyone and then the idea that perhaps they might allow it but only for a short while. There weren't a lot of laughs in Jam songs, but I liked that one. The defiance followed by the realism of the song perfectly captured that feeling of being a teenage boy. As for the rest, any album that ends with 'Down in the Tube Station at Midnight' and '"A" Bomb in Wardour Street' definitely has something going for it.

'Mr Clean' knocked me sideways. The tune was great and I was impressed by the slow, confident way that it started. This felt like a band really getting into its stride. The song starts so matter-of-factly. Paul is singing about a regular bloke. Nothing to get too worked up about, just a happily married guy getting a bit of breakfast before commuting to work. If she'd have been listening, my mum would've loved the first few lines.

But it was the next lines where things took a turn for the worse. Where Paul warns the protagonist to look away if he ever sees him in the street. And I'm thinking, 'Hang on, Paul doesn't seem so keen on this bloke. Who is this man and what has he done to Paul'? And then this: 'Cos I hate you and your wife, and if I get the chance I'll fuck up your life.'

I cannot describe how taken aback I was by the violence of these lyrics. I understand the concept of an ironic title now, but I certainly didn't in 1978. Not only does Paul hate the man, he also hates his wife. Why I don't know. And then to say that he'll fuck up his life if he ever gets the chance. Bloody hell. He really emphasised the 'fuck up your life' as well. He meant it. I actually found it more shocking that Paul is saying that he'll fuck up the man's life as opposed to just beating him up. And then the threat of 'Mr Clean, is that seen' really chilled me. There was something so visceral about the whole thing.

Back then, very few people would've lived lives like Mr Clean. Certainly no one we knew. But for me, it was never about the bitter resentment that seemed to be the theme of this song. I was fifteen at this point and I partially identified with and aspired to be Mr Clean. I think it was a Jewish thing. That desire to be or at least appear to be respectable. To fit in. I'd got that from my grandparents. Perhaps if we try and become part of the establishment, they might sneer at us behind our backs but they won't round us up and march us into gas chambers again.

I couldn't understand Paul's utter contempt for this man and his, to my mind, blameless wife. What did she ever do to Paul? So he got drunk at the annual office do, so what? Didn't everyone? Having a smart blue suit and going to Cambridge, I never thought there was anything wrong with either of those things. I'd long understood that Cambridge was never going to happen for me but I didn't hate the people who went there. As for graduating from *The Sun* to *The Times*, that is something that I thought was a good thing. *The Times* might be slightly to the right of the political spectrum but it's hardly *Mein Kampf* is it? And as for his parents being proud of him, what's wrong with that?

I sang along with 'Mr Clean' just like everybody else. You could really get behind the lyrics. Shouting 'fuck up your life!' was great fun. Me and all the other boys and girls in the audience were going to fuck up Mr Clean's life if we got the chance. Not that there was much I could do to him. Perhaps not deliver his newspapers on time or knock on his door and run away before he answered it.

I learned later that Paul wrote 'Mr Clean' after a businessman behaved inappropriately to his then-girlfriend when they were in a hotel. The vitriol made sense at that point and I realised it was more personal than I'd first thought. Some stupid, lecherous prick thinking he can touch up a woman because that's what men did in the 1970s. I'm not surprised Paul was so pissed off.

Things We Didn't Have in the 1970s

Part Fourteen
The Internet

The internet is great. It's helpful and convenient and the choice of pornography is extensive. But it does rather limit conversation. In the 1970s, if an argument started about, for example, which prime minister took us into the Crimean war, the discussion would've been lively. Some would've suggested Gladstone, others Disraeli, these being the two Victorian PMs we'd have heard of. At some point, unless one of the group was a student of British political history, we may have given up. Or found out at a later date. Or not at all. Whereas now, if you've got Wi-Fi, you just look it up. In a way, it's a shame.[*]

There was, of course, no social media. I have mixed feelings about this. Watching the Eurovision Song Contest or England football matches while chatting on social media is great. You can have insane, funny conversations with people you've never met. I once got into a discussion with a famous political commentator about sex dungeons and why one never gets sex attics (it's getting the equipment upstairs that is the real problem). It was a tremendous way to pass the afternoon. But you would have had this book far sooner if I hadn't spent so much time doodling about on Twitter or Facebook. It does rather eat into your working day.

It's also possible that forty years ago, I was much more content not knowing what my friends were up to and not having the consequent feelings of jealousy or anger or upset or sympathy or, once in a blue moon, happiness. I also would've seen far fewer photos of food. If I wanted to show my friends a photo of my breakfast in 1977, I'd take the photo, then take another twenty-three photos to use up the roll, remove the film from the camera, put it in an envelope, take it to Boots the chemist, wait a week, collect it and take the photo round to each of my friends, show it to them and say, 'That's what I had for breakfast last Tuesday.'

---

[*] The Earl of Aberdeen – I'd never heard of him either.

Chapter Fifteen

Life is a drink and you get drunk when you're young

While I was following The Jam around the country or, when at home, playing them to death at a volume that would upset neighbours two streets away, I was also secretly in love with Kate Bush. I'd seen her on *Top of the Pops* singing 'Wuthering Heights' and I was instantly hooked. She was floaty and ethereal, qualities that the girls in my social circle didn't really possess. And when I say girls in my social circle, what I mean is girls that I used to see in the playground. Kate Bush played gentle songs with melodic harmonies. They were about literary heroines I'd never heard of and secret affairs with imaginary men. She had an otherworldly quality that I found intriguing. For a Jam fan, it was confusing.

Of course I didn't tell a single soul – it was my guilty secret. Nowadays, it feels like kids can like whatever they like. They can wear what they like and express themselves in whichever way feels comfortable to them and they're unlikely to be beaten up for it. But when *The Kick Inside* was released on my birthday in 1978, like it was personal gift from Kate to me, I took a solo trip into the West End to buy the album. I couldn't let Simon see me with a Kate Bush album, or really any album by a female singer songwriter. As far as he was concerned, I wasn't that sort of boy.

The Jam presented far less complications. I was more than happy to let people know I was a Jam fan. Every time they were played on the radio, I sang along. I knew all the words. I had an approximation of the look. And I wasn't alone. As each single and album appeared, there were more and more of us. Even as I was listening along to Paul singing songs about individualism, I was much happier as part of the herd. Paul Weller was angry, so was I. The Jam played songs one could jump about to. It felt like the sort of stuff that boys should like. I kept Kate Bush to myself.

I think my new sensitive side helped in me getting my first proper girlfriend. Her name was Susan and she was a year younger than me. I somehow plucked up the courage to ask her out; she said yes. I thought I'd misheard. I had to ask her again just to make sure. We went out. It wasn't terrible, so we went out again. We saw *Grease* at the Golders Green ABC. We'd go out to the cinema and then I'd walk her back to her house near Wembley and we'd snog and fumble about around the back of the garages beside her dad's house. Every so often, we'd be caught in the headlights of a car pulling in and we'd scuttle behind the garage door laughing. On more than one occasion, our braces* got tangled up and we were locked together for a short time. I tried my best to get my hand inside Susan's top, but she was having none of it. We'd kiss for a while and when I thought she was horny enough, I'd make an attempt and she'd push my hand away. After six frustrating weeks of this, on my sixteenth birthday, I thought I might be allowed a feel as some sort of birthday treat. Instead, she gave me a Parker pen and a birthday card and then she told me she didn't want to go out with me any more. This was not the present I was hoping for, although it was a very

---

* Teeth, not trousers.

nice pen. She later came out as a lesbian, although, before you make the obvious assumption, I should point out there were quite a few boyfriends after me.* Surprisingly, we're still friends. A few years afterwards, she married her partner and she asked me to be best man at the wedding.†

I recently watched the video of 'When You're Young'. It's charming. All the young kids around the bandstand, the band laughing and joking and looking not much older than the kids. Listening to the song again, I'd forgotten how bleak some of it is. There was the upbeat idea of life being timeless and the days being long when you're young. And then the realism of finding out life isn't like that, setting up your dreams to have them smashed in the end. I could easily see how that might happen. And then the fact that you've got time on your side and they're never going to make you stand in line, you're just waiting for the right time. Optimism, pessimism and then optimism again. It really jerks you around. But then I thought, that was exactly how things were back then. The line about tears of rage rolling down your face but still you say it's fun captured the feeling of that time perfectly. Veering wildly from delight to despair and back again. That's how it was for me. Sure, there were fun moments. Times when I would've been helpless with laughter. The time at primary school when I had a running race in the playground with a kid called Jonathan Dweck and I couldn't stop myself at the end; I crashed through the fence and almost gave an old lady a heart

---

* Including one guy who, she told me, had the tiniest penis she'd ever seen and presumably will now ever see.

† At which ceremony I got to do the following joke: 'Of all the women that have dumped me, Susan was the only one to whom I could legitimately have said, "You only broke up with me because you're a lesbian."' It got a big laugh at the time.

attack as she was walking past the school. Her face will live with me to the grave.

But most of the time, it wasn't fun. When I was trying and failing to chat up a member of the opposite sex. That wasn't fun at all. Or when I was twelve years old and I was at some family wedding in the Majestic Ballroom in Willesden and I've been put on the kids' table with seven- and eight-year-olds, that wasn't fun. Even though it was still preferable to being on a table with all my aunts and uncles who all spoke English with a slight Eastern European accent and were probably born in some village in Poland called Plodj or Bilj and lost forty cousins in the Holocaust. They were like characters in *Fiddler on the Roof*. What did I have in common with these people?

My parents were still nuts. I couldn't believe I was even related to them. It made no sense to me. Was this my future? Is this what I had to look forward to? When Paul sang about how the world is your oyster but your future's a clam, I was right with him. I dreaded the prospect of living either of my parents' lives when I got older. They seemed so domestic. My mother had a full-time secretarial job but aside from when she was working, she stayed in the house doing all the cooking and cleaning and anything else that required effort. She made sure that me and Beverley had food to eat and that we got to school on time wearing the correct uniform. For all this, she got no thanks whatsoever. I feel guilty about that. If she felt some bitterness, I can hardly blame her.

My dad had quite a bit of free time due to doing fuck all around the house. By this point, my mother was desperate for him not to be at home so if he'd have gone to the pub every night, it would've been fine by her. Sadly, he wasn't a drinker. He spent his time in his chair reading the newspaper or watching television. At the weekends, he went to watch sporting events and as I seemed keen, he took me along.* It wasn't that he felt the need to take me to lighten the load on Helena, it was just that he was going anyway and I was genuinely interested.

It was an excellent arrangement for both of us. It gave us some time together which I suppose was a positive thing. He's never been a great conversationalist and we didn't have a lot in common, but we could talk about sport for hours. Even though we had zero medical training, we'd spend a good proportion of bus rides to and from football grounds happily discussing David O'Leary's left knee or Brian Talbot's troublesome groin. I've rarely discussed a man's groin in such detail since then.

The trouble with being out with my dad was that he couldn't help making mischief. If we were on the bus, he'd openly listen to conversations and interrupt to give advice. It wasn't well received. A man told him to fuck off once. If he wasn't my dad,

---

* As well as all the professional football he went to watch, he would also come down to watch me play on a Sunday morning. Well into my twenties, he'd seen every (and I mean every) organised match that I'd played in. I used to play five-a-side at ten on a Friday evening and he'd come and watch that. He liked his football. He watched me so much, it was agreed (although not by me) that he be appointed manager of our Sunday team. There was literally no one on earth who exuded less managerial qualities than my dad, but he was always there. I think every single member of the team missed more games than him.

One of the team knew some Israelis and they put us in touch with a political group called Betar who gave us free home and away kits. Someone on the team pointed out that their political leanings could best be described as ultra-Zionist. The fact that they supported the illegal building of settlements on the West Bank and Gaza Strip should've caused us some hesitation. But by then, we'd taken delivery of two sets of brand new kit, one home and one away, and it seemed easier to just ignore the problem. I imagine that any Palestinians who happened to be watching us play football may well have been outraged. But seeing as we were playing in a Jewish Sunday league, we figured that was unlikely to happen.

My dad immediately tried to make his managerial mark on the team but his options for tinkering were limited. We only had thirteen players and one or two were almost always missing due to other commitments such as family dinners, holidays or massive drink and drug hangovers. He once tried to drop Simon for a game because he felt that he was too slow. We explained to Ken that what Simon

I might have done the same myself. He'd get into arguments with people when he'd loudly proclaim that something wasn't right. He once got into a furious row with Stan Flashman, the self-styled King of the Touts, about selling tickets at more than face value. He was banned from Barnet football club.

Ken took me to see Middlesex against Yorkshire at Lord's, in a county cricket game and because my dad was a midweek member, we could sit in the pavilion. Geoffrey Boycott was playing for Yorkshire and my dad was complaining loudly about his slow play. People were looking round. They weren't used to working-class people in the pavilion, loud or otherwise. My dad said he was bored and he was going to the loo. When he was gone, Boycott was bowled out and walked back past me. I thought it was a shame

---

lacked in pace, he more than made up for by being the person who ensured that everyone turned up on time at the right ground and it was possible that he might be somewhat demotivated if he was relegated to the subs' bench.

He also had very little influence on tactics. We all knew our best position and there would have been little point in changing things. Elliot Shaw was the striker because he was the greediest player on the team. Simon was the centre half because he was one of the tallest and he had very little pace (none whatsoever). I played in central midfield because I was a decent passer of the ball. And Pete Schindler played wherever he wanted because even allowing for the phenomenal marijuana intake, he was still the best player on the team.

At the end of the season, Ken walked into the dressing room and said that he wanted to make a little speech. We waited.

'I think you've done very well this season and I'd like to thank you for your commitment and effort,' he said.

There was a round of applause. I felt this was a good start and much saner than I expected.

'But one player has stood out,' he continued and I thought, 'He can't be talking about me. Surely even my father would not do such a thing to his only son.'

'Player of the year this year is Ian,' he said. This without the merest hint of embarrassment. There had probably been more awkward times in my life up to this moment but I couldn't think of any. There was a moment's pause and then the laughter and piss taking started. It still goes on to this day. Thirty years later, people who were in that dressing room still mention it to me if I see them.

that my dad had missed it. I then heard shouting from behind me and turned round to see my dad furiously berating Geoffrey Boycott for his slow play. Boycott was having none of it and was angrily remonstrating with my dad. I honestly thought they were going to come to blows. Stewards were called and they had to be separated. My dad was told to leave the pavilion and we had to go and sit in another part of the ground.

The worst incident was at the football at Hendon. My dad thought it was amusing. When I was at primary school, we used to go there most weeks. Hendon played in the Isthmian League and were semi-professional. If it was cold or windy or wet, there were no large stands or terraces to shelter us from the worst of it. Everything was open to the elements. The crowds were small so there were never enough people to huddle together for warmth.

This particular week, I was standing on the terraces trying to get some circulation in my feet. The game had started and my dad was chuntering away as usual. He had a go at the opposition goalkeeper who was most definitely not amused by the stream of consciousness emanating from the terraces behind the goal. He had a go at our left-back for a series of wayward passes. He had a go at our manager for choosing to play the left-back in the first place. He had a very loud voice and it carried a long way. I can still see the manager's pained 'not him again' expression as he recognised my father's voice. He looked like he wanted to say something back but he knew that wouldn't end well.

My dad saved most of his ire (there was more than enough to go round) for the referee. As the tackles would fly in and fouls that nowadays would elicit a sending off and a long ban were not even penalised, my father kept up a non-stop stream of abuse and catcalls. He had a point. The standard of refereeing was consistently terrible, way worse than it was in the first division and my dad was not slow to let them know. And as bad as it must have been for someone to have their parentage questioned by forty thousand people, there was something much more personal to get it from a couple of hundred, particularly if my dad was one of them.

'What was that, referee?' he shouted, loud enough for people in the neighbouring postcode to hear. No answer came forth.

'How the bloody hell was that play on?' he asked.

As I looked down at our centre forward lying in a crumpled heap on the ground, I thought this wasn't unreasonable. But I was, as always, slightly embarrassed. 'Dad, leave it,' I pleaded. It made no difference. Nothing ever did.

'Stevie Wonder could've seen that, ref!' he shouted. That was a funny one. We'd recently watched a *Top of the Pops* where he'd appeared, and the singer must have been in his head.

'You're useless, ref. You should be taken round the back and shot.'

We all laughed at that one too. My dad was nothing if not harsh but that sort of punishment may have made referee recruitment even more problematic than it already was.

'You're absolute rubbish, ref,' he screamed, and I could see the vein in his neck throbbing. I thought he might have a stroke.

The final straw came when, right in front of us, one of their thuggish defenders scythed down our fleet-footed winger for the umpteenth time and the referee waved play on.

'How is that not a foul?' said my dad.

'You're blind, ref. You need glasses.'

And then my father, realising that he was wearing glasses, shouted, 'In fact, have mine,' took his glasses off and ran on to the pitch and up to the referee.

The game was still going on for a short while but at some point, the players cottoned on to what was happening and stopped. There appeared to be a crazy man berating the referee and offering him glasses. The referee looked grim. He kept blowing his whistle and pointing to the touchline. My dad was having none of it and gave him a thorough piece of his mind.

As it carried on, almost every single person inside the ground started laughing. The players were laughing. The managers were laughing. The stewards were laughing. The linesmen were laughing. The tea lady was laughing. The only people who weren't laughing were the referee who felt his authority draining away and one boy, standing and watching in abject horror as his father argued with the referee and praying for a bolt of lightning to strike him, his father, or both of them.

After what felt like a week, my father accepted that he was not about to change the referee's mind and walked slowly off the pitch. All the players clapped and everybody cheered. He walked towards me grinning from ear to ear. I pointedly moved to another part of the ground. If it was possible, I'd have moved to another country, changed my identity and entered the witness protection programme.*

---

* Years later, my sister told me that Ken had upset Alan Sugar. Ken had been walking through the West End with Beverley when he'd seen him coming out of a building and getting into his car. This was just around the time when he was Chairman of Tottenham and had recently sacked Terry Venables. My dad ran over to him shouting his name.

'Alan, Alan.'

Alan Sugar looked up with a start. My father grabbed him by the hand.

'I'd like to thank you, Mr Sugar.'

He was shaking his hand with some force. The word my sister used was 'vigorously'.

Alan Sugar looked uncertain.

'Thank you,' he said although he didn't know what for.

'Yes, you sacking Terry Venables has ensured that Arsenal will finish above Spurs for the next ten years.'

My father was howling with laughter at this point. Alan Sugar wasn't. He snatched his hand away, got in his chauffeur-driven car and sped off.

Things We Didn't Have in the 1970s

Part Fifteen

Teeth and Tonsils

Of course we had both of these but members of the medical profession seemed very keen to whip them out at the slightest hint of a problem. People no longer seem to have their tonsils removed. Back then, everyone I knew had had their tonsils out, usually before secondary school. It was just a thing that was done. Even though tonsils had developed and evolved over millions of years, the 1970s was when we decided we didn't need them any more. Often, they took the adenoids as well. I don't seem to have missed either of them although it's difficult to miss something when you never knew what they did.

As for teeth, with all the sugar being added to food, they began to suffer. Dentists weren't quite as brutal as they had been (in the 1950s, people had their teeth removed as a twenty-first birthday present to save them aggravation later in life — my mother only recently went to the dentist for the first time in fifty years because of the trauma of her last visit) but visiting the dentist was still an ordeal. NHS dentists were paid more money the more drilling and filling they did. Rarely would you leave a dentist without an intervention. It's also possible that we just didn't brush our teeth.

Chapter Sixteen

What chance have you got against a tie and a crest?

I think I first heard 'The Eton Rifles' at a soundcheck before one of the gigs at the Rainbow Theatre. There was a very close bond between the band and the fans and quite often, fans who didn't have tickets would be allowed in to watch the soundcheck. This was highly unusual for massively successful artists, and probably still is. It's one thing being a member of a fan club and getting regular newsletters telling you what the band are up to. It's quite another to be allowed into a half-empty hall four hours before a gig to watch a band tune up and play some songs and then to have a chat with the drummer afterwards. There's probably a direct connection between the number of albums sold and the number of small but significant conversations that Paul, Bruce and Rick had with star-struck teenage boys and girls and it's almost certainly why The Jam are so well loved even today, thirty-five years after they split up.

This particular afternoon, we were hanging around outside the stage door when John Weller popped his head out. He recognised a few familiar faces. He might have seen us in Birmingham, Poole, Norwich or Bracknell. We'd been all over. I wasn't paying much attention at school but my knowledge of Britain's geography improved no end thanks to Arsenal and Paul Weller. John was always very pally. Over the years, he'd provided us with cups of tea on cold afternoons and tickets for a few gigs.

'Alright lads. Bit chilly out. Wanna come in for a bit?'

We didn't need a second invitation. I'm not sure there was another band in the world where the lead singer's father came out beforehand to chat to the fans. I couldn't see Mick Jagger's old man popping out before a gig. Mainly because even back then, Mick's dad would've been in his nineties. It happened for me on a couple of occasions and it occurs to me now that there was a period in my life when John Weller was more interested in my wellbeing than my own father. If that was the only cup of tea he made for me, it was definitely one more than my dad ever did.

There were about two hundred of us in the hall. Rick and Bruce wandered on. We started cheering. They nodded to us and got on with their work. Rick was adjusting his drums, Bruce was doodling around on his bass. You got the feeling that if they weren't up there playing, they'd be down with us watching. Bruce was testing his microphone.

'Two, two, one two.'

There was a shout from the sound desk at the back of the stalls.

'Can you do that again?'

'Two, two, one two.'

He stepped away and starting playing the guitar. He played a few bass riffs. His fingers moved so fast. We gave him a round of applause. He looked pleased.

The roadies were humping stuff about. We nodded hello to them as well and although they were busy, they vaguely acknowledged us. In the early days, they were a bit gruff and offhand but as time went on, they got a bit friendlier. Kenny Wheeler was the main man; he once got told off by Paul for being a bit rude to some of the fans. By the end, they were letting the regulars who hadn't managed to get tickets to gigs in through the fire exits.

As we got more familiar, the roadies became sort of like our second family although no one in my family looked anything like them. For a start, they were doing manual work, a form of labour unknown to anyone I was related to. They were a group of men who, if you didn't know what they did for a living, you would have guessed were either long-distance lorry drivers or roadies. These men all wore the standard roadie outfit of a tee-shirt, jeans and trainers. They had large sets of keys. They had beards and tattoos and they were all overweight. They all spoke in the most glorious cockney accents. They all smoked roll-ups and, even though I didn't see this personally, I have no doubt that they ate a full English breakfast every day. I'd be amazed if any of them are still alive.

They also seemed to swear more than was necessary. One of them, I'll call him Terry although it might have been Dave or Kev or Bill (it definitely wasn't Sebastian), swore incessantly and in inventive ways that I'd never imagined up to that point. I watched him shifting gear from one part of the stage to another. He had a roll-up cigarette hanging from the side of his mouth

'Oy Dave,' he said to a junior roadie who was carrying some cables across the stage. The roll-up teetered precariously on his bottom lip. Dave looked like all the other roadies except he was marginally less overweight. 'Where the fuck are you going with those fucking cables?'

'Bill told me to fucking move 'em,' said Dave. He was also smoking a roll-up.

'Never mind what that cunt told you to do,' said Terry. 'Leave the fucking cables there and give me a fucking hand lifting this fucking sound fucking desk onto the fucking stage.'

I'd never heard a sentence containing five swear words. Including the insertion of a swearword between sound and desk that seemed superfluous, yet necessary. This was epic swearing. Poetic swearing. Olympic standard swearing. The Mark Spitz of swearing. Dave looked unsure. Bill was no doubt the same size and seniority as Terry and would probably have sworn just as much. And if he was a cunt, you wouldn't want to get on the wrong side of him. But he was nowhere to be seen so Dave duly put the cables down and helped Terry lift the fucking sound fucking desk onto the fucking stage. For a boy still making his way into the adult world, it couldn't get any fucking better than that.

At some point, Paul wandered out onto the stage. We started cheering.

'Alright?'

We were indeed alright.

Paul plugged his guitar in, and said, 'This is a new song.' He looked at Bruce and Rick, said, 'One, two, three, four,' and the band launched into 'The Eton Rifles'.

Paul Weller wrote 'The Eton Rifles' in 1979, probably around the time that Margaret Thatcher became Prime Minister. It tells the story of some working-class lads who get beaten up by boys from Eton but, as the man said, what chance have you got against a tie and a crest? David Cameron once claimed that it was one of his favourites. 'I was one, in the corps. It meant a lot, some of those early Jam albums we used to listen to,' he once said. 'I don't see why the left should be the only ones allowed to listen to protest songs.' Perfectly fair point I suppose. You can listen to whatever the fuck you want even if you're exactly the sort of person the song is protesting about. I guess arms dealers could listen to 'Masters of War' by Bob Dylan if they fancied it. I suppose Cameron didn't take it personally. Bully for him. I wasn't built that way. If Paul Weller had written a song called 'Fuck you, Jews!', even if it had an insanely catchy chorus and a great hook, I may not have been that keen.

Asked about it, Paul said that Cameron couldn't have been listening to the song and more pointedly, 'It wasn't intended as a fucking jolly drinking song for the cadet corps.' Personally, I think it's entirely possible that David Cameron liked the song because of the fact that the boys from Eton gave those working-class oiks a jolly good thrashing. Not really the mood that Paul was trying to convey but once art is out in the public domain, it's not the artist's property any more.

The class struggle was obviously a subject close to Paul's heart. He went to Sheerwater Secondary School, not far from Eton College, so he would have regularly bumped into some of their pupils. It must have been quite something for a working-class boy at a bog standard comprehensive school to be confronted by that level of privilege on an almost daily basis. It can't have been a pretty sight and I'd guess that the song was cooking up for quite some time.

Because of Paul, I imagine that hundreds of working-class kids like myself started thinking about these issues. Living in West Hendon, I never encountered anyone rich or privileged. People had money and privilege so that they didn't have to live in or even pass through places like West Hendon. Aside from the Baddiels and Robert, my family and friends were solidly working-class and while I could see that some of their parents were better off than others (and almost all of them were better off than mine), I didn't differentiate. None of them sounded vastly different to me.

I certainly never mixed with the establishment or any members of the landed gentry. They might as well have been on the moon. I knew there were posh people, I'd seen them on TV doing three-day eventing from the Badminton Horse Trials. We'd all heard of Lucinda Prior-Palmer, the second person I'd ever encountered who had a double-barrelled surname (after Ian Storey-Moore, a footballer who played for Nottingham Forest). There were also posh people in the black-and-white war films my dad watched. And they'd turn up on *University Challenge* with their corduroy jackets and their impossibly wide-ranging knowledge answering questions on music and books I'd never heard of. But I didn't resent them, I just thought they'd paid attention at school.

My parents' generation would have still looked up to them. It was expected that the people in charge would do the right thing. The Profumo affair had scandalised the nation fifteen years before but it was still thought of as an isolated incident. The upper classes knew how to behave didn't they? Of course, forty years later, we all know that the establishment are no more trustworthy than the rest of us and given the opportunity, can behave as badly as anyone. Paul Weller knew that then and because of that, so did the large number of disillusioned and disaffected young boys and girls who followed him. The things he wrote about had a profound effect on us, and continue to do so.

My parents knew their place. It wouldn't have occurred to them that things were unequal. The education system that they'd been through had been designed to tell them just enough to keep them from hurting themselves or others but not much more. It certainly didn't equip them for in depth analysis. Even if my parents had wanted to fight the power, they wouldn't have known where to start. Plus they'd have had to stop fighting each other for a couple of hours.

Our house was not one where intellectual thought was encouraged. The TV was always on. There were almost no books. There was the odd novel by Jean Plaidy, a cut-price Jane Austen that my mother liked but I wasn't going to pick up any ideas about political theory from them.* The only other things my mother read were *Reader's Digest*, *Woman's Realm* or if that wasn't available *Woman's Own*. I once popped round to the corner shop to get one of the magazines and both of them had sold out so I bought a *Woman's Weekly* instead. She was genuinely disappointed even though it appeared to me to be exactly the same as the other two, only with the stories and knitting patterns in a subtly different order. I never saw my father read a book. He read *Titbits*, a sort of adult comic similar to *Viz* but without the humour, *The Sun* (see *Titbits*) and the *Sunday People* (see *The Sun*). He sometimes took the *News of the World* but he didn't read what would be considered a broad range of political opinions. That was it for reading for the Stone family. If there was a copy of *Das Kapital* lying around the house, I never saw it. It might have been holding up one of the legs of the dining table.

When I was at school, class warfare never came up. My form teacher Clive Lawton was known as a bit of a hippy in that he looked how we imagined a hippy would look: long hair, clogs, no tie, and I assumed he was left-leaning but I didn't know for sure. Jews may have invented the whole idea of the class struggle, but at the Jewish Free School, they told us that if we were being oppressed for anything, it was for being Jewish. That was enough oppression to be getting on with.

---

* The Jean Plaidy books inspired my mother to try and write a romantic novel based in the eighteenth century. She showed me the twenty or so pages she'd written. This was brave on her part; I probably wasn't the target audience. The very first sentence read, 'Gerald walked into the drawing room, looked around and was struck by the excellent furniture.'

I started laughing. She looked slightly put out.

'What's funny?' my mum asked me.

'The way you've written this, Mum, it basically says that Gerald was smacked round the chops by a mahogany writing desk.'

My mother started laughing as well. It still tickles us both today. The novel remains unfinished.

Of course I could see that Britain was deeply divided, but until I heard 'The Eton Rifles', it hadn't really hit home what we were up against. Not only was Paul Weller unhappy about all this misery and injustice, he was articulate about it. He was writing vitriolic songs about class warfare, urban deprivation and social injustice, things that I'd never thought about up until that point. I'm not surprised he's angry at David Cameron for liking 'The Eton Rifles'. If you wrote a song which was to all intents and purposes a massive 'fuck off!' to the privileged classes and then, thirty years later, a very successful representative of that class said how much he liked the song, that would be upsetting.

Things We Didn't Have in the 1970s

Part Sixteen

Fancy Tea or Coffee

Perhaps David Cameron and his Etonian friends, when not smashing up expensive restaurants or plotting their way to the foreign office, drank fancy tea. Earl Grey or Lapsang souchong or perhaps a herbal infusion. For the rest of us, tea was either Tetleys or PG Tips. When someone asked if you wanted a cup of tea, they didn't then ask if you wanted normal tea. All tea was normal tea. And everyone took sugar.

As for coffee, it was still considered exotic. There were almost no coffee shops in London. Bar Italia and a couple of others, that was it. Getting a decent cup of coffee was nigh on impossible. Most of us would not have known the difference anyway. No one I knew had been to Italy. We'd never heard of cappuccinos or lattes or espressos. As for mochaccinos, frappuccinos and any of the hundreds of other variations of coffee we now have available, they were but a distant dream. Coffee came in a jar and was instant. It might not have been very good, but you got it straight away.

Chapter Seventeen

The public gets what the public wants

The 1979 general election was held on the third of May. It was the first election I really paid any attention to, and it felt like there was a huge amount riding on it. There had been a lot of industrial unrest throughout the 1970s, strikes, go-slows, work-to-rules, sit-ins, walkouts. We'd had power cuts and the three-day-week. My father said it was the fault of the unions. At least in part in this case, for one of the few times in his life, he may well have been right.

It seemed to be on the news every night. One evening, I watched striking workers from the Grunwick factory in Willesden amass in their thousands outside the gates. There had been a dispute involving Asian and Afro-Caribbean women regarding union recognition and things had taken a serious turn. A line of over-stretched policemen struggled to hold back the crowd and allow workers into the building. The next afternoon, I witnessed it all happen from the top deck of a bus. We got stuck in a traffic jam at the end of the road and I watched the very same scene live. It was tremendous entertainment for the journey home from school.

The Prime Minister James Callaghan was in serious trouble. Paul Weller had already put the boot in the year before when he wrote 'Time for Truth'.* Callaghan's avuncular style was wearing a bit thin and the Winter of Discontent of 1978–79 had felt like a watershed moment. There are all sorts of privations the general public will put up with but if rubbish isn't collected and the dead aren't being buried, it feels like things are starting to fall apart.

I wasn't old enough to vote but even if I had been, I was indisposed for the entire day. There'd been an issue with my FA Cup Final ticket application for the following Saturday's game against Manchester United, so I spent fourteen hours queueing up around Highbury waiting to buy one. I finally got my hands on one around eight-thirty that evening and I got home just in time to see the BBC project Margaret Thatcher as the likely winner of the election. And there she was the next morning standing on the steps of 10 Downing Street doing the 'Where there is discord, we will bring harmony' speech. I didn't believe her for a second. She seemed like the most discordant and unharmonious person I'd ever seen. I could understand why people might want a change, but I still couldn't work out how anyone could actively vote *for* Margaret Thatcher. She sounded more patronising than anyone I'd ever met which, considering the way adults spoke to children in the 1960s and 1970s, was quite an achievement. Plus I looked at the people who seemed happy about her winning and they looked and sounded unlike anyone I knew. I definitely wasn't a natural Conservative.

In office, Margaret Thatcher turned out to be an even more divisive figure than was feared. She had radical plans to transform Britain no matter the cost. She had it in for the unions and it felt like a storm was gathering, although no one knew quite how bad it was going to get. The opposition was in disarray and one rarely heard anything from them. It was a dark time. (Two weeks after she was elected, The Comedy Store opened in Soho and by the

---

* 'I think it's time for truth and the truth is you've lost Uncle Jimmy'.

time I got down there with Simon and made my (mercifully) short debut, it had become a centre for left wing dissent. There was very little balance. Tony Allen was the MC and he didn't try to hide his left wing credentials. I saw Alexei Sayle doing a set and he walked on stage and said, 'My name is Alexei Sayle. I'm a Marxist Leninist comedian. If you don't find me funny, you're a fucking fascist shitbag.' This was a *long* way from *Terry and June*. Andy De La Tour delivered a stunning anti-Thatcher rant to a very pissed-up crowd very late one night. There were regular appearances by a chap called Jim Barclay who railed against nuclear submarines. (The message was slightly diluted by the fact that he was wearing orange tights and he had deeley boppers on his head.)

I never talked politics at home. My parents never told me who they voted for, or if indeed they voted at all, and I never asked them. Judging by the newspapers my dad read and knowing his negative views of unions (not unusual in 1979), it's possible he was a Thatcherite. My mum worked for the GMB Union so I thought she probably voted Labour. Whatever the case, reasoned political debate was not at the top of the agenda in our house. I was in two minds as to whether either of them should be allowed to vote at all.

At school, there may have been whole lessons about British politics and the power of the unions and why people had voted for Maggie, but I'd stopped paying attention by then. There might have been discussions about how annoying it was that no one was collecting the rubbish, or a few years earlier, we might have bemoaned the fact that the electricity kept cutting out. But I don't think many of the kids were cognisant of or actually that bothered about the root causes. Most of those that were seemed to have picked up a watered down version of their parents' ideas. This meant that the school population was a touch more conservative than one would expect from that age demographic.

Being a Jewish school, we did discuss Middle Eastern politics and how it affected Israel. Again, almost everyone adopted their parents' views so there was a lot of anti-Arab rhetoric from kids who'd never met an Arab, shuttling as they were between Camden, Golders Green and Edgware. This was when Israel was still a socialist haven bravely defending itself against attack from hundreds of millions of Arabs hell bent on its destruction. As opposed to the trigger-happy, armed-to-the-teeth aggressive nuclear state with territory-expanding tendencies it is now. We had quite a lot of Israeli kids at school and they were a mixed bunch. They ranged from the quiet and unassuming[*] to the rude and arrogant.[†] I had some sympathy with the Arabs.

I'd joined a Jewish youth group called Habonim (meaning 'friends' in Hebrew) a few years previously. Habonim was a socialist Zionist organisation that existed mainly to persuade young Jewish boys and girls to emigrate to Israel and work on a kibbutz. Because of this, I was a little bit more au fait with Israeli politics. Quite a few of the kids did eventually go and live over there although what news emanated from Israel seemed to suggest that they spent most of their time diving into bomb shelters to avoid rocket attacks. I wasn't sure it was for me.

Habonim used to arrange summer camps to the English countryside. They tried to re-create as near as possible the life on a kibbutz, so we'd sing songs around a camp fire and do domestic chores. It wasn't an exact re-creation as they didn't have Arabs intermittently break into the camp and kill some of the campers; that might have put the parents in two minds as to whether to send their offspring. I went on three different summer camping

---

[*]   One really nice boy in Year Seven.

[†]   All of the others.

holidays to different parts of England. It was miserable. My distant ancestry may have spent many years in tents but that was in the Middle East where it's warm and dry. In all the years wandering the desert looking for the promised land, they probably didn't have to contend with unremitting drizzle.

One surprisingly dry evening, after a day spent learning camp craft (different knots and suchlike) and activities based around a Jewish historical theme (I was assured in all seriousness that there was one time when, in order to represent the Holocaust, late one night, teenagers dressed as German guards invaded the tents and made the other kids line up in the centre of the camp), we were having our late night cocoa and doing a dance which involved one of the girls skipping round the tent and giving her scarf to a boy that she liked. Like all activities that involved girls, this was massively depressing for me. I might have been one of the first chosen at football but I more than made up for it by being one of the last boys left awkwardly standing around while Jewish girls plumped for the least Jewish looking boy they could find. I stood there clapping along with everyone else but really, I wanted to slink back to the tent and wallow in self-pity.

But this night, for reasons known only to her, Amanda Shipson stopped in front of me and offered me the scarf. As much as I admired Amanda Shipson, I never for one second thought she felt the same way about me. She stood there coyly holding out the scarf. I looked behind me to see if she was offering it to someone else but no, out of all the boys in the tent, she had chosen me. As one hundred pairs of frankly bemused eyes looked at the two of us, I've never felt so self-conscious in my life. I took the scarf and pecked her on the cheek. Everybody cheered. It was the only moment out of all three summer camps that I didn't hate.

Simon and I were full blown Jam obsessives by this point. He told me that on the way to school one morning, he'd sung all the words from the first three albums while waiting for a particularly late bus. I wasn't surprised by either the fact that he knew all the words or the lateness of the 253. He'd pre-ordered 'Going Underground' from HMV and I followed suit. It was always a big moment when a new single appeared. They were never album tracks, so it was always a new song. We had to have their new stuff the moment it came out. It went straight in at Number One and we knew instantly because Simon had bought a radio into the sixth form common room and we listened as they read out the charts. We cheered when it was announced. The single was released ten months after Margaret Thatcher was elected Prime Minister. It absolutely cannot have been a coincidence. To my generation, and particularly those who were nominally on the political left, the song felt so relevant. In a three-minute burst, Paul had managed to capture exactly why we were so pissed off. I wanted to play it to everyone, point at the record player and say, 'This! This is what I'm trying to say!'

The Jam were phenomenally successful by this time, but even by the extraordinarily high standards set by Paul Weller, 'Going Underground' was a brilliant song. It was incredibly catchy for one thing. Paul emphasised the 't' in hate and plate a bit like he did with ouT on 'Non-Stop Dancing'. And the ending with the sort of wah wah sound from Bruce's bass was fantastic. On top of all that, like 'Mr Clean', it had irony, a form of expression I was only just beginning to get to grips with.* I played it incessantly for months until I knew every note (I was in the car with my son last year when the song came on the radio. I hadn't forgotten any of it.)

The song also had more overtones of impending nuclear doom and the video was pretty stark. The three boys playing the

---

* There wasn't a lot of irony in my house. When my mother told my father to fuck off, that was exactly what she wanted him to do.

song, Paul wearing a beautiful paisley scarf, intercut with photos of world leaders (including Thatcher) and nuclear detonations. It did not paint an optimistic picture of our future. I could see that the public got what the public wanted, and that Paul wanted nothing from society. It made perfect sense and I felt the same way. We were in a minority. Whatever Paul Weller or I might have wanted, what the public wanted at this point was Margaret Thatcher. And they got her. I found it very hard to come to terms with the fact that only a few months after 'Going Underground' came out, the government agreed to keep nuclear weapons at Greenham Common. It was all very depressing.

I'm sure there are plenty of people who say that protest songs (which is what this is) never change anything but I'm also sure that there are millions of fans of The Jam who've never voted Conservative in their life (or at the very least felt a pang of guilt when they did) because of this song. In a strange way, I think that Paul Weller and Margaret Thatcher had a lot in common. They were both stubborn, on a path from which they would not deviate. They both energised and engaged a large number of supporters. They were both obsessed by class and they both appeared to be permanently angry. Paul definitely had the better politics and I preferred the way he dressed, and, in fact, everything else about him.

The government may not have actually used kidney machines to pay for the rockets and guns but even if they had, we probably wouldn't have been told. We figured that if something really major happened in the world, something that could affect us, our betters would let us know. We were trusting like that. It may be overstating it a bit but in 1980, we all knew a lot less than we do now. I include myself and my entire family in this gross generalisation. I don't mean that people were thick, although there were plenty who were. There were people who thought *On the Buses* was funny, for a start.

It's not that people didn't care about the issues. They did, sometimes passionately. There was plenty of lively political debate and hard hitting investigative journalism. *Panorama* had been around for years. ITV had *World in Action*, *Newsnight* made its debut on BBC2. *Yes Minister* started. I thought it was funny although when I heard it was Margaret Thatcher's favourite sitcom, I felt conflicted. People were definitely interested in the workings of government and global events. But as opposed to the twenty-four-hour news culture we live in in 2020, there was just a lot less news about back then. I don't think there was any less going on in 1980. It's just that there was only so much news we could be told and famines or wars or natural disasters going on elsewhere were not things we could do anything about, so why bother us? Broadcast news consisted of a couple of bulletins a day on BBC and ITV. If you missed the six o'clock news, you had one more chance at ten.* On the radio, there was some news on Radio 4 but we never listened to that. And there was an hourly bulletin on Radio 1. And that was that.† Five thousand people might have died in an earthquake in the southern hemisphere on the same day that there was an election on the Indian sub-continent but if you were away from a TV and radio, it completely passed you by. I'm sure in some cases nowadays it still does but there's less excuse for not knowing.

The tabloid papers were *the* dominant news sources. There were broadsheet newspapers that I'm sure contained well written and considered pieces on all sorts of news events. But the majority of people didn't read them. Most people read *The Sun* or the *Daily Mirror*. Over seven million people bought one of those two. Plenty more read them. Another four million bought the

---

* It seemed more than enough at the time.

† John Craven had a kids' news show called *Newsround*. It was still more highbrow than most of the national press.

Daily Mail or the *Daily Express*. A million people bought the *Daily Star*. I'm amazed they could wash and dress themselves, let alone make it safely there and back from the paper shop. Five million people bought the *News of the World* on a Sunday, including my dad. I used to read it and I didn't need Paul Weller's (actually Bruce Foxton's) help to see that it was rubbish.

Information was out there but you had to dig a little deeper. For example, around the time that 'Going Underground' was Number One in the charts, Robert Mugabe had just been elected leader of Zimbabwe. If you wanted to know some of the background, there were options for finding out but they were limited. For some, that might include asking your parents but that was not an option open to me. There might have been some grainy footage of Mugabe in front of cheering supporters on TV. If you were interested, you could go to a library and read about Zimbabwe's political history and culture. There was probably an extensive entry in *Encylopaedia Britannica*.* The point is that if you needed to find out anything, you could but it required a more determined effort than just typing words into a laptop and hoping that the Wi-Fi worked.

Life was less complicated. We went to school, left as soon as we could, got a job and did that until we were sixty-five, retired and died around ten years later. We went to the pub most weekends and on special occasions we'd take a trip up West to see a show. We'd take a two-week holiday in Margate or Blackpool or the Norfolk Broads or, for the adventurous, a Spanish seaside resort where we ate full English breakfasts and talked loudly at

---

* According to the blurb, the *Encyclopaedia Britannica* contained all the knowledge you would need. And an enormous amount you never would. It was like the internet only heavier and without the porn. There were twenty-four densely packed volumes and you could buy a set for the price of a small family car. The joke being that *Britannica* would take you further. My friend Ivor sold encyclopaedias door to door for a while. I'm not sure he ever actually made a sale.

foreigners. We'd take a break at Christmas, watch Morecambe and Wise and eat and drink more than was good for us. And that was it. The rest was family and kids and general maintenance. Our horizons were fairly limited, but it didn't feel like a bad way to live.

From my middle-aged perspective now in 2020, while it is definitely a good thing to have the entirety of human knowledge available at the click of a mouse, it does rather increase feelings of inadequacy and impotent rage. It's all very well having all the news but it's very upsetting if one can't a) keep up or b) do anything about it. Whereas when I was a teenager, I felt massively angry but I didn't have a clue why. With songs like 'Going Underground', Paul Weller articulated and distilled that anger and gave a direction to my life that I hadn't had before.

Things We Didn't Have in the 1970s

Part Seventeen

More Than One Type of Cheese

In truth, there was only one or two of almost any item. No one ever said 'We have a wide selection' of anything. But the lack of choice for cheese was a scandal. I love cheese. I find the arguments for a vegan lifestyle compelling but the prospect of no cheese is just depressing beyond words. I really don't know how we got through the 1970s with only Cheddar cheese but as far as I could tell, that was pretty much the only cheese available. There was Red Leicester, but that was just red Cheddar. We could get Dairylea cheese triangles but anyone over the age of ten who ate them probably needed to take a long hard look at themselves in the mirror. There was also Primula, which was cheese in a tube. Like toothpaste. With a similar taste. A few years later, adverts for Boursin soft cheese appeared. It was eaten by sophisticated people at dinner parties. I was definitely not sophisticated enough to go to dinner parties, but I consoled myself with the fact they'd all have garlicky breath. (I'm hopeful that Brexit will not result in less 'continental' cheese. I worry that in years to come, my kids will go into a shop, ask for brie and be met by puzzled looks and 'We haven't had brie since we left the EU').

Chapter Eighteen

Loch Lomond

Simon had the rather excellent idea that he and I and a guy he'd recently met called Warren should go to see The Jam at the Loch Lomond Rock Festival in Scotland. Warren was a bit older than the two of us and lived in Kent. He'd seen The Jam quite a few times before we had, at Ronnie Scott's and the Greyhound and at the Marquee. Him and Simon had met in the Chelsea club shop when Warren had spotted Simon's Jam badges and they'd got talking. Warren was, if anything, funnier than me or Simon. We took this as a challenge. It got very competitive; we were like three drowning men with only one lifebelt.

I hadn't been to a festival since Rock Against Racism in 1978 and I was keen to give it another go. Although if I'd have thought about it, I may well have questioned the wisdom of holding an outdoor event north of the border. They do have warm, sunny days in Scotland, the difficulty is in predicting when those days might happen. And as much as we've all had fun at festivals when it's rained, it's way more fun when it doesn't.

I told my mother I was going to Scotland and she acquiesced with barely a hint of protest. She knew it wasn't worth the argument. Even if my father had been there he wouldn't have backed her up, but he'd left the previous summer. It had been building up for some time and even someone as impervious to other people's feelings as my dad could tell that my mother had had enough. The gaps between their arguments had got shorter to the point where one couldn't tell where one ended and another one began. Things came to a head one weekend afternoon. The football season was over and my dad was at home, always a recipe for disaster. There were no international tournaments to distract him. If there had have been a World Cup or a European Championship in 1979, my dad might have hung on for another year. He and my mum had had a four-hour-long shouting and screaming match, during which he'd sobbed saying, 'I'm not leaving my kids' over and over whilst holding tightly onto Beverley. I noted that he wasn't holding onto me.

Whatever his protestations, he moved out shortly after. I sort of missed him, but it's not like we talked every day even when he was at home and it was nice not to have to listen to the arguments. He'd moved in with his aunt Annie. She had a house on the Hendon Way near Cricklewood and since her husband had died, she'd lived alone so was glad of the chance of a bit of company. My dad may have shed a lot of tears when he left but when I went to see him in his new place a couple of weeks later, he'd settled in very nicely. He had his own room and his own telly and Annie made all his meals. That was all he needed. As long as one of the women in the Stone family was cooking for him, he'd have been happy living on the central reservation of the M1.

Even with my dad no longer there, I was keen to get out whenever I got the chance. The atmosphere at home was only marginally better. It was like he'd peed on the rug and we couldn't quite get rid of the smell. He lingered. He left me his collection of 3,000 football programmes and I spent all my time in my room reading and rereading them. If you need to know how far it is by car from Highbury to any of the big stadiums in

England, I can help you with that information. For example, it is 284 miles to St James' Park in Newcastle. I didn't need to look this up.

For most of the games, my dad had been in attendance. We had programmes from the entire Spurs double season in 1960/61. He used to go to Arsenal one week and Tottenham the next. And also a game during the week. On one Easter weekend, he'd been to five games, three in one day. He had watched a LOT of football. Even when he was living at home, he wasn't there that much.

The programmes would've been worth an absolute fortune but for the fact my dad had written the score on every one of them. And all the substitutions. And any other extraneous detail he might have felt relevant that day. Like the referee's performance, the attendance and the weather (Arsenal v Tottenham, 23 February 1963, was cold apparently. More pertinently perhaps, my father went to football six days after I was born, there being, in his mind nothing to help with at home.)

In the end, they took up too much space and I sold them as a job lot at a programme fair. A man looked disdainfully through the boxes.

'They're all written on,' he said.

'Yes,' I said. 'My dad did that.' As if in mitigation.

He sighed. 'It really affects their value when they've been written on. I'll give you forty quid for the lot,' he said.

'OK,' I said.

He looked at me with pity. He expected me to put up more of a fight.

'OK, fifty pounds,' he said.

'Brilliant,' I said. I had no idea haggling worked like this. I was an idiot.

We took the overnight train to Glasgow. It was only £6.50 for a day ticket to the festival and I can't imagine the train ticket cost much more than that either. We may even have bunked the fare, something we all did whenever we got the chance.* It took eleven hours and we stopped almost everywhere, whether we were at a station or not. We stopped in Rugby and sat for fifteen minutes. Not a soul stirred on the platform. Even the driver didn't get on or off. He may have been having a nap. In the early morning, we were jerked awake when the train stopped by a field. A herd of cows looked at the train. We looked back at them. We were there so long, I felt like I was watching one of the calves grow up. We stopped at places I'd never heard of. Leighton Buzzard, Lancaster. We stopped at Kendal and someone mentioned their famous mint cake. I dozed fitfully but when I was seventeen, I could manage on very little sleep. Strangely, my seventeen-year-old teenage son can, and will, sleep for twelve or thirteen hours at a stretch, get up and play tennis and then go back to bed.

We got to Glasgow late that morning and took a taxi to the

---

* Everybody I knew bunked the fare. Some people jumped over the barrier, if there even was one. Some flashed what looked like a ticket but was in fact a bus pass or a cinema ticket or just the palm of their hand. My thing was to tell the ticket inspector that I'd only got on the train the stop before even though I'd travelled seven stops. This felt a little less like stealing and more like negotiating a fare reduction. This worked out fine until one morning when I got off at Ruislip and casually told the inspector that I'd boarded the train at Harrow on the Hill, only for a man behind me to start shouting that I'd actually caught the train at Baker Street. The ticket inspector looked at me to see if I would deny it; I made a half-hearted attempt to do so, but I could not have looked more like I'd got on at Baker Street than if I was wearing a cape and a deerstalker hat and smoking a pipe.

I was told to report to a London Underground office in Lambeth the following day. I duly turned up and it was grim. Everybody looked at you with disdain, nobody smiled, you were kept waiting in featureless, badly lit rooms for what felt like weeks, there were endless forms to fill in. I was given a stern lecture in community responsibility. The whole place was designed to make you feel guilty. That was the point. At the end, I vowed not only to never bunk the fare again but to feel suitably pissed off at anyone else who did.

festival site. The driver wittered on about something, we didn't know what. We understood about one word in three. This was my first time in Scotland and I was struggling with the accent. There were very few regional accents on TV and broad Glaswegian was definitely not one of them. The main thing was that he understood us and he knew where we going. We got out and he gave us the change in what we thought was foreign currency.

'What's this?' said Warren.

The driver may have said something about it being legal tender but it was impossible to tell for sure without asking him to repeat it half a dozen times so we took the money and went on site. The festival was held in a place called Bear Park. We had read that there were actual bears living there, although we never saw any. We spent the day watching bands, drinking beer and eating terrible food. This was before the days when festivals had a wide selection of culinary choices. It was essentially burgers, chips and hot dogs. If there was a vegan option, I didn't see it. And all the while, we tried to avoid running battles between various youth sub-cultures. The skinheads and the mods had a grievance. They didn't like our sharp suited attire. We didn't like the fact that they wanted to kill us. Basically, it was a free-for-all. There might have been one steward to look after the entire event but essentially we were on our own. It would've been safer putting us all in with the bears.

The three of us were used to seeing fighting anyway. Like me, Simon and Warren had already developed that sixth sense that streetwise fans in those days acquired to avoid serious trouble. With the fearsome mob of hooligans that used to roam the area around Stamford Bridge, they needed to.

The festival line-up was a mix of well-known and newer, local bands. Some of them, I have no recollection of watching. The Cuban Heels, The Only Ones, Ra Bears, The Regents, Punishment of Luxury. I remember jumping around to Stiff Little

Fingers. I bought their single 'Alternative Ulster' and I felt like I was very well versed in the situation in Northern Ireland, what with knowing all the words to the song and the fact that my dad had been arrested for terrorism related offences.

Bad Manners came on and they were a laugh. I always loved their version of 'Wooly Bully' and when they played 'Special Brew' (a love song to a lager that only alcoholics would drink) the whole field went crazy when the song speeded up. Their lead singer Buster Bloodvessel seemed to have a very long tongue. I'd never seen a tongue that long. I could see it from forty feet away.

There was a mod band called The Chords. The Tourists played (the band that eventually became Eurythmics) and then, finally, Paul Weller and the boys closed the show. I've just looked up the set list for the show and their last eight songs were: 'When You're Young', 'The Eton Rifles', 'Down in the Tube Station at Midnight', 'Strange Town', 'The Modern World', '"A" Bomb in Wardour Street', 'All Mod Cons' and 'David Watts'. Most bands would kill to have written one of them. It was also the first time they played 'Going Underground'. They were so good that everyone stopped fighting for ninety minutes.

Our sleeping arrangements at the festival were rudimentary. Simon had brought a two-man tent between three of us. Maths was never his strong point. In tent terms, two into three does go, but only if one of you knows how to put a tent up. None of us did. This was a problem. If there's one thing you require in Scotland, even in 'high summer', it's the ability to ensure that you don't have to sleep outside.

It was dark. It started to rain. We fiddled about for a while but it soon became clear that unless we had help, we were sleeping under the stars; not that you could see any. We asked for help but discovered very quickly that having broad London accents was not a positive when it's three in the morning and you're asking insanely drunk Scottish teenagers. It was interesting to learn how

many different ways there were to be told to fuck off. More than
we thought, it turned out. Finally, two young men from Dundee
took pity on us and let us squeeze into their tent. As we lay in the
dark, we could hear songs about killing and burning the English;
thankfully not from the two guys in the tent. We felt very welcome. I didn't need to use the toilet but I would've happily wet
myself rather than go outside. The two lads from Dundee tried
to reassure us that we were fine with them but we were not reas-
sured. Mainly because we had not the first idea what they were
actually saying. The Dundee accent makes the Glasgow accent
sound like the woman who reads the news on Radio 4. It's virtually impenetrable even to other people from Scotland, so what
chance did we have? But they were not beating us up in the tent,
so we figured their intentions were friendly.

I didn't get a lot of sleep and I woke up in the morning feeling
as cold as I've ever done. It was almost as if Scotland was not
conducive to camping. I poked my head out of the tent. Aside
from the mist, everything was quiet. The songs about killing and
burning the English had stopped, possibly because all the English
that had been located had already been killed and burnt.
Although I have no idea how they got the fires to stay alight what
with all the rain. We left shortly after. I slept all the way back.

Things We Didn't Have in the 1970s

Part Eighteen

A Wide Range of Fresh Fruit

Like everything, for most people the choice of fruit was limited. There were places where you could get all sorts of exotic delights; the newly arrived immigrants set up shops selling stuff you couldn't get in the supermarket, but very few people outside of these communities shopped there. If my parents had seen a papaya, they'd have stared at it like pre-historic man coming across a combine harvester. In the winter, we had bananas, apples, oranges and pears. There were no easy to peel satsumas. People might have had satsumas in the 1970s but it's possible they never managed to peel one. In the summer, we might get strawberries and the odd peach but that was about it. Any other fruit came in a tin. Some of the fruit I ate during my childhood may well have been older than me.

Chapter Nineteen

Here comes the weekend,
I'm gonna do my head

As I moved through my teens into supposed adulthood, I went out whenever I could. Most weekends (and midweek if I could get time off work), I'd be travelling the length and breadth of the country watching either Arsenal or The Jam. Arsenal had just endured a heartbreaking end to the season and I'd seen most of it first-hand. We'd lost the FA Cup Final to West Ham at Wembley and then four days later, my dad and I trooped over to Brussels to watch us lose the Cup Winners' Cup final on penalties to Valencia FC. We then lost 5-0 at Middlesbrough which ensured that we didn't even qualify for Europe. It was grim. Going to see The Jam was a lot more fun.

Like everything in Britain back then, the transport system was a bit frayed at the edges and getting around proved challenging. I slept at train and bus stations. For one show in Manchester, the last train home was cancelled and a replacement coach back to London was laid on instead. The coach stopped at every station the train was meant to visit. And possibly quite a few others just for the hell of it. In every town, we'd have to leave the motorway, make our way to the centre, drop off and pick up stragglers and then head back out on the road. It was excruciatingly slow. There were very few people on the coach and after Milton Keynes, I was the only person left. The last stop before Euston was Watford Junction. We pulled off the motorway at Watford and drove to the railway station. No-one got on and I didn't get off. We waited for five minutes because we were running ahead of schedule and just in case someone turned up at Watford station at a quarter past two in the morning to get a train to Euston. We finally got going and drove the last few miles to London. As we turned off the motorway in North London, we stopped at some traffic lights less than three minutes' walk from my house. I walked to the front of the bus.

'Can you let me out here. I only live a couple of minutes away.'

'I can't do that.' He wouldn't even look at me.

'Why not?'

'Because it's dangerous.'

I looked at him. I thought he meant because it was late at night. 'I'm seventeen. I'll be fine.'

He turned to me. 'You say you'll be fine but what if you injure yourself getting off the bus?'

I genuinely didn't know what he was on about. 'I'll be careful. I haven't been drinking and I have total control over my legs.'

He didn't appreciate the sarcasm. 'What I meant was, what if a cyclist was coming up the inside and you stepped out without looking. If you were injured, I'd be in trouble.'

'I'll make sure I look. It's three in the morning. There are very few cyclists about.'

'Can't do it. Sorry.' He started straight ahead.

I couldn't believe it. He caught me looking at the emergency exit handle. He threateningly revved the engine. I genuinely think he may have driven off if I'd have gone for it. I looked at him but he was immovable. I went and sat back down in a huff until we got to Euston. I'm absolutely certain that he took an extended time to park the coach before he opened the doors. He silently smirked. I silently wished for him to have a painful and protracted death. I had to wait forty-five minutes to get a night bus home. Two hours and ten minutes later, I passed the exact same spot where he could've dropped me off. Prick!

I'd go and see other bands as well, any gigs I could get tickets for – the live music scene was thriving. Gigs were cheap and plentiful and I had a broad range of things that I listened to. I went to see Dexys Midnight Runners at the Old Vic in Waterloo. I'd recently bought their album *Searching for the Young Soul Rebels* and I loved it. I think it still stands up forty years later. 'Tell Me When My Light Turns Green' has always been one of my favourite tunes. It contains, in my opinion, the best trombone solo of all time, a sentence one doesn't hear very often. There was a point during the gig when the music stopped and the lead singer Kevin Rowland started asking if we could see 'the bridge'. Kevin was prone to moments like this. I honestly think that he believed that he was the white James Brown. He wasn't, he was just a bit of a berk in a cardigan. I think he was talking about a musical bridge but he kept asking, 'Can anyone see the bridge? Can anyone see the bridge?' so insistently, it was hard to tell. Aside from Kevin, the only sound came from a single, continuous note from the keyboard. It was meant to be moving but most of the audience were bemused. We just wanted him to play 'Geno'.

He looked up at the balcony to where we were sitting.

'Can anyone up there see the bridge?'

At this point, Warren couldn't help himself and shouted down to the stage, 'Hang on a minute Kev, I'll ask.' He then turned around to the audience on the balcony. 'Anyone seen a bridge?' he said, loudly enough for Kevin and indeed everyone else to hear. People started laughing, even the band stifled a few chuckles. Warren turned back to Kevin.

'We've looked high and low and there's no bridge up here mate. We'll let you know if we see anything.'

Kevin was not amused. Everybody else was.

Most of the time, I went to these gigs with Simon. We saw The Piranhas at the Hammersmith Odeon. They did a lively version of 'Tom Hark' (you'd know it if you heard it) and other songs of which I have no recollection whatsoever. We saw The Rezillos, a Scottish punk band that had a couple of hits in the late 1970s, the best known being a song called 'Top of the Pops'. Their lead singer, Fay Fife, sang in the most beautiful Scottish accent. We saw The Lurkers at the Lyceum ballroom. They played plodding punk rock. It was really miserable, but it suited my mood at the time. We went to see the UK Subs at the Michael Sobell Centre and it was strange pogoing around to 'Stranglehold' in the same hall where a few years earlier I'd played badminton for the school. We saw The Ruts at the Marquee. Simon and I went with Steven Wilson, another boy in our year at school who we'd kept in contact with. He had the worst bad breath we'd ever encountered but as long as you kept upwind of him, he was quite a laugh to hang out with. He used to do amazing impressions of all the teachers which was funny but niche. He also had an enormous train set in his loft. We met the band after the gig. Steven went up to Malcolm Owen, the lead singer.

'Are you Malcolm Cohen?' he said.

'Owen,' said Malcolm Owen, irritated. 'Malcolm Owen.'

'Oh,'said Steven.

We went to see The Clash at the Lyceum Ballroom (now the Lyceum Theatre and the current home of *The Lion King*) which was memorable not just for seeing a band I knew that Paul Weller loved, but also for them playing 'Safe European Home' and

'Tommy Gun', two songs I was very into at the time. It was also the first time I heard 'Rock Lobster' by the B52's, a song I love to this day. We saw The Members and 999* at the GLC headquarters. We saw Secret Affair. I liked their look and their attitude but they didn't have a large back catalogue. They played 'Time for Action' five times; it should've been called 'Time to Write another Song'. We saw The Undertones, The Adverts, The Boomtown Rats and for some reason, Toyah Wilcox. We saw Iggy Pop in Brixton and he stage dived into the audience seven times at one gig. The band kept having to wait around while he was fished out. It was hilarious.

Simon wasn't that into rock or heavy metal but I liked Status Quo so I got a ticket on my own to see them at Wembley Arena.† To hear the first bars of 'Caroline' ring out and see ten thousand people nodding their heads was great. I saw Motörhead and Saxon at Stafford Bingley Hall. I hitchhiked up the motorway to that one. I told my mum I was going out, wandered the half a mile down to Staples Corner where the M1 started and stuck my thumb out. I was barely seventeen. Ten minutes later, a large motorbike pulled up.

'Fancy a ride on one of these?' said a bearded man wearing a leather jacket. He had a broad Black Country accent. He opened a box on the back, pulled out a helmet and offered it to me.

I wasn't sure. I'd never been on a motorbike before and this was a big bastard. I told him.

---

* Years later, I got a gig opening for 999 at Rock City in Nottingham. I wandered out twenty minutes before they were due on and did twenty minutes of material to a couple of hundred punks sitting cross legged on a dancefloor. The whole thing was surreal but it sort of worked.

† I later heard that Quo were the first band that Paul Weller saw live. He said it was the loudest thing he'd ever heard and his first thought was, 'This is what I want to do.' When I heard this, it made me very happy.

'Never mind that. When I lean, you lean the same way. Where are you going?'

'Stafford Bingley Hall. To see Motörhead.'

He started laughing. 'It's your lucky day.' He turned round; he had a big Motörhead logo on the back of his jacket. 'Come on.'

I could hardly refuse. It was a bit of a struggle getting the helmet over my nose but I managed it in the end. He gave me a lift all the way there. I have no idea how I got home.

My two favourite music venues were the Rainbow Theatre in Finsbury Park and the Hammersmith Odeon. The Rainbow is now the UKGC Help Centre and it's owned by an evangelical church. I often see Christian people milling about outside waiting to go in. They look a lot less excited than we did when we were going in and there's never that many of them. The Rainbow has a capacity of two and a half thousand and I don't think they fill it. I guess there are a lot more entertainment choices around nowadays but it's also possible that Jesus doesn't pull the numbers he used to.

For a period in the late 1970s and early 1980s, I used to go to the Rainbow almost every week. In one glorious week late in 1979, I saw The Jam three times, The Police and Queen. Seeing Queen play 'Bohemian Rhapsody' was pretty cool. The band would go off for the operatic middle-eight and the stage would be alive with smoke and flashing lights. And then there would be a big flash of light, the rock guitar would kick in and the band would jump back on stage. I was sixteen. It was incredibly exciting to watch.

I'm gutted that the Rainbow is no longer a music venue although I understand the reasons why. Club culture became the dominant entertainment choice in the late 1980s and a lot of the mid-size venues were sold off. When live music made a comeback, it was as part of the festival experience and the owner-ship of the building had changed. And once a venue is in God's hands, it's hard to persuade Him to give it back.

Hammersmith Odeon was a bit bigger than the Rainbow but had a similar feel. We went there less often but still at least once a month. We tried to buy tickets to see The Police there one evening but it was completely sold out. Simon, Warren and I turned up anyway thinking that we could bunk in. This was quite common back then, security being much less sophisticated in those days. But for some reason, things were proving more difficult than we expected and we mooched about outside hoping for inspiration.

We were just about to give up when someone said we should follow them. They didn't look like they were there in any official capacity but we were almost out of options so we duly trooped round the side of the venue and climbed an emergency staircase attached to the outside of the building. And that was how seven of us ended up on the roof of Hammersmith Odeon. It's a long way up and not very well lit, the owners of the building rightly not expecting rooftop visitors late at night. We looked around for a bit, but we could hardly see anything. This was before the days of torches on mobile phones, or indeed mobile phones, but it didn't stop us creeping about one hundred feet above ground level with very little visibility. I'd somehow assumed the role of leader and I'd managed to find what seemed like a way back in. I felt my way around the structure and located the door. It opened and I found myself leading six teenagers down some stairs and along a pitch black walkway about one hundred feet up above the stage. We could hear The Police on stage directly below us. I couldn't see six inches in front of me and I slid my foot along the floor so I didn't suddenly step into thin air and fall one hundred feet directly on to Sting's head, which would have definitely cur-tailed the show.

From behind us came a commotion and a flashlight shone in our direction.

'Hey! What the fuck are you doing up here?' said a voice from the darkness.

'Trying to bunk in to the gig. What the fuck do you think we're doing up here,' said no one. I'm not sure they wanted an answer anyway.

'Get the fuck out of here now before we call the police.'

I wish I'd said that I didn't think the band would want to be bothered with having to deal with stupid teenagers just before they went on stage. But the security guards may not have appreciated the humour. We sheepishly followed them down ten flights of stairs and were unceremoniously turfed out round the back. We all found it hilarious and a relief to be on solid ground and not arrested for trespass, but it still didn't solve the problem of how we were going to get in. We wandered back round the front and were hanging around disconsolately by one of the exit doors when it suddenly opened. Someone had a mate inside and he'd come down to let him in. About fifteen of us barged through the door before anyone could stop us. We ran up the stairs, and we were in just as the first bars of 'Message in a Bottle' rang out.

Aside from when we managed to bunk in for nothing, all these gigs required money to buy tickets and I started looking for what my mother called a 'proper job'. I wasn't good at very much, but I had an aptitude for maths and physics, so engineering seemed like an option. I went to my local job centre and was told that the civil service were running a training programme. With my recently acquired fourth 'O' level in Sociology (actually a CSE Grade 1 but it meant the same thing), I applied for and, following an interview, was accepted onto their trainee draughtsman scheme. I was told to report to a drab office in Croydon. I discovered that there were no other sorts of office in Croydon. I was given various geometrical drawing aids and a selection of pencils. My workmates were uninspiring. I'm sure they felt the same about me. There was a Turkish guy called Bulent Hourshid, who we called bowl of horseshit. As you can tell, the level of banter was very high. There was one guy called Duncan who used to constantly take the piss out of my nose. He'd put his fist over his own nose and say 'Don't worry about the money' to me. I later learnt it was a thing that Spike Milligan did in his comedy shows. It didn't make it any funnier when Duncan did it. I fervently hoped that Duncan would be hit by a truck.

Within a couple of months, having learnt to draw straight lines, I was posted to an engineering office in Ruislip. The journey by public transport was a bit arduous. Two of my co-workers, a guy named Bill and his then girlfriend Stevie rode motorbikes and suggested I get one and for some reason, I thought this was a good idea. They took me to the bike shop and half an hour later, I was the proud (and terrified) owner of a second hand Honda CB125 Super Dream (now and forever known as a Wet Dream). They gave me some basic lessons around a car park and then I was off. I rode unsteadily home and proudly showed it to my mother. She went a funny colour. If she was Catholic, she would've been furiously crossing herself. I somehow survived for two weeks before it was stolen from outside our house, which I saw from afar as I was walking home late one night. I'd been into town and taken the train. As I turned the corner, I noticed two men lifting a motorbike that looked a lot like mine onto the back of a van. The van drove off. As I got nearer, I realised that the reason it looked a lot like mine was because it was. When I told my mum, she tried to be sympathetic but she couldn't have looked happier.

With the bike gone, I was back to taking a bus, a train and another bus to work but at least I could start daytime drinking. I was never much of a drinker but I was keen to get started. I got a taste for beer.* We had a little gang who used to get pissed almost every lunchtime. There was an on-site bar so it was difficult not to. We got almost nothing done in the afternoon but because it was the civil service, nobody cared. A guy in the office taught me how to angle my drawing board and hold a pencil in such a way that even though I looked like I was working, I could nap when I needed to. If you're a taxpayer, I can only apologise. We were part of the Property Services Agency. One office wag called it the Proper Tea Services Agency which was mildly amusing the first time he told it but after hearing it four hundred more times, I wanted to stab him with a compass.

The office Christmas party took the drinking to another level. We'd start at lunchtime in the on-site bar, move to a pub and then graduate to a local restaurant. There was a lot of bad behaviour; I once snogged a woman in a stationery cupboard.† The choice of restaurant was always a hotly debated topic. One year, our boss decided to book Christmas dinner in the local Conservative Club. It was the first and only time I've ever eaten dinner with a six foot high photograph of Margaret Thatcher looking down on me. It didn't help the digestion.

---

* My experience of booze up to this point was almost non-existent. I never saw my parents drink, although in the latter stages of their marriage, they had every right to. There was rarely booze in the house. Once a year around Christmas, my dad used to mix lemonade with a sickly liqueur called advocaat in what he called a snowball. I used to like them back then but I tried one a few years ago and it was disgusting. At Passover we had Palwin, a brand of kosher wine. It wasn't totally clear to me how wine could not be kosher. Perhaps if a Muslim fundamentalist had trodden the grapes during Ramadan. Palwin stood for 'Palestine wine' although with the way things are going in the Middle East, they might call it something different nowadays. Back then, it wasn't seen as a bad thing to give a twelve-year-old a sip of wine. I remember a mild flushing of the cheeks and a warm feeling but I never got a taste for it. The joke was that it was a good table wine but only if you wanted to strip the table.

† Thirty-five years later, she reappeared at a comedy gig not far from the office – not, I hasten to add, with a big-nosed young son who looked a bit like me.

On Friday evenings, I used to go drinking at a pub in Chelsea. The pub was directly opposite Stamford Bridge, and Simon and Warren 'knew' a few people down there. These were proper blokes and hardened drinkers. I used to watch them drink pint after pint after pint. It didn't seem to have any effect on them, and it certainly didn't cheer them up. They looked like they'd been there since the war.

'I'm just going down the pub, Mum,' I'd say as I was going out the door, like a proper grown-up man, albeit one still living at home with his mother.

One night, we saw an advert for a stag evening and Warren suggested we go. The leaflet said that the evening was strictly for men only. The word 'strictly' was in capital letters, as if women would've wanted to go but needed to be discouraged. It was held in a function room at Crystal Palace football club. There were about two hundred of us and the atmosphere was raucous. The bar was rammed. There was a compere and three strippers. The compere told horrible sexist and racist jokes: 'This paddy walks into a bar . . .' or 'So I went to my local Paki shop' or 'I was shagging this bird up the arse . . .'. That sort of thing. He wouldn't be doing the Royal Variety Performance anytime soon. He also picked on members of the audience and utterly humiliated them. I silently gave thanks that Warren had guided us to seats near the back of the room.

After delivering a suitably brutal put-down of some poor chap which was passed off as banter but probably caused deep psychological problems for years to come, he'd introduced a 'beautiful lady for our entertainment'. And onto the stage would step a woman wearing something revealing. Who would then take it off to reveal quite a lot more. All the strippers had a different shtick, a bit like 'You Gotta Get a Gimmick' from the musical *Gypsy*.

One had a sort of floaty thing going on with lots of silk scarves, another was a bit more in your face, as it were. But it all came down to the same thing in the end. They'd end up standing in front of us in the altogether while we drunkenly cheered. It was pretty tame. We may have got the odd glimpse of pubic hair but mostly it was tits and bums and suggestive dancing. They weren't unattractive, but it wasn't what you'd call sexy.

Sometimes, they'd get a man on stage and there would be some simulated sex. There was some shaving foam involved. I had a brief-but-happy moment as I remembered being in Mr Cohen's Religious Knowledge class at JFS. I turned to mention it to Simon, but his attention was elsewhere. The women seemed very adept at choosing men who looked mortally embarrassed to be there. The guys who were sat there with their legs wide apart and, I don't doubt, quite visible bulges in their trousers were never selected.

Of the three strippers, my favourite was a woman who took her clothes off and then sat on a chair with her legs open hiding what little modesty she had left with a Kermit the Frog glove puppet. The puppet would sing along with 'Mahna Mahna', the tune from *The Muppet Show,* and the woman would alternately reveal and hide her vagina. It was hysterical but then I was very drunk. Around that time, I almost always was.

Things We Didn't Have in the 1970s

Part Nineteen

A Dim View of Drink-driving

There were laws against driving while under the influence, but people did it anyway. We disapproved of drink driving but only in the same way that we disapproved of dropping litter or public displays of nudity. We'd rather you didn't but if you do, we don't wish to know. The general feeling was that public transport was either poor (in the city) or non-existent (in the country) so how else were people meant to get home from the pub? And if you happened to run over a child at two in the morning, well, what the hell were they doing out at that time anyway?

There was an oddly prurient view of booze anyway. Getting a drink after eleven at night was almost impossible. Our licensing laws had been brought in during the First World War to make sure that munitions workers weren't *too* hungover when they were handling high explosives, which seems sensible enough. And even though, by the 1970s most people outside of IRA terror cells were not involved in munitions production, we still liked our workers safely out of the pub by eleven. Although it wasn't safe at all because all the violent drunken people who were irritated at not being able to drink any more emerged from the pubs at exactly the same time. There were one or two late night drinking dens in big cities, but aside from them, unless you had booze at home that was it until late the next morning.

Chapter Twenty

I'm going to put it in the fruit machine

Simon, Robert and I went down to Brighton to see The Jam. I was excited; so were Simon and Robert. There were plenty of other mods on the platform at Victoria and they looked excited too. This was what it was all about. A day out. We were off the leash, some of us for the first time in our lives. Fifteen years before, kids our age would have been making the same journey on a bank holiday weekend. Ten years after, we would've been driving around the M25 looking for an illegal rave and trying to buy drugs. And ten years after that and we'd have been humping camping gear off to a festival, also trying to buy drugs.

But in 1980, Brighton was the spiritual home for mods. Going there to see The Jam was a thrill and the nearest most of us would ever get to a pilgrimage.* We'd all seen *Quadrophenia* the year before. We all knew that Paul Weller looked up to Pete Townshend and the fans felt the same way. I loved The Who's music almost as much as I loved The Jam. I still do.

I'd taken a half-day holiday from work. I took the train from

---

* I did go to the Wailing Wall in Jerusalem a few years later but all I felt was hot.

Croydon and met the boys at Victoria station. Simon and Robert had worn their parkas. I'd gone for a Harrington jacket. I'd spent the evening before looking for suitable badges. I'd gone for one with The Jam and another with The Who. I was nothing if not imaginative. We jumped on the train to Brighton. It was the same one I'd just got off from Croydon. We managed to nab one of those six seat compartments that you used to get on the old style trains. (You can see one in the film when Jimmy goes down to Brighton for the last time and we hear The Who doing '5:15'). The train had seen better days. Overground trains were adequate at best. All of the rolling stock was over twenty-five years old and it showed. The British Rail tagline at the time was:

'British Rail, we're getting there.'

To which the response may have been 'eventually'.

For a while, we thought we were going to have it to ourselves but at East Croydon, some lads got in with us. They were older than us (nineteen?), slightly aggressive and they were keen to know which football team we supported. Simon tentatively said Chelsea and they looked a bit doubtful. By way of proof, Simon showed them his Chelsea lapel badge and they suddenly adopted a friendlier tone. For reasons of self-preservation, I decided not to mention that I was an Arsenal fan and, consequently, I couldn't contribute much to the discussion of Chelsea's season so far. I guess they thought I was the quiet one of the group. At some point, they got off and it was only then that Simon noticed that I was wearing an Arsenal belt.

I'd never been to Brighton before, but because of *Quadrophenia* it felt very familiar. It didn't look quite as good up close, but it was November and British seaside towns are never at their best in winter. We stayed at a friend of Jackie's, Simon's sister. I was glad we didn't have to stay in a bed and breakfast. I'd stayed in one or two of these establishments over the years and they were grim. They were the most passive aggressive places on earth. There were 'polite' notices all over the place: 'Breakfast served only between 7:30 and 8:30' and 'Please leave the communal bathroom in the same state you found it' and 'If you get back here after midnight and you haven't got your key, you're sleeping on the beach you wanker.'

We dumped our bags in the flat and headed back into the centre of town. We wandered about pointing places out from the film.

'That's where Sting parked his bike.'

'That's where one of the rockers got thrown onto the beach.'

And of course, 'That's the alley where Phil Daniels shagged Leslie Ash.'

We wandered about some more. I spent a lot of my teenage years wandering about. At least I was getting some fresh air. We bumped into Warren. He'd made his own way down. At one point, out of the blue, Robert stopped at a phone box and said he was going to phone his mother. It seemed a very odd thing to do. We were all seventy-odd miles away from our respective mothers and to the rest of us, it seemed like a great time not to think about them for a while. But we understood that no one gets between a Jewish boy and his mother, so we let him get on with it. We couldn't hear the conversation but Robert didn't appear to be adding much to it. There seemed to be a lot of shouting from the other end. After a time, Robert emerged ashen faced from the phone box. We all thought something terrible had happened.

'Christ Rob, what's up? Is everything alright?' I asked him.

'I have to go home.' He looked very upset.

'What? Why?'

'My dad says I have to. He didn't know I was here. He's very upset and so is my mum.'

'I'm not surprised.' I looked at Simon and Warren. They weren't surprised either. When it came to our parents, we operated on a need-to-know basis. We couldn't understand why

Robert, on his arrival in Brighton, felt they needed to know. I said that to him.

'That might have been a mistake,' he said dejectedly. 'Could you sell my ticket?' We said we would. He wandered back up the hill to the flat to pick up his stuff and then on to the station. We waited until he'd got a fair distance away and then pissed ourselves laughing.

We were all getting a bit hungry. This was way before Brighton became a gourmet heaven with overpriced vegetarian restaurants and sushi bars. There were takeaways selling fish and chips or saveloy and chips. That was it. Saveloys were large sausages that looked, and indeed were, very unhealthy. I'd once seen someone at football with a saveloy in one hand and a cigarette in the other. He took alternate bites out of the saveloy and pulls on the cigarette. It's possible that fitness was not top of his priority list.

I bought fish and chips covered in salt and vinegar. Simon had the same and a pickled onion and a gherkin as well, even though we were all sharing a room at the flat and things would get pungent later on. Warren had a saveloy and chips. We went down to the beach and ate our food, and talked about football and music and clothes and girls and whatever nonsense teenage boys talk about. We tried to skim stones into the sea. Brighton beach doesn't offer much in the way of comfort but if stone skimming is your thing, you're in luck. We looked on in amazement as an old man stripped off and dived into the water. It was November. We couldn't believe that he didn't have a coronary on the spot. He probably looked at Warren eating his saveloy and thought much the same thing.

We wandered along the seafront. There were shops selling saucy seaside postcards. They featured, for example, busty women carrying two dogs and sexually frustrated men making double entendres about what a lovely pair they are and what a handful they must be. There were kiss-me-quick hats, snow globes, bits and pieces for the beach and large sticks of Brighton Rock. For the uninitiated, rock is a stick of sugar with the name of the town running through it. It has the same consistency as an uncut diamond. We all ate them a lot as kids. If anyone ever wondered why dentists live in such big houses, try eating some rock.

We went on to the pier. There was a woman in a booth with a sign outside offering a glimpse into the future. We considered asking her if the boys were going to play greatest hits or some new material, and who was going to win between Chelsea and Arsenal. There was an enormous amusement arcade. Personally, I've never been convinced of the amusing properties of amusement arcades but if they were called 'disappointment arcades', it may put the kids off going in. They were a relatively cheap way of passing the time. We fed pennies into the Penny Falls and waited in vain for the mountain of pennies to fall over the edge. If we lent on the machine too much, an alarm would go off and a stern security guard would come over and wag his finger at you. We played pinball and tried not to tilt the machines. We played air hockey. We wasted cash in the fruit machines. They promised a 75% pay out, how could we lose? We looked at posters advertising 'traditional' seaside entertainment featuring comics like Mike Reid and Jim Davidson. We had a couple of drinks in a pub. I was only seventeen but no one seemed in the least bit bothered. Warren bought me a pint of beer. It seemed like an enormous amount of liquid but it went down easily enough.

The gig was in the Brighton Centre. I've since been there for the Labour Party conference but there was a better atmosphere at Jam gigs and I definitely preferred 'Going Underground' to 'The Red Flag'. We looked around for a tout so we could sell Robert's ticket. They weren't difficult to find. They were quite familiar figures, and we recognised quite a few of them from football. They were burly men with a shifty air about them who were twenty years older than anyone else at the gig. At Arsenal, I once saw a whole group of them getting out of the same van. If there had been a crash on the way to the game, there would've been a lot more empty seats.

Dealing with a tout was always fraught. It was illegal after all, although the police didn't seem concerned. We tried to find the one who looked the least criminal. A guy walked past us in a sheepskin coat. 'Anyone want seats for the gig. Buy or sell.'

We let Warren approach him as he was the oldest. We watched from a distance as he did the deal. Once it was done and Warren had the cash, we went in and took our place in the crush as near to the front of the stage as we could get. Support that night were The Vapors who had a hit with 'Turning Japanese', a song that I later found out was a hymn to masturbation. They went off, the familiar soul tunes played and then the lights went down, John Weller came out and introduced the band. Here they were. It felt like a homecoming but then, it almost always did with them.

I've always been amazed how much noise emanated from just three blokes but that's amplification for you. The setlist was a mixture of old and new. They played 'Modern World' and 'Going Underground'. They played 'Start'. Warren told me that Paul had nicked the riff from 'Taxman'. (I started listening to The Beatles because of this song. They'd always been in my life – some of my earliest memories are of hearing 'Strawberry Fields' on the radio when I was five – but now I dived a bit more fully into their back catalogue. This is one of the reasons I love music, the fact that through listening to stuff, you get to discover other stuff.) They played 'It's Too Bad', the first song I'd ever seen them play live. The new album *Sound Affects* was just about to come out and they played some of the tracks from that. I always liked 'Pretty Green' played live. Bruce would kick off with that bassline and all of us would clap along. And then the drums would kick in. There was nothing too complicated about the lyrics; a fairly simple message about how having money was essential if you wanted to do anything. And then a line about power being measured by either force or money. This was self-evident. Not that I could do anything about it; I wasn't powerful or rich. No one in my family had ever had much money or power and I didn't know anyone who did.

The whole night was exactly how we hoped it would be and we were suitably drenched with sweat as we emerged into the cold night air. Somebody said that the band were staying at The Grand just up the road and that we should go along and see if we could catch a glimpse. Even though we'd just watched them for an hour and a half, no one had any better ideas so we trundled down to the hotel. It was either that or go back to the flat and we were way too pumped for that.

We walked the four hundred yards back down along the seafront and went into the bar. This was the poshest hotel I'd ever been in. A man opened the door for us and eyed us suspiciously. He was wearing a military style jacket with braiding and epaulettes. The three of us could not have looked less like residents but there's nothing to stop anyone over eighteen going into a hotel bar, though neither Simon nor I were over eighteen. We mooched about for a bit. Simon bought three beers and we chipped in when he told us how much they cost. We'd paid less for the tickets for the gig. Warren saw some Chelsea mates and he and Simon went and spoke to them. I sort of tagged along (as well as wandering around and mooching about, I did a lot of tagging along) and we found ourselves part of the group. There was a lot of Chelsea talk; I was once again reduced to the role of silent but nonetheless engaged bystander. I nodded as they mused on the relative merits of Mike Fillery, John Bumstead and Ian

Britton. Simon looked over at me but I was ahead of him and made sure my jumper was covering my Arsenal belt.

Nearby, there was a table of businessmen talking very loudly and telling rather sexist jokes. They were laughing a lot. It was horrible. Everyone was trying not to listen but it was difficult to avoid it. Warren wasn't having that.

'A man walked into a bar with a newt on his shoulder,' he suddenly said, loudly enough for the businessmen to stop talking.

'"I'll have a pint for me and a vodka and tonic for my friend Tiny,"' he continued. The businessmen were all paying attention at this point.

Warren continued. '"Why do you call him Tiny?" said the barman.' The whole bar seemed to be listening now.

'"Because he's my newt,"' said Warren. Not the funniest joke, but it upset the suits so we all laughed anyway.

At some point, because we obviously looked like we didn't belong there and possibly at the behest of one of the businessmen who didn't like the way we'd taken over the conversation, the man with the epaulettes asked us to leave. We protested but he had epaulettes and one can't argue with them. As we were being escorted out, we bumped into Paul Weller and the band coming in. We blurted out that we were being removed and Paul said to the man with the epaulettes, 'Let them stay, they're with us.'

It was one of the best moments of my life up to that point. I was part of an entourage. A very small part, but a part nonetheless. 'I'm with Paul Weller and the band,' I would've have said if anyone had asked. No one did of course and that was the last word Paul said to any of us. We weren't complaining, we were just happy to be in his general vicinity. We clubbed together to buy three more beers and we nursed them for an hour while watching Paul and the band and their actual mates sit around at another table. The businessmen looked like they wanted to kill us, the man with the epaulettes eyed us suspiciously, but there was nothing any of them could do. We listened in for a bit and talked about the gig and at some point we decided to go back to the flat. I lay down on the sofa but I couldn't sleep. I was, albeit for a brief moment, 'with the band'. It wasn't exactly Keith Moonesque, but it felt enough at the time.

Things We Didn't Have in the 1970s

Part Twenty

Safe Toys

There were numerous ways in which toys could kill or maim a child. A lot of the toys were highly flammable and they were often held together by pins. They contained lead or cadmium or arsenic or other toxic substances. There are industrial paints today that are less toxic than children's toys in the 1970s. If there was a collection of asbestos toys but they were good value for money, people may have been tempted. At some point, I acquired Klackers. These were two rock hard plastic balls attached to each other with some string. One clacked them together as fast as possible, hence the name. Originally, they used to shatter and the small pieces would find their way into the eyes of unsuspecting children. Later on, they were made of something more solid. They no longer shattered, but any bones they touched were very likely to. They could render the user unconscious or break wrists or knock teeth out. Bruce Lee could've killed people with them. Our parents gave them to us as presents.

Chapter Twenty-One
We'll always have Paris

In Britain in the early 1980s, the same lack of opportunities still existed for a large proportion of the population. The only people who seemed to be enjoying themselves were City traders. It felt like the wankers had taken over. I hadn't noticed any particular changes to my life, but the effects of Thatcherism were still in their infancy. It was obvious she was spoiling for a fight with the unions and in order to keep the people onside, they were now given the option to buy, at a large discount, the council houses they were living in. We couldn't purchase our place and I'm not sure we would've done if we could, my parents having never made a sensible financial decision in their lives. But a lot of people did and, suddenly, we were a nation of property owners. And also massively in debt for the next twenty-five years, but no one wanted to think about that back then. And so the spending spree began.

Paul continued to rail against the way things were going. We knew that he didn't hate the country, just what it was becoming. I always thought The Jam were quite a patriotic band, from the Union Jack jackets of the early days to all the mentions of English culture. I never felt that they were parochial – anyone with Paul's vision of how society ought to be would never be so narrow minded – but they were such an English band, so grounded in the minutiae of England. Look at some of the lyrics in 'Saturday's Kids'. References to *half time results* and *Afternoon tea in the light-a-bite* and *Tescos* [sic] *and Woolworths and Babycham* and *Capstan non filters* and *Selsey Bill or Bracklesham Bay, and Cortinas*. What did foreigners make of any of that? As it turned out, they loved the band as well. The Jam gigged in Holland, Belgium, Germany, France and Sweden. They sold thousands of records in Japan. What did the Japanese make of 'Sunday's roast beef' and 'The Co-Op'? You'd have to ask them.

It never quite worked out for the band in the United States. On their first tour, they supported Blue Öyster Cult, a pairing that was only marginally more compatible than my parents. I'm sure they would've liked success stateside but it never seemed like a good fit. A lot of people looked with envy across the Atlantic, but Paul wasn't one of them. From reading some of the interviews, Paul was ambivalent about the country and it doesn't seem to be the sort of place that welcomes ambivalence. Not that much music went westwards anyway. The Beatles and The Rolling Stones and one or two others but very little else. Certainly not a lot of the punk stuff which felt *so* English (although the Americans had their own thriving punk scene).

In an interview with the fanzine *Positive Energy of Madness*, Rick Buckler told the story of when The Jam were touring in the States and things weren't going particularly well. 'It was a shock when we got to Number One, otherwise we wouldn't have been in the States. We knew "Going Underground" would do well. We had a good drink that night. However, everyone wanted to be back in Britain. We made out we had all come down with a virus. We cancelled the rest of the tour of the States. We flew back to Britain on Concorde, to record "Going Underground" on *Top of the Pops* for the following week.'

I was still working at Ruislip at this point and because we were working with the US Air Force, Americans would regularly turn up in the office. They were very different. Their teeth were excellent and they were incredibly friendly. We all mistrusted their dental work and their positivity. One day, I was introduced to an enormous man with a perfectly trimmed beard and shiny white teeth. We shook hands. My hand disappeared into his.

'Hello, I'm Ian Stone.'

'Hi. Dick Phallus.'

Only in America.

Warren had somehow managed to get a couple of tickets for the Jam gig in Paris from John Weller and he suggested we go over there to see them. I thought this was a splendid idea. I told my mum I was going to Paris. She may or may not have been concerned but I was indifferent either way. I was smoking so much dope by this point, I was indifferent to most things. I ate and slept at home but at all other times I was elsewhere. I paid my mother a little rent but came and went as I pleased. The phrase, 'You treat this house like a hotel' would be a perfect description of me at this time.

My passport had run out so I had to get a temporary one. I had to collect all the relevant documentation including a photo signed by a professional person. Our family doctor, Dr Collins, signed mine with 'I hereby declare that this is a correct likeness of Ian Stone' just in case someone else wanted to steal my identity and live my life. If someone did, he was welcome to it.

I queued up at the passport office in Petty France for a few hours. I was very excited and I told the lady behind the desk why I needed a new passport. She smiled sweetly, the way one does when a five-year-old manages to tie their shoelaces for the first time.

'You have a nice time, dear.'

'I will, thank you.'

The night before the gig, we found ourselves on an overnight ferry from Dover to Calais. It was only the third time I'd been overseas. The first time was for a family holiday to Majorca when I was ten,* and the second was with my dad to watch Arsenal lose in Brussels. This was the first time I'd been unaccompanied and the first time I'd ever been on a ferry. The crossing was rough. I wouldn't say I'm a natural sailor, but I wasn't sick over the side of the boat which, considering the amount of alcohol I'd consumed, was a positive. In this, I was in the minority. I'd never seen so many people puking up at one time. One man was sick just as a particularly strong gust of wind picked up. The vomit was lifted and propelled fifty feet down the deck where it hit another man leaning over the side. The language was choice. We slept fitfully on the crappy plastic seats they provided, but it wasn't restful. There was also trouble on the boat between different sets of football fans. English people will fight anywhere, even in stormy weather.

We docked at Calais in the morning and took the bus to Paris. After what felt like an interminable journey but was in fact just over three hours, the Eiffel Tower hove into view. We disembarked at the central bus station. Paris looked exactly as I'd imagined. Even at the tender age of eighteen, I had a vague notion that I was wandering around the most romantic city in Europe. A city full of art and culture and history. Not that it made any difference to us. We weren't there for art, history and culture, we were three young lads on a mission to see the best band in the world. As for romance, the women may have all been impossibly glamorous but I couldn't even talk to women in my own language let alone a foreign one. I had enough issues trying to

---

* That hadn't gone well at all but if you're in the middle of a loveless relationship, the temperature pushing thirty degrees in the shade doesn't help.

decipher the street signs which, amazingly to me, were all written in French and were therefore not pronounced correctly if read phonetically in a broad North London accent. There was a place called the 'Shom Sellisay' that I'd been told to visit but all I could see were signs saying 'Champs-Élysées'.

We went to a restaurant and tried to order food and drink from a waiter. He was the most French waiter I'd ever encountered, not that I'd encountered many up to that point. He could not have looked down on us any more if he'd served us from the balcony. We practised our limited French on him.

'Deux bières s'il vous plaît.'

He looked at us as if we'd been speaking Cantonese and made us say it three more times. In the end, Warren pointed at a waiter carrying beers past and held up two fingers. Unless he thought we were ordering two French waiters, our recalcitrant server could hardly say that he didn't understand; he sloped off grumpily. When he returned, we ordered pomme frites and something called a croque monsieur and felt very grown up.

On the streets, we tried to avoid the large gangs of French skinheads looking to pick off any stray English mods (to be honest, we wouldn't have felt any less threatened by English skinheads). Warren suggested that we keep a low profile by speaking quietly and not walking down main streets singing 'We are the mods' loudly in English which he felt might be a bit of a giveaway. Once we were inside the hall, we tried not be too conspicuous.

The gig itself was like any Jam gig. There weren't a lot of allowances for the fact that we were in Paris. They played the same soul tunes they always did before the band appeared. John Weller did not walk on and say, 'S'il vous plaît accueillir le meilleur groupe de baise dans le monde. La Confiture!'

The band came on and it was apparent that Paul was angry about all the trouble outside. He draped a Union Jack over the mic stand. The English boys and girls all cheered and promptly identified ourselves as a possible target. There was a bit of pushing and shoving but once the band started playing, we all got lost in the moment. They played a few songs you didn't hear live that often. 'Butterfly Collector' was great, if a bit bleak; I really liked the harmonies. After the gig, we hung about. Sometimes at Jam gigs, if you managed to avoid the bouncers trying to move you out of the venue, the band would come back out and you'd have a brief chat with them. It was like the players coming out for a warm down after a match and coming over to the fans.

The French bouncers kept asking us to leave. We kept saying we would and then we'd move to another part of the hall. We found ourselves chatting to a journalist and a photographer from the *Melody Maker* magazine. He asked if it would be OK if we answered a few questions and they took a few pictures. We were happy to oblige. Anything to hang about in the venue for a bit longer, and the bouncers were more likely to leave us alone if there was someone with a microphone in front of us. It was my first interview with the national press and all I can say is that I've improved. This is not a verbatim record of the interview but it'll give you a gist of what was said.

Journalist : So I'm talking to two fans of The Jam. Ian and Warren. Lads, how comes you decided to come all the way to Paris?

Warren : It's the Jam, innit. We love The Jam.

Journalist : Did you have an easy journey over?

Ian : Well, we ran into some geezers on the ferry. They might have been Tottenham.

Warren : No, they were West Ham.

Ian : I thought they were Tottenham.

Warren : We had to run otherwise we'd have had our heads kicked in.

Journalist : Have you been to Paris before?

Warren : No. We met these geezers when we got here. There were a load of French skinheads knocking about . . .

And on and on like that for what seemed like hours.

On our return, we waited until the following weekend and bought the *Melody Maker*. They'd printed our interview. They hadn't used a photo which was a relief. We came across as excitable but not that bright. I've since searched high and low for a transcript of the interview but I've had no luck. It's probably for the best.

THIS IS THE FIRST TIME I'VE BEEN PHYSICAL WITH MYSELF AND NOT FELT GUILTY!

Things We Didn't Have in the 1970s

Part Twenty-One

Affection between men

The general rule, at least in Britain, was that the male of the species was expected to show almost no affection to other males. Men had friendships in the 1970s, some of them deep and meaningful but any physical contact beyond a comradely punch on the arm would have been deemed unacceptable. The nearest men got to actual physical contact was sport; in rugby it was considered perfectly fine to grab a man between the thighs and stick your head very close to his arse. Unlike women who routinely hugged their good friends, men rarely did. It was seen as overtly continental and no one wanted that. As for men kissing other men, that was beyond the pale. If my dad had kissed me it would've been weird for both of us.*

---

*   When I was forty and I no longer worried about whether kissing my father signified homosexual tendencies, I kissed my dad hello one afternoon. There was a moment when we looked at each other.

'This OK now?'

'I think so.'

It's been fine ever since.

Chapter Twenty-Two

Lift up your lonely heart and walk right on through

One evening, just before Christmas 1981, Simon told us that he'd managed to obtain tickets through the fan club for us to see The Jam record the *Sight and Sound* radio programme at the Hippodrome Theatre in Golders Green. This was great news, as it would just be a select group of a few hundred Jam fans, some of whom had followed them from the very beginning. Plus, it was also only fifteen minutes from my house. I loved it when things were both exclusive and yet only a short bus ride away.

After Stamford Hill, Golders Green is the most heavily populated Jewish area of London. On any given day, ultra-religious Jews, wearing outfits unchanged for hundreds of years can be seen walking around the area. It's like an eighteenth-century Polish village has been transported to North London, where everyone has been taught to drive and park really badly.*

---

* I had an uncle who was a Chassidic Jew and used to wear one of these outfits. I asked him why.

He said, 'That's what our ancestors wore in Russia two hundred years ago.'

And I thought, 'Yeah, but was that a religious thing or just because it was freezing? If you started a religious cult on the equator where all you wore was a

The Hippodrome was an odd venue. In its early days it had played host to Marlene Dietrich and Laurence Olivier but by the 1980s, it was more readily associated with *Friday Night is Music Night* for Radio 2 with the BBC Concert Orchestra. But it also played host to AC/DC, so it had rock credentials. It was unusual inside as well. The ground floor was for artists and technicians. The audience sat upstairs but were still really close to the band.

We got a support band too. Department S had just had a hit with 'Is Vic There?' and they played it. And others, but I don't recall. And then the boys came out, gave us a wave and launched into the set. They played eleven songs that night including a few from the soon to be released *Gift* album. One of those was 'Ghosts'. It was unusual for a Jam song. For a start, it had horns. Also, it was slower than most of their output.

As for the lyrics – about keeping your feelings hidden, about being vulnerable – how many working-class men admitted to feeling like that? Of being unsure of who you were and your place in the world. I felt this way almost all the time but I could hardly tell my mates. Girls might have shared their feelings but boys rarely did. I don't recall ever meeting the boys in the pub and saying to them, 'Lads, I've got something to say. I don't know about you lot but I really can't take holding it in any more. I feel sad and lonely quite a lot of the time. Sometimes, when I'm on my own, I have a little weep at the pointlessness of it all.'

'Shut up and have a drink, you cunt.'

I read somewhere that Paul said that this song was about acting differently so that you're accepted into the crowd. I could relate to that. I knew I was desperate to fit in, I just wasn't sure

---

loin cloth and then some major trauma befell your people and you had to uproot to Siberia; you wouldn't walk about in your loin cloth saying "Fuck me, it's a bit parky. I wish our guru had chosen a long black coat and a big furry hat. That would be much more conducive to the conditions we now find ourselves in".'

where. I was still travelling up and down the country watching Arsenal but I was doing that on my own so that didn't count. Sometimes, when I'd travelled hundreds of miles and I was standing in the pissing rain on an open terrace watching my boys lose 2-1 to Notts County for example, I did question what on earth I was doing with my life.

I was watching all the England matches at Wembley, and some of the away ones as well. We went to watch England play Hungary in Budapest. My mother objected. She knew that at England away matches, violence happened with depressing regularity. I felt confident we'd be fine although I didn't share with her the reason I thought we'd be fine, which was that Simon and Warren vaguely knew the main thugs from the Chelsea hooligans so even if it had kicked off, I figured we'd be on the right side. She might not have found this information comforting.

I wasn't totally sure that I wanted to be friendly with the Chelsea hooligans. They were massively racist for one thing, and I thought that being Jewish I might not fit in. They were also one of the more fearsome bunch of hooligans operating in Europe. Our football teams might not have been up to much, but our gangs of thugs were some of the best on the continent. They had well paid jobs enabling them to wear expensive designer clothes and travel round Europe being aggressive towards foreigners. They went to every England away game. For people who hated foreigners, they travelled abroad a lot.

Their leader was a large, blonde-haired man known as Blonde Barry. Simon had told me about him but I must have misheard because I was under the impression that there were two men called Blondie and Barry. When I was introduced to Barry, I almost asked him where Blondie was, but Barry was the most blonde-haired man I'd ever met and at the last moment I thought better of it. Barry was frighteningly charismatic. Enormous thugs would do exactly what he told them to do. If he wanted sixty lads to rampage through a shopping street in Belgrade, they'd be there for him. He was the conductor of the most violent, racist orchestra of all time. He was racist but he liked me.

'You might be a yid, but you're one of us.'

It was nice to belong.

Budapest was the first Eastern European city I'd ever been to. The Iron Curtain was still very firmly shut and it was a shock to see how grey and monochrome it all looked. The Danube ran through the middle and that was attractive enough but there was very little colour elsewhere. It was only when I got back home that I realised that this was because there were no advertising hoardings. For a good reason: there was very little for the locals to buy.

We hung out with some of the less racist and violent members of the Chelsea gang. It was a fine distinction but even amongst hooligans, there were gradations. They might all be anti-social and racist but not all of them were criminals and thugs. Some of them were just thick. There was Flobby Phil who acquired his nickname because of the tremendous amount of phlegm he used to be able to summon up. He spent the entire time hawking and spitting. I've never seen someone spit quite as much as Flobby Phil. If you stood near him at football, a pool of spit would form at his feet. Most people tried to stand as far away from him as possible.

There was also a young guy called Nick, who's nickname was Nutty Nick. He was the same age as me but compared to him, I felt like a very responsible adult. Nick was tremendously excitable and also not very bright. He'd never stayed in a four star hotel before and was delighted to find that there was a minibar in the room. Having consumed the entire contents, he was less delighted when he found out that he had to pay for it. I think he may have absconded without doing so.

Like England fans in every city they visit, we found the main square, draped flags over the central fountain/statue of a war hero and settled down to drink and sing rude songs about our hosts, and also songs about the world war. *The Dam Busters* theme was a particular favourite. I wasn't clear which side the Hungarians had been on but sensitivity wasn't top of our priorities. I figured that most of them would never have seen the film anyway. This carousing took up most of the afternoon. The locals looked on impassively. In the evening, we were bussed down to the stadium and England won 3-1.

After the game, there was a dinner reception for the England fans. Around three hundred of us sat down at long tables and were served a stew of some sort, presumably goulash. We then had speeches. A representative of the Hungarian FA made a welcoming speech in broken English which we could barely understand. We duly listened as best we could considering we were blind drunk. At some point he stopped talking and we gave him a round of applause more in relief that it was over. And then Ken Bailey was asked to say a few words. Ken Bailey was the England mascot in the 1960s and 1970s. If you look at old pictures of England games, you'll see him there. A smiling old geezer wearing a red topcoat, a Union Jack waistcoat and hat, and often carrying a Union Jack or St George's Cross flag. He sometimes wore an England rosette as well just in case you had any doubts about his allegiance.

Ken started speaking and it became apparent that he had quite a bad speech impediment. Bad enough that we understood less of what he was saying than the Hungarian bloke. People started shifting in their seats. Some people started laughing. A lot of the guests had had more than a few by then. By the end of his speech, most of the room were either feeling painfully embarrassed or doubled up in tears of laughter. I was in the latter group but in mitigation, I was painfully embarrassed to be laughing so much.

*

The rest of the time I was lost. I hated living at home. My mother had recently found some dope in my room and being the calm, rational person she was at this point, surmised that I was addicted to heroin and made an appointment for me to see Dr Collins. After a fearsome row, I agreed to go although I didn't tell her I was taking my dealer with me. Dr Collins was very understanding. As we left, he gave us two pieces of advice. Firstly, he told us he'd prefer it if we didn't smoke it next time we were coming to see him as he could smell it when we were still in reception. Secondly, he advised me to hide it better next time.

My sister Beverley found all this very amusing which really pissed me off. What I didn't realise until much later on was the reason for her amusement, which was that while I was being sent to the doctor for supposed drug addiction, she, at twelve years old, was climbing out of her bedroom window, meeting up with mates, smoking dope and going to gigs at the Hammersmith Odeon. She obviously hated being at home as much as I did. (Over the next few years, she lied about a school skiing trip and went clubbing in Manchester, lied about going to her friends for the weekend and went to Reggae Sunsplash and lied about staying with another mate and went to the Castle Donington Rock festival on the back of a motorbike with her friend Sheila and her boyfriend who was a Hell's Angel. When she told me, I was jealous but also a little impressed at her independence. I guess neglect is a powerful driving force to sort your own shit out.)

I also hated my job. To make me a vaguely competent engineer, I was sent for six months site training. I started at a trades centre in Wallington, near Croydon, where I learned the basics of construction. It was so dull. I was given some overalls and I did stuff on lathes and drills. I picked it up OK but it was hot and sticky and I vowed never to work in heavy industry. I got a thin cut on my hand from some sheet metal that was sore for weeks. While I was there, trainee hairdressers were brought in and we were offered free haircuts. I had one and I realised there was a reason they were free. I wore a woolly hat for two weeks. Every lunchtime, I'd go over to the work's canteen and eat food that was only a couple of steps removed from gruel. I had some soup once that tasted of absolutely nothing. It was just tepid grey water. If I put salt in it, it tasted of salt.

Once I'd completed the course, I was sent to Enfield to work installing pipes in greenhouses on the site of an agricultural college, from September to February. I have rarely been so miserable as when I was getting up on a bitterly cold November morning to travel to Enfield in North London to be the personal slave of a gang of pipe fitters, freezing half to death, making lots of tea and humping large stainless steel pipes around a building site. My workmates took the piss out of me constantly. If they weren't sending me for buckets of tartan paint, they were making comments about my nose. It was not a happy time. One of the gas fitters was undoing a stand pipe and making the noise of gas escaping. I went and hid behind a wall. They all thought it was hilarious.

I still saw Simon quite a bit but he'd fallen in with a Jewish crowd and I didn't like them much. They were spoiled, arrogant and wealthy, not a good combination. They were demanding in restaurants. They used to order off menu.* They had expectations and I fell way below them. They used to hang out at either Golders Green or Edgware station. Sometimes, we'd go to Hampstead. On warm evenings, the boys would cruise around

---

* This is a *very* Jewish thing to do. I've lost count of the number of conversations I've heard like this:

'Could I have the chicken please but could you grill it rather than bake it? And I know it comes with broccoli but could I have it with green beans instead? And would it be possible to have sauté potatoes as opposed to mash?'

The waiter pauses.

'This is a Little Chef mate. It comes how it comes.'

the narrow streets with the windows wound down. They'd have 'Body Talk' by Imagination blaring out over the sound systems. There were a couple of cafes where we would congregate. One was called The Milk Churn which had a modern American style feel. The other was the Coffee Cup which was a bit more old Hampstead. The last time I looked, it was still there.

Everyone seemed obsessed with money. With the boys, I could at least talk about football but when they started talking about their futures in business and how quickly they were going to make their first million, I lost interest. As for the girls, none of them wanted anything to do with me and the feeling was mutual. They compared clothes and jewellery and cars. They were Jewish princesses but we called them Becks (short for Rebeccahs). It was like a meeting of wanabee Mariah Careys. One young woman drove up in a brand-new Nissan. Everybody crowded round.

'That's beautiful,' said someone.

'It's not,' said the driver, pouting. 'I specifically told Daddy I wanted the blue one and he got the green one by mistake.'

There was a lot of sympathetic billing and cooing. I was thinking that if she didn't like the colour, I'd be happy to take a key down the door and remove some of it.*

Simon straddled these worlds much better than I did. We both had a working-class upbringing but he's always liked a bit more comfort than me. He still does. He lives in a much bigger house, his car is relatively new, he has more expensive tastes. He's never camped at a music festival or used a chemical toilet. Jews don't do that, at least not his sort. Whereas I never felt like one of those

---

* I met one of these women years later at a comedy gig. She was very nice and I felt terrible thinking the way that I had. She felt terrible that she'd ignored me. We were getting on very well. She asked me if I fancied meeting for a coffee. I told her I was in a relationship. She looked disappointed. I thought, 'Where were you when I needed you?'

Jews. The Jewish kids who hung out in Hampstead had parents who were aspirational. They wanted to get on, take nicer holidays, have bigger cars and house extensions. My parents only aspiration was to be as far from each other as possible.

Like at every Jam gig, we hung about afterwards. I always wanted the evening to keep going but the houselights would go up, the roadies would move in and start dismantling the gear and you'd know it was over. We never saw Paul, Bruce or Rick. They scooted back to Woking. It was a shame really,' as Golders Green was my manor; I could've shown them around the nightspots. It was a Saturday night and because the Sabbath ended early during the winter, everything would've been open. We could've got a bagel and then cruised up and down the high road. And then got another bagel. We could've driven up the hill to Hampstead with the windows down playing 'Body Talk' on the stereo. But they were nowhere to be seen and we were ushered out of the venue.

Outside, I found myself standing next to Vaughn Toulouse, the now sadly deceased lead singer of Department S, and Siobhan and Keren from Bananarama. I think one of them was going out with Vaughn.

'I like the new single,' I said to him for want of anything else to say.

'Thanks,' he said and then looked over at the Bananarama girls. 'You hungry?'

'Erm, yeah.'

'Know anywhere to eat round here?'

No one did. I chipped in. 'There's a McDonald's just over the road.'

'That'll do,' said Vaughn.

I tagged along. I didn't know if I was meant to tag along but it was my suggestion so it would've been weird if I hadn't. Which is how I ended up going to McDonalds with the lead singer of Department S and two-thirds of Bananarama. It was without doubt the coolest moment of my life. Up to that point, there hadn't been a lot of competition.

Chapter Twenty-Three

A Whole Street's belief in
Sunday's Roast Beef

The Jam had their summer exhibition at Somerset House in 2016. Of course Simon, Warren and I had to go. We thought it would've been funny if, in homage to that trip, Robert had come along with us and then had to go home just before we went in. He probably wouldn't have found it as funny as we did. It was a brilliant exhibition, but then we were the perfect demographic. There were a lot of paunchy balding middle-aged men – we fitted right in. It was gratifying to note that I had less paunch and more hair than most of the other visitors. We looked around at the memorabilia, the clothes, the ticket stubs and the posters. We swooned over some of the old guitars even though none of us could play so much as a note. We pored over Paul Weller's school reports looking for clues to his later success. None were apparent. There were no comments from teachers saying he'd be nothing. I guess it's not the sort of thing you put in a school report. We went for dinner afterwards and talked about gigs we'd seen, songs we'd loved, adventures we'd had. The years between then and now instantly melted away.

There was an accompanying TV documentary. I watched it on the night it was broadcast and then again a few days later.* There were all sorts of facts that I wasn't aware of; I was never a Jam geek. For research for this book, I've had to look up information about gigs and albums and B-sides and what have you. I never kept that stuff in my head, I just loved the tunes.

Near the end of the documentary, they asked the boys the question that everyone always asks. Would they ever get back together again? Rick and Bruce seemed ambivalent but not wholly against the idea. There's been a lot of water under the bridge in the thirty-five years since they split up, but I imagine the money would come in handy. Tickets would definitely be in demand. Bruce had played with a Jam tribute band so I guess he's well-rehearsed if things ever got going again. Warren tells me they're excellent.

When Paul Weller was asked the question, he said three words. 'No fucking way.' It was the most unequivocal answer I'd ever seen anyone give to anything and the more I think about it, the more it sort of feels like the right thing to say. Sure I'd like to see the band again, sure I'd like to spend more money than is sensible to revisit my youth one more time, sure I'd like to shout 'I don't give two fucks about your review' when/if they played 'Modern World'. Having been poorly reviewed quite a few times, it might well feel more resonant. I might even venture into the mosh pit for the encore. It would be tremendous fun. Plus, I could take my kids and maybe they'd have some insight as to what it was like. But if Paul's not feeling it, what's the point? And also, playing 'Boy About Town' or 'When You're Young' when you're in your sixties does seems a bit ridiculous.

Seeing the concert footage at the exhibition took me right back. When I was sixteen, going to a gig could be a life changing

---

* I've watched snippets again. I will in the future.

experience. I don't know where it was filmed but I may well have been there. All those young faces, squashed together at the front nodding along to all the songs.* Kids would sometimes faint from dehydration or just general overexcitement, get passed over the crowd into the orchestra pit, be taken round to the side of the stage, revived and then chucked (willingly) back into the crowd. It definitely wasn't a comfortable experience. You went to worship. Comfort didn't come into it.

On the footage, they were playing 'Town Called Malice'. It remains a brilliant song, possibly their best. I'm still stunned by how good it is. The tune is fantastic. That bass at the beginning and then the keyboards and the rest. I remember seeing them play it on *Top of the Pops*. The audience look like they're actually enjoying the song. (Not always the case on that show. Take a look at the earlier *Top of the Pops* video for 'Tube Station'. Most of the crowd are just standing there looking vaguely interested.) I don't think Paul ever sounded better on a Jam song. And the lyrics, about disused milk floats dying in the dairy yard or lonely housewives clutching empty milk bottles to their hearts, were beautiful. This is songwriting of the highest quality. This is poetry. The fact that the subject matter, the dislocation of working-class communities and the slow erosion of so much of English life, is so grim makes it even better. I knew exactly what Paul was singing about. Travelling up and down the country watching football and gigs, I could see that not everywhere looked as affluent as North London (even the parts of North London I'd lived in) and it didn't take a genius to see the country was divided.

This was before the worst effects of Thatcherism even kicked in, the miner's strike was still two years away, but Paul could see the way it was going. There was a lot of anger and, as ever, Paul

---

* And knowing every single word. If Paul had lost his voice, any one of us could've filled in.

was out front telling it like it was. Quite a lot of kids in his audience would've lived in those towns and felt the frustration and anger he was feeling. If anyone could lay claim to being spokesman for a generation, it was Paul.

We weren't to know that we were nearing the end for the band but there's no doubt that Paul does not look happy in this video. Perhaps once you've written a song this good, you might start to wonder where you can go from there. As for the hundreds of thousands of new fans of the band, I might have resented them but I probably should've been more irate with anyone who was still unconvinced. How could you *not* like that tune?

'Town Called Malice' went straight in at Number One. By then everybody was into them. If you wanted to see them live, you had to queue for hours with people who'd only got into the band in the last year or so. I was outraged. We'd been fans since the first album. We should've had a special queue. A sort of priority-boarding lane for long-term fans.

Like three-tour veterans of Vietnam not wanting to get too close to the new recruits just in case they led the company into an ambush, we wanted nothing to do with them. Had they driven up to Manchester in Simon's clapped out old car and broken down just past Birmingham? Had they, like Warren, travelled back from Birmingham after a gig and slept on the tube for an hour before going straight to work? No, but we had.*

I moaned to Simon and Warren.

'Who are all these people buying Jam records?' I asked them.

They looked at me like I was mad. 'People who like the band?'

'Yeah, obviously, but where were they five years ago?'

'Listening to something else, I guess.'

Which was exactly what they were doing but it didn't make

---

* I say we although, for reasons unknown, I hadn't done either of these things. But I'd paid my dues.

me feel any less contemptuous. The Jam bought out a sense of ownership in me. I know Warren and Simon felt it too but they would never forgo a chance to take the piss. That's why I liked them.

By the time 'Town Called Malice' came out in 1982 I'd still not left home. I was earning enough money to look after myself and I definitely didn't want to be there, but for a nominal rent, I was fed and I had somewhere to sleep. Taking the final step was proving much more difficult than I imagined it would. I guess I took after my father more than I cared to admit.

I spent all my spare time at my friend Steve's flat. I smoked a lot of dope, listened endlessly to Pink Floyd's *Dark Side of the Moon* and David Bowie's *Low* and talked shit about politics. For those of a vaguely left wing persuasion, it was a terrible year. Shortly after 'Town Called Malice' came out, the Falkland Islands had been invaded by the Argentinians. Thatcher, who at that point was not popular at all, saw her chance and sent a task-force to the South Atlantic. I was vaguely against the war, but only because it felt like I should be. I couldn't for the life of me understand how anyone could want to live in the Falklands and also what the fuck they were doing living there in the first place but I could sort of see why we went. It was touch and go whether we'd win but in the end, the islanders were liberated and Maggie soared in the polls. The warships sailed back into Portsmouth harbour and there were Union Jack flags everywhere. I didn't like how it affected the country. I didn't feel at home at all.

And then in October of that year, Paul announced that The Jam would be splitting up. This came as a monumental shock. There had been rumours for weeks but no one could believe they were true. It didn't make any sense. They seemed to be at the very top of their game. Eight months earlier, they'd had a huge number one hit. They were the biggest band in the country. Who quits while they're ahead?

Now I completely understand. That feeling that you've taken something as far as it can go. But it's different when you're a fan. I'd spent that period of my life eagerly awaiting the next single, the next album, the next interview. And then suddenly, it was gone. I couldn't believe it. Paul wouldn't do that to us. To me. I was hurt and shocked. Everybody was, particularly the other two members of the band. Rick Buckler said he and Bruce were completely taken by surprise and it took them a long time to recover. I'm not surprised. For them, it was a matter of income. For me, after Susan, it felt like only the second major rejection of my life. Paul didn't need me any more. It was a painful moment and I knew I'd miss him. I didn't even get a pen.

Paul said that they would do a short tour at the end of the year and that would be it. We scrambled to get tickets for the Brighton Centre for the last ever gig but they sold out in about ten minutes flat. I was OK with that. I'd seen them enough and they weren't going to play anything I hadn't heard before. The problem I had was trying to work out what I did next. Paul's songs had signposted all of my supposedly adult life up to this point. It looked like I was going to have to take some sort of responsibility. Shit!

Epilogue

When The Jam split up, I was nineteen years old. For six years, they had been a central part of my existence. I have a theory that when you're young, the band or artist you choose to follow reflects your inner needs. If you grew up in the 1970s and gender or sexual fluidity was your thing and you felt like you didn't quite fit in in that way, you would probably have been into David Bowie. Some of the black kids I went to football with listened to pirate radio and bands like Steel Pulse, or poets like Linton Kwesi Johnson. This may well have been partly to make some sense of the harsh urban environment they found themselves living in. I guess hip hop and grime does the same thing for the generation nowadays.

But for me and thousands of other city and suburban kids back then, pissed off with our lives and worried about our future prospects, The Jam filled that gap. They spoke the same language as us and gave us hope. They showed us that slavish acceptance was not the only way. You felt like you had something to hold onto.

It gives you the feeling that you belonged.

And then they were gone. I'd only had two heroes in my life, Liam Brady and Paul Weller. Liam Brady had left Arsenal to go and play in Italy. Paul Weller had left The Jam behind and formed The Style Council. They played sweet, melodic pop songs. They wore casual clothes (jumpers loosely tied round the neck for Christs sake!). They didn't seem angry at all. It wasn't for me, at least not at that time. (A few years later, I did start listening to them. They were really good. The songs still stand up today. 'Walls Came Tumbling Down!' is great.) But I had to grudgingly accept that Paul had moved on. Perhaps it was time for me to do so as well.

So I did. I got on with my life, not that there was much happening. I left home and moved into my friend Steve's flat. During the day, I was an apprentice engineer designing heating, ventilation and air conditioning systems for office buildings. And in the evening, I smoked dope so I didn't have to think about the fact that I was an apprentice engineer designing heating, ventilation and air conditioning systems for office buildings. At some point, I even stopped listening to The Jam. I didn't need Paul Weller any more. I was less angry. The songs didn't feel relevant to me at that time.

I met my missus, Rosie, in 1984 and we moved into a flat share. We were just mates at this point. Not long after we moved in, she told me I was wasting my time being an engineer and suggested that with my compulsive need to make people laugh, perhaps I should try stand-up comedy. I thought she was insane. She might as well have said that I should try Olympic high hurdling. But I was also intrigued. Who was this woman? Why was she telling me this? I'd spent the last seven years singing along to 'Away From the Numbers' and about breaking away and taking control but I'd never met anyone who had a plan, however crazy, for how I might actually do this. I wanted to know more.

From that moment on, there was this nagging feeling that something was missing. I could feel the straitjacket of nine-to-five getting ever tighter but stand-up comedy? Really? Finally, seven years later (I was very slow on the uptake), I mentioned to

Rosie that I was thinking of going travelling in India. She barely missed a beat. 'I think that's a great idea,' she said.

I thought she'd put up more resistance.

'I'll be gone for a year.'

'Have a great time.'

'Won't you miss me?'

'I'll manage somehow.'

It was almost like she wanted our flat to herself. I started saving money and in March 1990, I resigned from my job and got on a plane to Delhi. A week after that, I was lying on a beach in Goa in thirty-two-degrees heat, with a cup of chai in one hand and a very strong joint in the other watching as the waves of the Indian Ocean lapped gently onto the shore. It was paradise and it may have occurred to me that if I could get to be in this place, I could do pretty much anything with my life. It might have been the marijuana talking.

While I was backpacking round India and 'finding myself' (essentially, you get on a plane and nine hours later, you find yourself in India), Paul was getting on with life as a solo artist. Apparently, it wasn't all plain sailing. A couple of years before, the record company had rejected the fifth The Style Council album and Paul was without a record deal. He had to release a single on his own label and there were no decent offers forthcoming. For someone who was used to being feted wherever he went, it must have been hard to take.

When I got back from travelling, I half-heartedly tried to get a job but the arse had fallen out of the design engineering business so there was nothing going. I had to do something. I did some hospital radio (Sample jingle: 'You've got a friend at your bedside, Radio Northwick Park 945'). Sometimes, I was quite entertaining.

I took a creative writing class. There were people who wanted to write historical fiction. There were aspiring poets. One chap called Jeremy, a lugubrious man with a very soothing voice, wrote some rather beautiful romantic poems. When he read them in class, I watched the women melt. I tried to write romantic poetry. When I read mine out, they laughed. I didn't try again, but I did write a poem about Saddam Hussein (not a romantic one) that went down very well. Inspired by this reaction, I started writing jokes with Ivor Baddiel and on 14 August 1991, I stepped on stage at The Comedy Cafe in Shoreditch.

Wildwood came out in 1993 and it contains some of my all-time favourite Weller stuff. 'Has My Fire Really Gone Out' and 'The Weaver' are two of the best things I've ever heard him do. He followed that up with *Stanley Road* and 'The Changingman', another bit of brilliance; it was like he'd never been away. It was good to have him back and, at least in my mind, doing what came naturally.

As a fledgling stand-up comedian, I guess I was doing what came naturally as well, although in the early days it didn't feel like that at all. The first gig was bad. Aside from my five-minute humiliation at The Comedy Store twelve years earlier, I'd never been on stage before and it wasn't what you'd call a sparkling performance. The gigs that followed were slightly better. I got laughs, but things were unpredictable. Sometimes the audience stared; it was the looks of pity that got me the most. The heckling was also challenging. I died regularly. With all the years of being ignored as a child, my first instinct was to be needy. This does not work for stand-up comedy (or life in general). When things started to go south, my body language screamed 'please like me'. Audiences who've paid money for a good night out are, unsurprisingly, resistant to desperation. But every so often, I'd be standing there talking and people would be laughing and I'd have a momentary feeling of control, of knowing what I was doing and I'd think,

'This is good, I want more of this'. And slowly, oh so slowly, with Rosie's help, I started to get it.

Since then, things have improved and for the most part, it's been tremendous fun. I love performing live and at this point in my career, the interaction is part of the fun. I performed in Canada a few years ago and there were signs all around the club saying 'strictly no heckling'. I was talking to the promoter about this and about how different gigs in England were. He was incredulous. 'So, people heckle in England?'

'Yes,' I told him.

'Doesn't it spoil the show?' he asked not unreasonably.

'Sometimes, yes,' I said. 'But, sometimes, something magical happens and the whole gig plays at a higher level from then on and people feel like they're watching something unique.'

He thought for a moment. 'I never saw it that way.'

If a few years before he had been at The Comedy Store in London one night when I was MCing, he may have understood. This particular evening, in their usual seats in the front row were two regulars, a couple. They were both somewhat overweight. I waved at them before the show started. They waved back. I went on, chatted to various people in the audience and then I looked at the overweight man and asked him what he did for a living.

'I'm a cake taster,' came the reply. Everybody laughed.

'That's very funny,' I said. 'That's one-nil to you but this is not over.'

The second half starts and I'm doing a routine where I'm talking about listening to people when they tell you not to do something. I say, 'For example, if someone tells you "Don't come round for dinner" you probably wouldn't.' I then look at the man and say, 'Well, you probably still would.'

Everybody laughs again, even him.

I continue. 'OK, that's 1-1, now we need a decider. Let's have a race.'

There's a big laugh. His missus looks up at me. 'You'd win by a nose,' she says.

The place erupts. She looks slightly surprised at the reaction and looks at me as if to say I am *so* sorry and please don't be too hard on me. I'm not about to. I say that, once in a while, I don't mind audience members being funnier than me and sometimes, the heckles are so good, one has to just take it on the chin. ('Or "chins", in your case,' I thought but didn't say. A little humility can go a long way.) I introduced Marcus Brigstocke who was on next. As I pass him in the doorway, he says, 'That was brilliant.' He wasn't wrong.

It's not always that good natured. Punters in this country seem very keen to tell comedians what they think of us, our acts, our clothes or our general demeanour. This is very particular to comedy clubs as opposed to theatres where crowds are much more respectful. In a club, late at night, it can get very messy very quickly. The booze might have something to do with it. For example, even if there had been any doubt before (and there hadn't), I have been made very aware how big my nose actually is. Someone has told me every week. I find one can never be reminded enough. I've also been told I was shit, racist, sexist, anti-Islamic, an apologist for Israeli aggression and anti-Christian (that was one tough gig!). That I'm as funny as cancer and had no soul and an evil heart. I once did a show on a cruise ship that went so badly I was constantly tutted at for the rest of the voyage. I ended up staying in my cabin. And at one gig, I so upset the locals that I had to leave by a side door and be smuggled into a taxi under a makeshift blanket and driven out of town. One of the main lessons I've learned is that if people don't like your comedy, they really don't like your comedy.

But at least it feels like I'm alive. One Thursday night, I was at The Glee Club in Birmingham, a purpose-built comedy club and one of the best rooms in the country. I've been playing there for over twenty years. The staff are fantastic and if there's anything the comics need (within reason), they'll get it for us. (Once, very late at night, when many drinks had been consumed, Griff the manager (RIP) came into the dressing room with an enormous cheeseboard. While this would not be what everyone would want, at the time I thought it was a tremendous gesture.)

I was on stage doing my thing, mentioned I was Jewish and a man stood up, started making gas noises and did a Nazi salute. It was unexpected. I hadn't encountered a Nazi salute for quite some time. The last time I'd seen one was at the Sham 69 concert in 1979 and before that by the Holloway Boys in the playground at school. I told him to fuck off and tried to continue doing the show but it's hard to do comedy when the ghosts of uncles and aunts that you're never going to meet are swimming about in your head. After no more than a couple of minutes, I decided to call it a day, put the microphone back in the stand and politely said goodnight. The MC, a friend of mine called Dave Johns (who has since gone on to play the title role in *I, Daniel Blake* at the cinema) bounded up on stage.

'That was Ian Stone, ladies and gentlemen, Ian Stone.'

As I walked off stage, my head was pounding. I passed the heckler and he gave me a look. That was all I needed and the red mist descended. I grabbed him from behind and, still in his chair, dragged him backwards out of the room. I had a hold of his shirt and I remember the buttons flying off in all directions. I was swearing and shouting that I was going to kill him. This was not how gigs usually ended for me. Or him I imagine.

'Fucking hell,' said Dave. The audience turned as one to look at me attacking the heckler.

Dave is nothing if not a pro. 'There's nothing to see, ladies and gentlemen,' he said. The audience disagreed.

I was pulled off the heckler by the bouncers and shoved against a wall. The heckler was summarily thrown out of the venue and I was told to go into the dressing room and stay there until further notice. A bouncer was stationed outside my door. I paced up and down like a caged animal. I was given a cigarette. I didn't smoke but I had it anyway. A short while later, a man knocked at the door and introduced himself as the heckler's boss. He apologised profusely for his employee's behaviour and told me he'd be sacked in the morning. I appreciated the gesture. I went back to the hotel but sleep was not easy to come by.

I spent the next day expecting a call from the venue saying that perhaps I should go home and they'll get someone else for the next evening. I didn't hear a thing. When I got there no one seemed too bothered. It was odd. As I was waiting to be introduced and go on, the DJ played the *Rocky* theme and the words 'Let's Get Ready to Rumble'. No Jew wants to be confronted by a Nazi salute, but it's hard not to love a job where you can (justifiably) attack a member of the audience because he's done one and when you come back the next night, you've got your own theme tune.

(This all happened around fifteen years ago. Anti-semitism went quiet for a bit after that but in the last few years, there's been a resurgence. It's become quite popular in certain quarters and for a topical comedian like myself, there's been plenty to talk about. With prejudice, as with so much else, it seems that what goes around comes around.)

There's a film called *Dying Laughing*. Various well-known comedians talk in some detail about what it's like to do stand-up comedy. Gary Shandling talks about how unpredictable and painful it can be and therefore how you only do stand-up comedy if you really need to. I've been doing it for twenty-seven years so I must fall into that category but I've often wondered why I chose to do a job where there was a decent chance that I would be humiliated, insulted, hated or even physically attacked. Partly, I blame my parents. Also, I need an outlet. If a major world event has taken place, I can stand on stage that evening and have something relevant to say. It happened with 9/11, Brexit, Trump and the 2017 General election. I don't know how other people cope with these events but getting up and ranting about them is probably the only reason I'm still relatively sane. I'm sure Paul could relate to that.

I obviously like the attention as well. And I love getting laughs, but I have plenty of mates, Simon and Warren included, who also have that need and none of them ended up doing stand-up comedy. But if anything keeps me getting back up, aside from having to pay the mortgage and put food on the table, it's that desire for that moment of inspiration, that thing that comes out of your mouth that surprises you as much as it surprises them. That flash of insight that hits the audience with something totally unexpected that they know is unique to that night. At that point, you've got them literally in the palm of your hand and where you go after that is completely up to you. All artists are looking for that moment and it's wonderful when it happens. It doesn't happen that often.

When it's like that, when I've captured, albeit briefly, that 'lightning in a bottle', I feel like I'm connected to the entire audience on the end of hundreds of silken threads and I'm just effortlessly swooshing them around the room. They're laughing and they feel giddy, but there's nothing they can do. They're helpless. At some point, I'll let them slowly float back down to their seats where they eagerly await another moment when I swoosh them around again. Others have used the analogy of surfing and that moment when you catch a wave and you're completely in control and it's smooth from then on. That also works for me, not least because there will be times when you terribly misjudge the whole thing and an enormous wave thuds down on top of you and drives you into the ground.

But that's the chance you take. And I don't know about you but if I'm part of the audience, that's the chance I want you to take. It's why I watch live performance. That unpredictability, that sense of being on the edge. I get the same feeling watching Arsenal come from behind to beat Spurs (insert your own teams here). It's not a passive thing. I'm involved, I'm invested. Live music, when it works, feels the same way to me. Sometimes, like when Sham 69 played the Rainbow, it can all go wrong and a skinhead will put his boot through the drumkit (personally, I think that's taking audience interaction just a bit too far). But when you get just the right mixture of tension and intensity and excitement, it's the best thing in the world.

As much as I love pretty much every tune The Jam ever recorded, live is where you saw them at their very best. John Weller may have been biased but for me, then, they *were* the best fucking band in the world. The gigs were so special. Getting into the venue as early as I could, getting as close to the front as possible and just feeling that excitement building up. And when the band were on, and I'm ten feet away from Paul and he's singing a song he's sung a thousand times but he's doing it like it's the very first time, I was totally with him. We all were.

When I first saw Paul Weller, he was this skinny kid in a suit. He was only five years older than me but he seemed to know so much. He sang songs about youth and the city and school and violence and the media and the establishment. He cut through all the bullshit and he meant every word of what he said. It blew me away.

As I write this, forty years later, Paul has just celebrated his sixty-first birthday. He's The Modfather, respected and loved and with a back catalogue and cheekbones to die for. His credibility is entirely intact, he does what he wants when he wants, he's got all his own hair and he's pretty much the same shape he was when he was nineteen. The lucky bastard.

I think he's mellowed a bit. I watched a TV documentary about Paul McCartney a few years ago and it included a little gig and a Q & A. Paul Weller was there and he asked Macca whether he got annoyed when people asked him to do Beatles songs. Macca said that that was what people wanted so he was happy to oblige. Weller said, 'That's probably why you play stadiums and I don't.' It was a very funny line. I'm glad his humour is a bit more out there.

But that fire in his belly is still there. You can see it. He still has that need to try new things, to get better. That relentless desire to move in a forward direction. To produce a piece of music, put it out there and move on. To keep working, to keep plugging away. In the end, he understands that fundamental artistic truth: You can only do what you do. Whether they like what you do is entirely up to them.

I don't give two fucks about your review.

It took me a long time to get it. To feel that feeling. To be confident enough to express myself. To be unafraid to fail. To be totally honest with myself. To tell people what I think and be prepared to take the consequences. To care deeply about what I do but to not care at all what people think of it. To be passionately indifferent. To be like Paul Weller was at nineteen, for fuck's sake! To be someone.*

---

* Work in progress.

About the Author

IAN STONE is a stand-up comedian, broadcaster and podcaster. He won Comedians' Comedian of the Year for 2018 and a Sony award for his Absolute Radio show with Ian Wright and he has been part of two hugely popular Arsenal podcasts, The Tuesday Club with Alan Davies and Handbrake Off for the Athletic. He lives in London.

www.ianstonecomedian.co.uk

Acknowledgements

My agents David Luxton and Rebecca Winfield were incredibly positive and supportive throughout the process. David helped with pitching the original idea and then he and Rebecca babysat me every step of the way. It's been a total pleasure working with the two of you. I hope you feel the same way. Thanks to Mark Brend at Unbound for agreeing to publish the book. Thanks to Ella Chappell and Anna Simpson for putting up with my endless idiotic questions with endless patience as we went through the process and thanks to everyone else at Unbound including Alexander and Lauren who helped get it all together. Once I got over my initial irritation at having to do more work, I realised that Gary Budden and Ian Preece provided some very sound editing advice. It really helped – thanks. Paul Weller's manager Claire Moon put me in touch with Luca and Tom at Universal to arrange the use of Jam lyrics in the book. Otherwise there'd have been a lot more rewrites so thanks for getting me out of that. Thank you to Matteo Sedazzari for agreeing to let me use a quote from the fanzine he wrote. Thanks to Saba Salman who I met on a 'how to get people to pledge' workshop and who's been very encouraging ever since. She's been through the same process and her book is out now.

To the people who pledged, you're listed separately but you know that none of this happens without you. Your regular 'what's happening with the book?' or occassionally 'where's my fucking book?' inquiries really 'motivated' me. Thanks for your incredible generosity in buying this book before it had been written. I appreciate your faith in me and I'm sorry it's taken a while. I hope it's worth the wait.

When I started writing this, my first book, I knew I'd spend long hours on my own staring at a blank screen. I was prepared for that. What I wasn't prepared for was the enormous amount of assistance, constructive advice and small but significant snippets of encouragement I was given. I'm genuinely humbled by the sheer number of people who, just because they liked me or the idea of the book were prepared to give their time and energy to help make it happen. Thanks to Alan Davies who read one of the drafts, took me to lunch (it probably should've been the other way round) and gave me a whole heap of incredibly helpful and positive notes and advice. This book is more concise and readable because of you. (Also, for clearing up the Fay Fife/Fay Wray mix up. No-one else noticed it.) To Phill Jupitus who drew the fantastic illustrations within, thanks mate. They're beautiful and even more than I'd imagined they might be. As you said, my face is eminently cartoonable. Thanks to Matt Lucas who got an initial draft to Paul Weller because that's what mates do. You're a mensch. Thanks to Ivor Baddiel, Simon Carne, Robert Fraser, Warren Filmer and Stevie Hatten for giving me permission to use stories and photos from our shared past. And thanks to others who shall remain anonymous. Thanks to Matthew and Caroline for the photos from the Marquee. Thanks to Susan for the pen. I wish I could say I'd written this book with it but it's 2020. Whatever, you obviously sensed that I might be able to write. I hope you like what I've written. Thank you to Joy Lightman who helped with some of the JFS stories. Thanks to Tom Wilkinson and Diana Hardcastle for our excellent evenings out. Your huge positivity for the promo video was a major boost just when I needed it. Thank you to Ayesha Hazarika, Jen Brister, Susan Murray and Amy Lawrence for helping me through countless minor and major wobbles. We got there in the end. Thanks to John Moloney for directing me towards Paul's appearance at Hoxton Hall which led to me having a sit down chat with him before the gig. Thanks to Kate for listening. Thank you to Ian Moore for helping to connect me with a lot of mod culture I wasn't aware of. To my parents Ken and Helena, I hope you're not too upset by some of the more brutal passages in the book. To my mother, thanks for putting up with the moodiness and the loud music. Without that, you wouldn't be holding this. To my father, thanks for the stories. You know there are plenty more and perhaps they'll feature in another book. Or two. To Beverley, my sister, thanks for the lunch and also the rather shocking stories. I guess you never completely know anyone and you might have some explaining to do when our parents read this. Thanks to my sons Elliot and Alexander for help with jokes and sentence structure and for listening to me read passages to you. Whether you wanted me to or not. You know I'd throw myself in front of a train for you guys. Particularly on a Sunday because there's often a rail replacement bus service.

Finally special thanks to Paul Weller for the music and the gigs and the energy. It was brilliant fun. And when you phoned me to tell me how much you liked the book, that was one of the best and most surreal moments of my life. And to my partner Rosie, this book was your idea and I wouldn't have got anywhere near this point without your insight, optimism and love. Thanks for always pointing me in the right direction.

Unbound is the world's first crowdfunding publisher, established in 2011.

We believe that wonderful things can happen when you clear a path for people who share a passion. That's why we've built a platform that brings together readers and authors to crowdfund books they believe in – and give fresh ideas that don't fit the traditional mould the chance they deserve.

This book is in your hands because readers made it possible. Everyone who pledged their support is listed below. Join them by visiting unbound.com and supporting a book today.

Special thanks to
Lee Dixon
Patrick A Gallagher
Matt Lucas
Ken Stone

Supporters
John Addis
Ant Adeane
Clive Ades
Debi Allen
Patricio Alvarado
Clive Anderson
Michael Anderson
Annie
Peter Antenen

Peter Armitage
Dave Ashby
Stuart Auld
Sam Avery
Chet Aziz
Nigel Bailey
Rebecca Baird
Charlie Baker
Andrew Ball
Irene Barbari
Jon Barnard
Kev Barnes
Colin Bartoldus
Tim Barton
Rich and Shilpa Beale
James Bearcat

James Beech
Nick Belton
Phillip Bennett-Richards
Morten Berger Karlsen
Marc Bernstein
Ian Bigley
Malcolm Birch
Neale Blackburn
Chris Blacklay
Nick Blake
Claire Blume
Ashley Bond
Gary Boocock
Peter Borsey
Adam Bourn
Michael Boyd
Mark Brend
Jen Brister
Simon Brodkin
Jo Brookes
John Brooks
Jonathan Brooks
Mathew Broughton
Chris Brown
Graham Brown
Mike Brownstone
Steve Butler
Lloyd Calegan
Scott Capurro
Neil Carlin
Simon Carne
Margo Carr
Tim Carrigan
Alison Carthy
Kelly Cates

Jo Caulfield
Kevin Cawley
Paul Chamberlin
Lynn Chambers
Gopinath Chandran
Scott Chapman
Robert Christie
Adrian THFC Cimino
Dave Clark
John Clubb
Gabriel Codreanu
Dave Cohen
Chris Coleman
Gary Colman
Mick Colsey
Pat Condell
John Connor
Anne-Marie Conway
Caitie-Jane Cook
Jason Cook
Caroline Cooke
Alex Coric
Andrew Costa
Phil Cotton
Tony Cowdrill
Ian Coy
Archie Creasey
Simon Crosse
Phil Crossland
James Crowe
David Crowther
Hal Cruttenden
Jon Curl
Rob Curry
Oliver d'Souza

Jeremy Danks	Philip Flint
Steve Day	Christine Flynn
Tony De Meur	Michael Flynn
Ruth Deacon	James Friel
Christopher Dean	Elaine Frost & Martin Jennings
Mark Dederer	Matthew Fuller
Ivor Dembina	Dominic Furey
Martin Dempster	Stefano Galli
Stephen Dinsdale	Eric Galzi
Les Dodd	Scott Gibson
Mark Dolan	Lynn Gifford
Todd Dorigo	Dominic Goacher
Chris Dougan	Simon Godley
Paul Dredge	Kerry Godliman
Rob Dunn	Nick Gold
Catherine Duxbury	Paul Goodes
John Earls	Chris Goodstone
Juliet Edwards	Big Dougie Graham
Tania Edwards	Ivo Graham
George Egg	Albert Grant
Chris Eldridge	Lucy Grattan
Rob Emmins	Glen Gray
Kathryn Enwright	Joe Gray
Andy Everett	Rachel Green
Simon Everett	John Grey
Andy Exley	Ray Griffiths
David Faber	Perry Groves
Nick Fairweather	David Gubbins
Jönfs Fändango	Martin Haddrell
Said Farah	Tony Hagdrup
Noel Faulkner	Ben Hall
Warren Filmer	Raymond Halpenny
Arlene Finnigan	Cathy Halstead
Tim FitzHigham	Scott Hamilton
Neil Flint	Richard Hancock

SUPPORTERS

Colin Harbett

Diana Hardcastle

Jeremy Hardy

Paul (Miserableolgit) Harley

Jen Harris

Pete Harris

Steve Harris

Ian Hartley

Ian Harvey

Tim Hassall

Zoe Hassid

Richard Hayter

Ross Hazard

Ayesha Hazarika

Colin Heath

Graham Heath

John Hegley

Matt Hellyer

Richard Herring

Ralph Hillier

Richard Hillier

Jamie Hindhaugh

Rob Hitchmough

Emma Hobin-Brady

Dom Holland

Pierre Hollins

Sally Holloway

Paul Home

Tina Hooker

Keith Hore

Simon Houlihan

Paul Howell

Steve HS

Gregory Hughes

Michael Isaacs

Steve Iwasyk

Adam Jackson

Paul & Helen Jeffrey

Simon Jerrome

Jo & Liz

Andrew Jobbins

Avis Johns

Dave Johns

Derek Johnson

Steve Jolliffe

Charlie Jones

Chris Jones

Craig Jones

Fran Jones

Gavin Jones

Miles Jupp

Russell Kane

Claire Keenan

Des Kelly

Andy Kempster

Ian Kendall

Dan Kieran

Glyn King

Martin King

Christian Knowles

Hardeep Kohli

Karen Koren

Hannah Lacey

Lloyd Langford

Lois Langton

Robert HP Laversuch

Marcial Lavina

David Law

Amy Lawrence

Danielle Lawrence

Michael Lawrence

Dan Lawton

Jimmy Leach

Bernie Lee

Ethan Lee

Simon Lee

Mary Leeds

Adam Leeves

Max Lever

Geoff Lloyd

Sean Lock

Gabby Logan

Steve Lomax

James Long

Ian Longbottom

for Cliff Lorenz

Steve Lount

Matt Lowman

David Luxton

Gerard Lyons

Zoe Lyons

Fred MacAulay

Ravi Mani

Johanna Mann

John Mann

Mike Mann

Charlotte Mannion

Alison Marrs

Paul Marshall

Darrell Martin

Simon Mason

David Matkins

Bev Maxey

Heather Mayfield

Kevin McCarthy

Peter McCowie

Lawrence McCrossan

Judy McGuire

Steven McLellan

Ian McTigue

Kate Medlin

Jonathan Meth

Robert Middleton

Steve Millar

Andy Millicheap

Jem Milner

Richard Minnis

Mort Mirghavameddin

John Mitchinson

Ian Moore

Justin Moorhouse

John Moran

Mark Morfett

Stewart Moritz

Richard Morton

Andry Moustras

Rufus & Martha Mowatt

Karl Mueller

Susan Murray

Paul Murrell

Paul Napthine

Carlo Navato

Henry Naylor

John Nicosia

Geoff Norcott

Ben Norris

Paul Northeast

Mike O'Brien

David O'Doherty

Jeremy O'Donnell

Mark O'Donnell

Ardal O'Hanlon

Johnny Oliver

Simon Oliver

Andi Osho

Dave Overall

Stefano Paolini

Gareth Parker

Andy Parsons

Phil Peberdy

Andrew R Pemberton

Alan Penfold

Nigel Pennington

Clifford Penton

Damon Pettitt

Dawn Phillips

Nick Pitt

John Plumridge

Lisa Plumridge

Danny Plunkett

Justin Pollard

Tayo Popoola

Alex Porter

Ian Porter

Mark Pougatch

Martin Poyntz-Roberts

Richard Purchase

Andy Quinnell

Bradley Quirk

Colin Ramsay

Mark Randall

Simon Randall

Stephen Rashbrook

Nick Reeve

Nick Revell

James Reynolds

Ri Ah

Simon Richards

Geoff Rippon

Brian Ristau

Neil Roach

Chris Robb

Yvette Robinson

Michael Rose

David Rosenberg

Mark Rothman

Darren Russell

Roy Russell

Andrew Ryan

Ian Ryder

Saba Salman

Miranda Sawyer

Richard Schaller

David Schneider

Hermann Schultebeyring

Dave Seager

Andy Sharp

Paul Sherry

Anthony Shipman

Larry Shulman

Amy Silvers

Supriya Sinha

Paul Slaney

Philippe Smailes

Nick Smallman

Andy Smart

Clive Smith

JoJo Smith

Matt Smith

Petri Somerkari

Phil Sorrell

Steve Stadalink

Dean Standerwick

David Starkey

Andy Stedman

Graham Stephen

Paul Stevens

Helen Stone

Roy Stone

Paul Stubbings

Claire Sturgess

Trevor Tall

Mark Taylor

Becky Thomas

Rick Thomas

Nick Thompson

Paul Thompson

Mike Scott Thomson

Paul Thorne

Mark Thorpe

Eleanor Tiernan

Richard Tiltman

Mish Toszeghi

Amanda Triccas

Jonathan Turner

David Turvey

Dave Vickers

Brett Vincent

Peter Vincent

Mark Waldron

Sophia Walker

Steven Walker

Neil Walters

Don Ward

Sebastien Ward

Wendy Wason

Hugo Wastnage

Ken Watkins

Paul Watson

Julian Watts

Michael Watts

Guy Weaver

David Webber

Jim White

Mark Whitehouse

Jon Whiteoak

Miranda Whiting

Kirsten Whitworth

Geoff Wilkinson

Ian Williams

John Williams

Steve Williams

Rich Wilson

Martin Winch

John Winstanley

Christopher Worrall

Anthony Wren

Debbie Wythe

Shane Youngs

Philip Yoxall

Imran Yusuf